THE
TECHNOLOGY
OF PRAYER

REEXAMINING THE BIBLICAL PURPOSE, POWER, AND PRINCIPLES OF PRAYER FROM A KINGDOM PERSPECTIVE

ROBERT G. PAUL

THE TECHNOLOGY OF PRAYER
Copyright © 2013 by Robert G. Paul

Note regarding capitalization: "Church" or "Community" is capitalized when referring to the global or universal, many-membered body of believers or saints in Christ. When these words are not capitalized, they are referring to a localized body of believers or smaller subset of the global whole. The word "Kingdom" is capitalized when referring only to God's Kingdom, as are certain pronouns that refer to any member of the Godhead. The name "satan" and all related forms are not capitalized according to standard grammatical rules because we choose to degrade, diminish, and disregard him in light of Jesus' finished work on the cross.

ISBN-10: 1493511637
ISBN-13: 978-1493511631

For Worldwide distribution, Printed in the United States of America.

DEDICATION

This book is dedicated to my wife, Alicia Paul, our five wonderful children—Jadorian, Jielle, Jireh, Jenaya, and Jedidiah—and to every Kingdom citizen who is in genuine pursuit of our Eternal Father's will and pleasure here on earth. I pray that the words written upon the pages of this book will impregnate every heart with true Kingdom architecture and heavenly technology, causing a mighty birthing and acceleration of God's eternal purpose within every sphere of our human existence. May the sound of His voice cause us to shift from old patterns and paradigms of prayer, where we have been motivated by our own personal satisfaction and comfort, to a more Kingdom-focused and Christ-centered biblical pattern.

ACKNOWLEDGMENTS

When I first began writing about *The Technology of Prayer*, it was intended as an article (series) for our ministry website. I was encouraged by my wife to consult an editor about making it into a booklet of some sort. This is when I contacted Wendy Anderson, the editor of this project. Through her wise consultation and guidance, I was encouraged to add some "meat" to the core skeletal structure of principles I was seeking to present so that it could be better appreciated and understood by a wider audience. What you are now holding in your hands is the result.

I want to give special thanks to my wife for her encouragement and godly patience throughout this trying process as I dedicated many long hours and late nights toward completing this project. To my editor, Wendy Anderson, thank you for your wisdom, effort, and expertise. What you have contributed to this project in terms of counsel, hours of editing, and suggested revisions is priceless. But most importantly of all, I wish to thank God for giving me the grace, wisdom, and insight to address this topic. He is the Source of true wisdom and understanding. Therefore, He is the true Architect of this message, while I am only the messenger.

TABLE OF CONTENTS

FOREWORD

Welcome to *The Technology of Prayer* by Robert Paul. Robert takes a pragmatic approach to the topic of prayer. He attempts to address the principles, or technology, that drives prayer as a powerful part of our spiritual lives.

We find an example of the technology of prayer described in First Timothy 2:1 (NET)[1]: *"First of all, then, I urge that requests, prayers, intercessions, and thanks be offered on behalf of all people."* The list in this passage implies that there are "modes" of prayer. The three words in this list each carry specific connotations regarding what is happening when we pray. First, *requests*, or supplications, from the Greek word *deēsis* meaning "petition."[2] This is what most people mean when they say they are praying. They are making their requests known to God. This prayer is typically a monologue from man to God.

Second is *prayers* from the Greek word *proseuchē* meaning "prayer" but carrying the emphasis of "earnestness."[3] This is the word most commonly used for both private prayers and corporate prayers in the context of worship. This mode of prayer may be dialog, that is, conversation between God and man. Finally, the third word in the list is *intercession* from the Greek word *entugchánō* meaning, primarily, "to fall in with, meet with in order to converse"; then, "to make petition," especially "to make intercession, plead with a person," either for or against.[4]

Of these three modes of prayer, intercession may be the most misunderstood. This word is also a technical term for approaching a king with a petition or suit for or against someone. Intercession describes a court case where the person praying is acting as an officer of the court. Examples of the use of intercession in this way are: the suit against Paul

1

before King Festus, "made suit to (me)" (Acts 25:24); and Elijah "pleading" with God, "making intercession" against Israel (Romans 11:2). The Old Testament also has this concept of intercession in the Hebrew word *pāgha*. A clear example is in Jeremiah 7:16 (^NET1^), *"Then the LORD said, 'As for you, Jeremiah, do not pray for these people! Do not cry out to me or petition me on their behalf! Do not plead with me to save them, because I will not listen to you.'"* Jeremiah is instructed to stop interceding because the judgment had already been decreed.

Jesus acts in this way to intercede for us by the authority of His sacrifice having made payment for our sins (Hebrews 7:25). Now we also see the intercessory work of the Holy Spirit for the saints "to make a petition" or "intercede on behalf of another," as used in Romans 8:26-27. This same authority is given to us to execute the judgments written. But to be officers of the court of heaven we must be able to know what God is declaring. Even Jesus said that He had to hear the voice of God (John 5:30 ^NET1^): *"I can do nothing on my own initiative. Just as I hear, I judge, and my judgment is just, because I do not seek my own will, but the will of the one who sent me."* If Jesus must hear the Father to intercede properly, how much more must we depend on the voice of God to know how to intercede for God's will to be done on earth as it is in heaven.

The Technology of Prayer by Robert Paul explores prayer principles and challenges us to truly understand how prayer is intended to work to bring change. Robert confronts misconceptions where he sees them and tries to bring strength and light to our prayer lives. I hope you enjoy this journey of discovery with Robert Paul.

Dr. Timothy Hamon

CEO

Christian International Ministries Network

ENDNOTES

1. NET Bible – First Edition
2. *Strong's Greek & Hebrew Dictionary.*
3. Ibid.
4. *Vine's Expository Dictionary of Old Testament and New Testament Words.*

INTRODUCTION

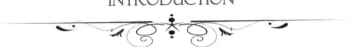

Very few topics in the realm of religion—especially Christianity—have been devoted more time, focus, and attention than the topic of prayer. Countless sermons have been preached, lessons taught, books and articles written, and seminars or conferences held on the subject of prayer. The abundance of information that can be found just by doing a basic search on this topic is mind-boggling.

Yet, in spite of all the focus on it, prayer is—in my opinion—one of the most misunderstood, misapplied, and misappropriated biblical practices among believers today. This observation is in itself very puzzling and disturbing because prayer is supposed to be a very fundamental and elementary principle in the Body of Christ.

When Paul and the other apostles wrote letters (epistles) to the New Covenant Community of believers during the early ages of God's *Ekklesia*,[1] the purpose of their writing was never to establish a theological treatise on any particular subject. It is true that their writings did eventually become the basis of our theological beliefs due to their authoritative inspiration as what we refer to today as the New Testament Scriptures. However, this was not the writers' original purpose in writing. As apostles, like the prophets before them, their main objective and purpose for writing was to instruct and correct regarding prevailing issues in the respective Kingdom communities (churches) of their time. Their focus was correcting errors and meeting doctrinal needs, not teaching or expounding on their favorite subjects.

Similarly—but in no way equal to or as authoritative as our apostolic and prophetic forefathers—my primary concern in this book is dealing with common errors and abuses in the practice of prayer rather than painting a vivid theological picture as a scholar or mature teacher would do. Many others have sought to provide a formula for prayer or a theological dissertation on how to pray in various situations. Rather than attempting to replicate their efforts, the purpose of this writing is to bring a greater level of sight and understanding regarding the "technology" by which prayer operates.

Technology here simply refers to the art, science, or principles that govern the effective functionality of any field. For instance, there is an art, science, or technology to swimming, singing, or any earthly, spiritual, or religious practice. When we properly adhere to the technology of a particular field of endeavor, we maximize our potential and realize and establish an effective functionality in that area. When proper technology is ignored, the opposite occurs.

It is no different with prayer. When we truly understand and apply the biblical principles that serve to govern both the functionality and effectiveness of prayer from a renewed Kingdom mindset, we experience amazing (supernatural) results. We become confident that our prayers are not just heard *some* of the time, but *all* of the time. We are able to rest in the confidence that God *will* answer, not *may* answer. We experience true intimacy with God. We discover the hidden power of prayer to change us *first*, rather than delusively expecting God to change everything or everyone around us as His major priority. But most of all, we discover how to effectively partner with heaven so that God's Kingdom is advanced in the earth.

Conversely, when we lack understanding regarding the principles or technology of prayer, failure is the result. This ignorance or lack of understanding is the primary reason for the very apparent failure in our personal and corporate prayer initiatives today. We may choose to blindly disregard or ignore these failures by making religious excuses, but that only creates delusion. Unless we are brutally honest with ourselves and confess our failure and need for understanding to God, there can be no help for us. God can only fill an empty cup.

It is my belief that you are holding this book in your hands right now because you have a desire to learn—which in most cases will first require you to *unlearn*—so that your prayer becomes more effectual. It is impossible to build truth upon an existing foundation of error. Therefore, erroneous beliefs must be dismantled first before we can proceed into truth. If there is one basic principle we can take away from God's prophetic charge to Jeremiah (see Jer. 1:10), it is that it takes twice as many negatives to establish one positive. It takes twice as much effort to *root out and to pull down, to destroy, and to throw down* (that which is incorrect and false), than it takes *to build and to plant* (divinely given truth).

Throughout the course of this reading, especially in the earlier parts, you will encounter many negative observations or statements that may appear overly critical to popular Christian beliefs or religious practices. Do not become alarmed or offended by this. It is a necessary process in our migration towards truth. There is no other way forward. We must allow God to invalidate, destroy and remove the old rotting foundation— that which has deviated from Christ and His biblical pattern—before we can allow Him to build us a new one. Keep the Jeremiah 1:10 principle at the back of your mind as we move forward. We are about to embark upon a heavenly journey into *The Technology of Prayer*.

ENDNOTE

1. The word *Ekklēsía* is the Greek rendering of the original Aramaic word Jesus used to describe His Covenant Kingdom Community. It is often translated as "church" in our English Bibles, which is a poor and inaccurate rendering of the word since "church" applies more to a building or place of worship rather than to a Covenant Kingdom people.

CHAPTER 1

REDISCOVERING GOD'S ORIGINAL PURPOSE

Prayer is without question the most common and universally accepted spiritual activity known to man. It transcends race, culture, age, gender, religion, or any other earthly division. It is practiced by both the devoutly religious and non-religious alike. In addition, prayer is ancient, being one of the earliest mentioned biblical practices recorded in Scripture. This particular point should shed some light as to why prayer is so widely accepted and practiced across all races, cultures, and religions, and has been so for many generations. Ironically, it is also because the practice of prayer is so ancient that it is so misunderstood today. Purpose often becomes lost in tradition, especially when that tradition has been around for generations.

I remember hearing a story many years ago about a woman who would always cut a turkey in two and then cook each piece separately in the oven, one at a time, because doing so was part of a secret recipe that had been in her family for generations. After being questioned by her husband, one day the woman decided to ask her grandmother the reason behind this bizarre practice. The grandmother replied that there was no special secret or significance to this practice. It was the only way she could get the bird to fit due to the small size of her oven! While I am not certain as to the credibility of this story, being as there have been many variations of it over the years, the principle it communicates is certainly true: *Purpose gets lost in tradition*. If we keep doing the same thing long enough it becomes routine, and chances are we (or future generations) will forget the real reason why we began doing it in the first place.

Unfortunately, the practice of prayer has suffered the same fate. Its true purpose has become obscured or lost through generations of blind religious tradition or just plain misinformation. Misinformation can be twice as destructive as blind religious tradition. It is one thing to know that you *don't know* because a person who doesn't know can still be open to be taught. However, a person who has been misinformed and, therefore, *thinks that he (or she) knows* will often resist being taught something new, because in his mind he already knows. Can you imagine what could have happened if the husband had not questioned his wife and prompted her to question her grandmother? What if instead of acknowledging that she didn't actually know, the wife had taken the stubborn approach and became defensive to her husband's questioning? They would probably have continued a meaningless tradition for generations longer. We need to take a cue from this woman's husband and start asking the right questions. And, like the woman, we should be humble enough to acknowledge that we really *don't know*.

Prayer is a very popular subject. There is quite a lot that has been written and spoken about prayer. I remember reading a foreword recently written by a very reputable Christian leader who claimed that he has at least six shelves of books on the subject of prayer. I confess that I have nowhere near that many, but I would surmise that no other biblical subject comes close to matching the quantity that has been written on the subject of prayer. Yet, in spite of this, misunderstanding and error continue to be widespread with regard to its operation and practice, on a global scale and in every known religion, including Christianity. The questions we need to ask are: Do we really understand what biblical prayer is? What is the true purpose of prayer? What is its primary function? How do we pray? How did Jesus pray? What should we pray about? Who should pray? Why does my prayer fail? What is the correct science or technology that enables prayer to function? How should prayer operate within a corporate context? These questions and more will be addressed throughout the course of this book as we seek to wade through the hype and misinformation that often accompany this subject.

PURPOSE GETS LOST IN TRADITION.

Before we proceed any further in identifying these important core principles of prayer, it is important that we take some time first to redefine what prayer is and what God's intended purpose is for this very valuable spiritual exercise. Prayer was designed by God for a very specific purpose and function. Therefore, we will never truly be able to understand or accurately grasp the principle by which prayer operates until we first take time to comprehend the divine purpose for which it was given. Otherwise abuse and misuse are inevitable.

IT IS NOT ABOUT *YOU*

Contrary to what we may have thought, or heard taught, prayer was not given for the purpose of satisfying our own personal—or rather, selfish or carnal—wants, needs, or desires. Neither was it given as a means for us to escape from every affliction, test, hardship, adversity, or trial. This is not to deny the fact that there is substantial scriptural evidence to support prayers of a more personal nature. We can find many examples of such prayers in the Psalms, which in addition to being a scriptural songbook is the largest prayer book in the Bible. However, anyone who has carefully read the Book of Psalms will note that the prayers that take on a more personal nature in this book maintain an undeniably vertical focus of wanting to thoroughly please God. They mostly address internal issues, repentance, desire for God, praise and thanksgiving, confession of personal weakness with trust in God, and

11

deliverance from enemies. You will never find one instance of a prayer that focuses upon the petitioner's own earthly, selfish, or carnal physical wants or desires such as a new house, horse, property, wife, money, clothes, job, etc.

Long before David became the ruler of Israel, kingship was his prophesied calling. However, Scripture records not a single instance of David praying to become king or to live in a palace rather than in a cave as a fugitive and vagabond. The reason David never prayed this way was because he understood the true meaning and purpose of prayer. His heart was postured toward seeking and pleasing God rather than fulfilling his own carnal desires; therefore, he never used prayer as a license for making self-seeking requests. Also, we should note that David's prayers for help and deliverance during times of intense affliction, hardship, or trial were never focused upon God removing the affliction, hardship, or trial, but on God giving him grace, power, and help in the midst of it.

These types of personal prayers are acceptable because they function in unison with God's divine purpose. It is God's desire for us to seek Him in such a manner, or for such provision, and He has promised to sustain us during times of testing (Matt. 6:11; 1 Cor. 10:13). We will discuss these prayer issues in greater detail toward the end of this book. Notwithstanding, it would be incorrect to assume that the primary purpose or main objective of prayer is to serve you. In other words, prayer is not about you!

From a scriptural standpoint, the true purpose of prayer is not ambiguous. After all, it is visibly expressed through every righteous prayer recorded in the Bible. However, the corrupt influences of religious and secular education, television, media, peers, societal culture, man's natural tendency toward selfishness, and, unfortunately, incorrect religious doctrine or practice have effectively eroded that understanding. As a result, both children and adults tend to approach God as a big heavenly "Santa Claus" from whom we can request nice gifts. Many of us who consider ourselves "experts" at prayer approach God with the same mentality, bombarding Him with a long "grocery list" of personal (or rather, carnal) requests. Many won't approach God at all unless they have a personal crisis, need, or emergency. But prayer was not designed for our own personal comfort or happiness.

So if the purpose of prayer is not to get our personal (selfish or carnal) needs met, what is its purpose beyond the obvious communion with God? To effectively answer this question will require that we go back to the beginning when prayer is first introduced or mentioned in Scripture. We will discover the foundational purpose of prayer by examining a story from the life of Abraham.

THE PURPOSE OF PRAYER ACCORDING TO SCRIPTURE

Prayer in its simplest form is speaking or communicating with God. As such, this principle is embodied in Scripture from as early as the creation of man. However, the very first time that I can find the word *pray* or *prayer* mentioned from a practical standpoint of communication between man and God in Scripture is in Genesis, the twentieth chapter:

Now then, return the man's wife, for he is a prophet, so that he will pray for you, and you shall live. But if you do not return her, know that you shall surely die, you and all who are yours." (Genesis 20:7 ESV)

The context of this passage is Abraham's journey to a place Scripture calls Gerar. Accompanied by his wife, Sarah, Abraham sojourned in the territory of Gerar, which was ruled by a king named Abimelech. King Abimelech appears to have taken quite a fancy to Sarah and inquired of Abraham about her. Apparently Abraham feared for his safety, believing the inhabitants of this land would quickly terminate his life if they knew he was the husband of this beautiful woman, so he presented Sarah as his sister rather than his spouse. King Abimelech then sent for Sarah and brought her to his palace.

After Abimelech had sent for Sarah, God appeared to him in a dream. In the dream God informed Abimelech that Sarah was another man's wife and that He was going to hold Abimelech accountable for taking her, even though he had not yet touched her. God threatened Abimelech's life for something done in ignorance, while seemingly holding Abraham guiltless for his deception—but the latter is beside the point for the moment. Abimelech pled his case that his actions were done in innocence based on the false information provided by both Abraham and Sarah. God affirmed his integrity in this matter and commanded him to restore Sarah to her husband. God then identified Abraham as a prophet who had been given the authority to pray life unto Abimelech and his household. The dream made it clear, however, that failure to comply by returning Sarah to Abraham would mean certain death for Abimelech and his house. In other words, there would be no prayer or release of divine healing over Abimelech and his household until or unless he had been obedient to God's command.[1]

A number of interesting points can be made here. First off, not only is this the first official mention of the word *pray* in Scripture as it relates to communication between man and God, but it is also the first use and mention of the word *prophet* in Scripture as well. Is it merely coincidental that these two words are first mentioned together?

The word *prophet* here is used in the context of one who not only has the ability to hear from God as an intimate friend, but also one who has the authority to speak (pray or intercede) to and for God in the execution of God's purpose and judgments in the earth. Abraham was authorized to pray and release life over Abimelech and his household in a prophet-priestly fashion after God had afflicted them with a curse as a result of Abimelech having harbored another man's wife (Gen. 20:17-18).[2]

Bear in mind that God was the One who put the curse upon Abimelech's household to begin with. Yet instead of God promising to remove the curse by His own initiative when Sarah was returned, His requirement was that Abraham should *pray* for it to be removed. We can see here the tension and interconnection between divine sovereignty and

14

human responsibility in prayer. This suggests to me that if Abraham did not pray, or prayed incorrectly, the curse would not have been removed and Abimelech's household would probably have died in their affliction. God wanted Abraham to partner with Him in undoing what He Himself had done!

It's interesting to note that during the dialogue between God and Abimilech in the dream, Abraham was not present. Yet God still had complete confidence in Abraham that once his wife was returned, Abraham would pray life and healing over Abimelech and his household. Abraham's natural response may have been to take personal vengeance upon him for having taken his wife, even though he had deceived Abimelech by presenting her as his sister. Yet God had confidence in Abraham's response because He knew that Abraham heard God and would respond based on what he had heard rather than from a place of hurt or offense (Gen. 20:17-18).

> *ABRAHAM WAS ABLE TO PRAY EFFECTIVELY BECAUSE HE HEARD GOD ACCURATELY, AND HE WAS ABLE TO HEAR GOD ACCURATELY BECAUSE HE PRAYED EFFECTIVELY.*

In other words, Abraham was able to pray effectively because he heard God accurately, and he was able to hear God accurately because he prayed effectively. Based upon this principle, there is no fundamental difference between prayer and prophecy to the extent that they both require sensitivity to the voice of God in order to be genuinely functional or effective. Prophets and prayer are very closely related throughout Scripture because they are mutually dependent in principle—as two sides to the same coin. The activities of both are never self-focused.

This brings us to the main point of the text: The first time prayer—both the word *prayer* and the official, practical exercise or activity of prayer—is mentioned in Scripture, it is mentioned in the context of exercising God's divine will, purpose, or intent in the earth as its primary function. Secondary to this purpose is the function of ministering to or helping others as an expression of God's mercy and love. There is absolutely no indication of prayer being issued from a place of self-preservation, personal satisfaction, or self-gratification.

Another way of stating this is that prayer is first used as a means of executing God's righteous rule and judgments in the earth, followed by a clear emphasis on ministering help to others (mercy and compassion), bringing life and healing where there was death and destruction.. In fact, a careful study of the activity of prayer in Scripture as a whole will reveal an overwhelming emphasis on these virtues. Despite the occurrence of various petitions that appear to be of a more personal nature, prayer in Scripture is always focused upon fulfilling the will of God as its primary objective. In addition to this foundational purpose, we often find the horizontal expression of ministering, helping, or bringing healing and deliverance to others.

We live in a day and age today when everything has become about "me." Not only is this true in the world, it has also become the defining face of religious Christianity today. This perverse heart and mentality runs so deep in today's religion that it has corrupted the very definition and understanding of prayer. Many of us act as if we believe that prayer was given primarily as a means for serving or satisfying our own needs or selfish desires.

THE PRAYER OF JABEZ

The prayer of Jabez is a perfect example. Many of us will remember how the name of this obscure biblical character and his somewhat unique petition to God, nestled ambiguously in-between a long list of genealogical records, became immensely popular several years ago. I believe one of the reasons it became so popular was due to a misconception that Jabez's prayer seemed to legitimize, validate, or justify our own natural human tendencies toward selfishness. Nothing could be further from the truth!

> *Now Jabez was more honorable than his brothers, and his mother called his name Jabez, saying, "Because I bore him in pain." And Jabez called on the God of Israel saying, "Oh, that You would bless me indeed, and enlarge my territory, that Your hand would be with me, and that You would keep me from evil, that I may not cause pain!" So God granted him what he requested.* (1 Chronicles 4:9-10 NKJV)

It's unfortunate, and very alarming to me, that of the numerous Bible translations used to examine this text (over twenty), the New King James Version was the only one with a truly accurate translation of the text, for reasons we will see below. I have discovered that when there is confusion regarding the meaning of a Scripture text or divergence among translations, it helps to examine the text in its entire context.

PRAYER IN SCRIPTURE IS ALWAYS FOCUSED UPON FULFILLING THE WILL OF GOD AS ITS PRIMARY OBJECTIVE.

We can safely assume that the Holy Spirit, who inspired the writing of this text, understands the human tendency to look for a license for selfishness. Knowing that Jabez's prayer could be misconstrued in this way, He inspired the writer to first provide a description of Jabez's noble character as the defining factor for the prayer that follows. Jabez was

17

described as *honorable* for a reason, which leads me to believe that he was neither selfish nor self-seeking.

The word *honorable* in the Hebrew language basically means "weighty" or "heavy," but it can be used in a wide variety of applications. Its usage here can either imply outward riches, wealth, and respect or a rich and weighty substance of internal accuracy and inward character. In light of the context, I am inclined to believe that the latter is being described here rather than the former.

The unique circumstances regarding Jabez's life and birth are also foundational to the story. His mother named him *Jabez* because she bore him in pain, which seems to imply above normal pain, prolonged labor, or various complications during childbirth. Whatever the case, Jabez was given a name and identity that etymologically and contextually meant "one who causes pain, grief, sorrow, or distress." This meaning is very important to the text. In ancient Hebrew culture names were never given or chosen frivolously. Names were indicative of identity, character, and destiny. Therefore, Jabez was destined to live a life of causing others pain, even though he would do so unintentionally.

When these qualifying key points are taken into consideration as the basis for Jabez's unique prayer, it becomes quite apparent that the primary emphasis and overarching concern of Jabez's prayer was not selfish ambition or personal increase, but a desire to be a blessing to others rather than a perpetual cause for pain or sorrow. Thus the NKJV's translation of *"... that I may not cause pain!"* toward the end of verse ten is the only accurate one. Jabez's prayer was never about his own pain and sorrow because the very connotation of his name implied a pain and sorrow projected on others rather than upon him. He was the cause of the pain rather than the victim of it.

God answered Jabez's prayer because it was not self-seeking. It was a noble petition of a man who desired to live a life where he would cause blessing and honor rather than sorrow and pain. His prayer was motivated by love and compassion rather than by covetousness, lust, greed, or selfishness. Any personal dimension to this prayer is quickly overshadowed by a much greater emphasis on submission to God and genuine concern for others.

REFUSAL TO TAKE PERSONAL RESPONSIBILITY

Our failure to recognize or understand God's original purpose and intent regarding prayer has caused many today to place unrealistic expectations upon God. Due in part to the self-centered teaching that plagues churches today, as well as the narcissistic mentality that has become the spirit of this age, many believers today think and act like prayer operates in some kind of spiritual vacuum, void of any sense of personal responsibility. And even though most of us would deny it, we have equated prayer with some sort of *magic* that "attempts to control or manipulate the divine will in order to induce it to grant one's wishes."[3] We take the promises of God regarding answered prayer (Matt. 7:7-11, Mark 11:24) and try to use them as a spell for invoking immediate results for our own carnal desires. God either becomes our divine "sugar daddy" or a "genie in the bottle" whom we can command at will. But God never designed prayer to be a substitute for taking personal responsibility. In other words, God will never do for you what you have been given the power to do for yourself.

Having served on staff at Christian International under Dr. Bill Hamon for over ten years, I have had numerous opportunities to receive prayer calls from people all over the world desiring prayer from a "company of prophets." On one such occasion a gentleman who claimed to be a Christian called to request prayer on his behalf. When I inquired of him regarding the nature of his request, he proceeded to complain that the electronics and appliances at his home had started breaking down on him rather suddenly, one after the other. First it was his television, then his washing machine, and then it was something else. He wanted me to pray a prayer for him that would put an immediate stop to his stroke of "bad luck."

I further questioned him on his obedience to the requirements of God to be integrated into a Kingdom community (local church) and connected to other believers, and whether or not he had been faithful to honor God with his substance. He began to make excuses, but he still wanted me to pray. I told him that I was not a magician and that I could not help him until he was ready to help himself. At this point, he tried to argue with me.

This man wanted to continue in his disobedience, living his life as normal without taking any personal responsibility, yet have me wave my "magic wand" to immediately fix his condition. Sadly, this is the prevailing mentality of many Christians today. For this reason, I always take time to inquire of the petitioner whether or not he or she is making a legitimate request, and if he is, whether or not he is faithfully positioning himself for an answer to that request. In this particular instance he had failed on both counts.

GOD NEVER DESIGNED PRAYER TO BE A SUBSTITUTE FOR TAKING PERSONAL RESPONSIBILITY.

Another case in point happened several months ago when a woman called the ministry to request prayer for a "need" she had. As I inquired concerning the need, she said that she needed a job and she wanted me to pray that God would "move her" to fill out the applications she had gathered. I was so surprised by the request that I paused for a while—I was trying to determine whether the caller was really someone trying to play a joke on me! When I realized that she was serious and that it was not a prank call, I responded by saying that it would be a waste of everyone's time (including God's, even though He doesn't exist in time) to ask Him to do for her what she had the power to do on her own.

I told the woman that if it was motivation she needed to fill out the application forms, just wait a few weeks (or months) until all her savings had been depleted, the rent and bills were due, and she was facing eviction. Or when the refrigerator was empty and there was no food. She would find plenty of motivation then!

GOD WILL NEVER DO FOR YOU WHAT YOU HAVE BEEN GIVEN THE POWER TO DO FOR YOURSELF.

Had she called for prayer to obtain favor in securing the right job after diligently filling out and sending the applications, I would have responded differently. I still would not have prayed for her regarding this request because this was still a matter which required her to take personal responsibility and then trust God for the results. Biblically speaking, this was a matter that required simple trust and faith in God, not prayerful petitions, especially not from me. But not only was she too lazy to pray (regardless of whether or not her prayers would have been foolish or self-seeking), but she was too lazy to do everything within her power to secure the desired results. She refused to take personal responsibility for the job she desired. We will develop this principle a bit more later on.

Another self-seeking request that ignored this key of personal responsibility was sent to me by way of email. The writer said he had sexual relations with a woman who was not his wife, apparently the previous night. After committing this sinful act, he became fearful of two things: 1) that he had impregnated the woman, and 2) that he may have caught a sexually transmitted disease. His email sounded desperate and anxious, demanding that someone pray immediately and respond to his message so that he could have the peace that he was delivered from the possible consequences of his actions. I could sense no remorse, godly sorrow, or repentance for his actions, nor any sense of fear that he had violated the righteous commandments of God. Instead, his only concern was that he would escape unscathed from any unwanted outcomes. Due to the self-centered nature of this request, coupled with the unwillingness to take personal responsibility, I deleted the email!

If King Abimelech could not expect to receive any prayer, help, healing, or deliverance from God until or unless he had exercised complete obedience to God's clear command and taken personal responsibility, why should we expect prayer today to operate any differently (Gen. 20:7)? Abraham's anointing, calling, and function as God's prophet could not supersede this divine foundational principle. It must be recognized as the foundation for effective prayer.

KEY PRINCIPLES

1. Purpose gets lost in tradition.
2. Prayer is not about you.
3. Prayer in its simplest form is speaking or communing with God.
4. Abraham was able to pray effectively because he heard God accurately, and he was able to hear God accurately because he prayed effectively.
5. Prayer in Scripture is always focused upon fulfilling the will of God as its primary objective.
6. Prayer in Scripture often carries the horizontal expression of ministering, helping, or bringing healing and deliverance to others.
7. The prayer of Jabez is not a license for selfishness. True prayer is never self-seeking.
8. Prayer is not a substitute for taking personal responsibility. God will not do for you what you have the power to do for yourself.
9. Prayer is not magic and God is not our own personal "genie in the bottle" whom we can command at will.

ENDNOTES

1. This is a very important observation and principle which will only be alluded to here. This principle will be addressed in greater detail further on in this book.

2. Note that Abraham prayed on his own initiative as being divinely directed to do so by God. There is no mention in Scripture of Abimelech ever requesting prayer.

3. Dennis L. Okholm, "Prayer," in *Baker Theological Dictionary of the Bible*, ed. Walter A. Elwell (Grand Rapids, MI: Baker Books, 2000), 622.

CHAPTER 2

A HOUSE OF PRAYER

Jesus said, "It is written, *My **house** shall be called a **house of prayer**...*" (Matt. 21:13 NKJV; emphasis mine). If you're like most Christians, you've probably heard this clause quoted over a hundred times in various Christian religious gatherings and have probably even quoted it yourself. But what exactly does it mean, and where did it come from? Jesus quoted it, so He obviously didn't write it. But if He didn't, then who did? Where was it first "written"? Do we quote it in the way that Jesus and the original author meant it? And what exactly are the implications of such a bold declaration?

Jesus was actually quoting from the prophet Isaiah. Isaiah had prophesied concerning God's divine intent and promise to bless and welcome into His house, or temple, those who were previously rejected—the foreigners and eunuchs who honored and obeyed God and kept His covenant.

> *Thus says the LORD:*
> *"Keep justice, and do righteousness,*
> *for soon my salvation will come,*
> *and my righteousness be revealed.*
> *Blessed is the man who does this,*
> *and the son of man who holds it fast,*
> *who keeps the Sabbath, not profaning it,*
> *and keeps his hand from doing any evil."*

Let not the foreigner who has joined himself to the LORD say,
"The LORD will surely separate me from his people";
and let not the eunuch say,
"Behold, I am a dry tree."
For thus says the LORD:
"To the eunuchs who keep my Sabbaths,
who choose the things that please me
and hold fast my covenant,
I will give in my house and within my walls
a monument and a name
better than sons and daughters;
I will give them an everlasting name
that shall not be cut off.
"And the foreigners who join themselves to the LORD,
to minister to him, to love the name of the LORD,
and to be his servants,
everyone who keeps the Sabbath and does not profane it,
and holds fast my covenant—
these I will bring to my holy mountain,
and make them joyful in my house of prayer;
their burnt offerings and their sacrifices
will be accepted on my altar;
*for **my house shall be called a house of prayer***
for all peoples." (Isaiah 56:1-7 ESV; emphasis mine)

Notice the context from where this quote was taken. God is talking about the prerequisites for being integrated into His "house of prayer": justice, righteousness, obedience, keeping the Sabbath, departing from evil, pleasing God, holding fast to His covenant, cleaving to God, ministering to God, loving God, and serving God. Then He emphasizes again that "a house of prayer" is the name by which His house would be called. What exactly does this all mean?

Before we attempt to connect the dots, let's add a few more. When Jesus quoted the prophet Isaiah in making the bold declaration, *"My house shall be called a house of prayer,"* He also added—or more accurately, combined—a quote from the prophet Jeremiah: *"But you have made it a den of thieves"* (Matt. 21:13 NKJV).

> *The word that came to Jeremiah from the LORD: "Stand in the gate of the LORD's house, and proclaim there this word, and say, Hear the word of the LORD, all you men of Judah who enter these gates to worship the LORD. Thus says the LORD of hosts, the God of Israel: Amend your ways and your deeds, and I will let you dwell in this place. Do not trust in these deceptive words: 'This is the temple of the LORD, the temple of the LORD, the temple of the LORD.'*

> *"For if you truly amend your ways and your deeds, if you truly execute justice one with another, if you do not oppress the sojourner, the fatherless, or the widow, or shed innocent blood in this place, and if you do not go after other gods to your own harm, then I will let you dwell in this place, in the land that I gave of old to your fathers forever.*

> *"Behold, you trust in deceptive words to no avail. Will you steal, murder, commit adultery, swear falsely, make offerings to Baal, and go after other gods that you have not known, and then come and stand before me in this house, which is called by my name, and say, 'We are delivered!'—only to go on doing all these abominations? **Has this house, which is called by my name, become a den of robbers** in your eyes? Behold, I myself have seen it, declares the LORD."* (Jeremiah 7:1-11 ESV; emphasis mine)

27

Here is a prophecy of rebuke given by the prophet Jeremiah, at the Lord's command, to the children of Judah in denunciation of their corrupt religious practices. The core of this rebuke is aimed at their self-deception: They vainly trust in their repetitious, religious declarations made at the temple, while continuing to violate the righteous requirements and commandments of God, both vertically in their relationship to God and horizontally in their relationships with each other.

Despite their faithfulness in corporately gathering before God in His temple for worship (v. 10), and despite their faithfulness in offering burnt sacrifices and offerings (prayer and praise) before God (Jer. 7:21-22), they have unwittingly transformed God's house—a house of prayer—into a *den of thieves* (v. 11)! Keep in mind that a thief, otherwise known as a robber, is one who tries—often through violence—to secure or obtain something that does not belong to him or that he has never earned.

THE LINK BETWEEN PRAYER AND OBEDIENCE

The previous text from Isaiah makes little to no mention of prayer in its commonly used, practical sense of petitions, supplications, intercessions, or thanksgiving. In fact, the foreigners and eunuchs are identified as being occupants of this house of prayer through their acts of obedience, rather than through any oral exercises according to our traditional understanding of prayer.

In this particular instance recorded in Isaiah, the people of Judah, who are called by His name and should be the primary occupants of this "house," are completely disassociated from it through their willful acts of disobedience, despite their frequent prayers and vain, repetitious declarations. Do you notice the irony here? Are you beginning to connect the dots?

From these two passages of Scripture Jesus quoted, it seems quite obvious that from God's point of view there is a deep and profound connection between prayer and obedience. Whatever this *house of prayer* represents, it is used in a context that stretches far beyond the utterance of corporate prayers or any oral exercise of personal petitions, supplications, or intercessions. The house of prayer can only be accessed by, and identified with, those who live and operate from a place of covenant faithfulness and personal obedience.

PRAYER IS MUCH MORE THAN AN ORAL DECLARATION OR REQUEST; IT IS A LIFESTYLE.

The key here is that prayer is much more than an oral declaration or request; it is a lifestyle. From God's perspective, prayer has very little to do with what we actually say and everything to do with how we live and what we do. We cannot gain access to God's house of prayer without meeting the prerequisite of obedience. When we show disobedience or a blatant disregard for God's righteous requirements, we are no longer a legal or legitimate member of God's household (of prayer). Instead, we become thieves and robbers who are trying to gain illegitimate access to the resources of heaven without having any right to them.

This truth does not in any way diminish the doctrine of grace, but it establishes an understanding of human responsibility. Like the children of Judah, we can't just violate the commandments of God and then expect Him to answer our requests for divine protection (Jer. 7:9-10). It just doesn't work that way! Not realizing this, when we receive no immediate answer, we often try to "war" and "storm the gates of heaven" in order to violently seize the things we are petitioning for. The rude reality is that most often it is not the demons or devils we think we are fighting that are preventing us from what we desire; it is God! Thus, when we do this, we become violent robbers seeking to obtain from God something we have no right to because of our disobedience!

JESUS AT THE JERUSALEM TEMPLE

When Jesus quotes from Isaiah and Jeremiah in this particular context, He is responding in a similar manner as the prophets before Him to the disobedience and corrupt practices taking place at the physical temple in Jerusalem.

> *And Jesus entered the temple and drove out all who sold and bought in the temple, and he overturned the tables of the money-changers and the seats of those who sold pigeons. He said to them, "It is written, 'My house shall be called a house of prayer,' but you make it a den of robbers."*

> *And the blind and the lame came to him in the temple, and he healed them. But when the chief priests and the scribes saw the wonderful things that he did, and the children crying out in the temple, "Hosanna to the Son of David!" they were indignant.* (Matthew 21:12-15 ESV)

A detailed exegesis of this passage would take far too long, so I will try to condense it and address the high points briefly. Bear in mind that a lot of the information about to be shared was derived from extra-biblical, historical sources that add more understanding to the passage.

As you most likely know, Jesus was not a recognized priest in the organized religious order of the priesthood of His day. The temple He entered, known as Herod's Temple, was a structure (or series of structures) comprised of several "outer" courts preceding the main sanctuary where the priests ministered. It is widely believed and understood that the part of the temple being described here that Jesus entered into was the *Court of the Gentiles*—the lowest, outermost, and least sacred (based on the common perception) of the courts. Open access to the Court of the Gentiles was allowed to anyone, including the Gentiles and the ceremoniously unclean.

Since Jesus was not a priest in the literal, accepted sense, He was never allowed access into the temple proper (the main sanctuary) where the majority of the actual ministry was conducted by the priests. The farthest He could go was to the court known as the Court of Israel. However, based on the information given in Matthew's text, it seems highly unlikely that the Court of Israel was the actual place where the temple cleansing took place.

This outer court or Court of the Gentiles had become a place of commerce, somewhat like a huge marketplace or bazaar. The exchange of money and goods was actually necessary and permitted by law to accommodate foreign or proselyte Jews gathering at the temple from different nations, especially during the holy days. These visitors needed a means to exchange their foreign currency for the temple shekel, which was the only currency accepted. They were also required by law to purchase their sacrifices in Jerusalem. So the presence of the moneychangers and those selling the required sacrifices, such as doves, was very convenient. However, historical records give ample evidence that what began as a convenient service had become a means of extortion, extraction, and dishonest gain as the merchants charged overly high prices for their services.

Whatever the case, after Jesus enters the court, He proceeds to drive out everyone *"who sold and bought in the temple,"* as He overturns tables and disrupts the flow of business. Then He makes His famous quote from Isaiah and Jeremiah regarding the *house of prayer*.

Some critics view the scriptural account as somewhat dubious, considering the expanse of this great court and the heavy amount of traffic that would have been in it, including the numerous vendors. Some claim it would have taken an army to do what Jesus reportedly did. The opinion of such critics, however, is of no consequence. The purpose here is to provide context, and the fact that Scripture records that Jesus did these things should be enough for us.

Based on what we have already discovered from our brief examination of the texts Jesus quoted regarding the *house of prayer*, we have seen that Jesus is operating in a similar vein in this context. It should be quite apparent also that this Court of the Gentiles was not recognized as a hotspot for any liturgical prayer gatherings or significant religious activity of any kind. So Jesus' reference to a "house of prayer" has no logical application in this context if the word *prayer* here is understood in its conventional way. His main issue is not the lack of personal or corporate prayer taking place in this part of the temple because that is not what it was known for.

If, as we believe, Jesus' primary issue and concern is a lack of obedience, who exactly is at fault? If it is just the merchants and vendors who were taking unfair advantage of the people through price gouging, why then didn't He drive only them out? Why did He also drive out the buyers who were being cheated and defrauded? What was it about this entire activity that made Jesus irate?

Jesus' actions in this context, which is commonly referred to as *the temple cleansing*, appear to be prophetic in nature. They are communicating a much deeper and broader message than we have otherwise perceived. This message, however, would have been easily interpreted by Jesus' original audience, which was aware of the abuses and corruption taking place at the temple.

CORRUPTION IN THE PRIESTHOOD

The ruling priests and the high priest in particular were responsible for everything that took place at the temple. They were its stewards. Interestingly, they were not only the architects of this corrupt system of commerce, but the ones who stood to gain the most from it.[1] Taken as a whole, they had no mercy or compassion on the poor, but sought only their own welfare and benefit. They had become a selfish, self-centered, and self-absorbed priesthood.

When Jesus overturns the tables and expels both the sellers and the buyers from the temple, He is not attempting to clean the outside of the cup like the religious Pharisees (Matt. 23:25-26). By a powerful prophetic act, He is showing contempt for the selfishness and greed that fuels such profanity from the inside. By driving out both seller and buyer, Jesus issues a judgment upon a corrupt religious system, a corrupt religious priesthood, and a corrupt religious people who participate in it either as the perpetuating agents or as passive victims. Whether as an active (seller) or passive (buyer) participant, each one was partly responsible.[2]

The issue of disobedience that Jesus is confronting and contrasting with His house of prayer is mostly an internal dimension. He is concerned with the corruption of the people's hearts, and the priests are the primary offenders. Beyond the literal dishonesty and acts of thievery taking place by the sellers in the temple, the priests were primarily a band of violent robbers who were seeking to obtain or enjoy from God that which they had no legal right to due to their corrupt internal architecture and hearts of disobedience. They hid behind God and religion as a covering or camouflage for their own greed and covetousness like a robber in those days would hide out in a cave or den. These ungodly systems affected the people by extension.

It is no coincidence that when Jesus initiates a true prayer initiative, the chief priests are the first to become offended. Jesus ministers mercy and compassion to the blind and the lame—two categories of people who were previously forbidden from entering the temple and who represent the rejected and those with the greatest need (2 Sam. 5:8). This result is an exultant declaration of praise from the children. The chief priests become *indignant*, which is translated from a Greek verb meaning "to be stirred up in anger" (v. 15). They are enraged because of the hypocrisy and corruption that exists in their own hearts. Rather than becoming offended or indignant at the corruption that was permitted to continue at the temple, they become indignant at the accurate reformation initiative being displayed by Jesus.

Jesus doesn't just criticize and judge what was wrong; He corrects the error by giving a practical example of what is right. In this instance, the *prayer* Jesus has in mind is acted out through a practical (yet supernatural) demonstration of love, mercy, and compassion toward those who were rejected, spiritually deprived, and had the greatest physical need.[3] By allowing them access to come and receive healing, Jesus meets their spiritual, physical, social, and financial needs. This is the house of prayer that Jesus is seeking to emphasize.

THE HOUSE CONCEPT

The fact that God chose a *house* as the word picture or symbol with which to identify prayer is of great significance. It is indicative of something that is built or being built through a process of skill, effort, resource, and architecture. Constructing a house is a process of predetermined design, not wishful thinking or chance. The result stands integrated and connected as a whole, not isolated and separate. So what does all this have to do with prayer? Everything!

PRAYER CANNOT EXIST OR BE EFFECTIVE INDEPENDENTLY FROM THE FOUNDATION GOD INTENDED FOR IT TO BE BUILT UPON.

Prayer is associated with a house because both have form and structure. When Jesus teaches His disciples how to pray in Matthew chapter 6, He is teaching them the proper form and structure of prayer from a Kingdom perspective (Matt. 6:5-15). But more than a formula for prayer, which is how the vast majority of us normally view it, Jesus is actually releasing powerful insight and technology regarding the Kingdom of God being established in the earth. This model prayer of Jesus contains powerful Kingdom architecture that will totally

34

revolutionize your understanding of prayer. (We will discuss this in some detail toward the end of this book.)

The fact that God's house is *called*—which is indicative of its nature, character, and destiny—a *house of prayer*, with a clearly defined form and structure, alludes to the principle that it must also have a foundation. The foundation determines the strength and accuracy of the structure. A house is only as good as the foundation it is built upon.

In other words, prayer cannot exist or be effective independently from the foundation God intended for it to be built upon. Therefore, when Jesus boldly opposes the corruption that is taking place in the part of the temple complex known as the Court of the Gentiles, His main grievance, as we have already discovered, is not the lack of formal, private, or liturgical prayer taking place in the courtyard. His grievance is the lack of obedience—the missing foundation—which nullifies the accuracy and true nature of the house and instead causes it to conform to the nature of a *den of thieves*.

A TRUE HOUSE OF PRAYER IS NOT DEFINED BY ITS NUMBER OF PRAYER MEETINGS OR RELIGIOUS GATHERINGS, BUT BY THE LEVEL OF OBEDIENCE THAT OCCURS REGARDING WHAT GOD HAS COMMANDED OR REQUIRED.

Based on this understanding, and approaching this principle from a corporate dimension, it should be clear to us that a true *house of prayer* is not defined by the number of prayer meetings, prayer gatherings, prayer services, prayer vigils, prayer walks, or all-nighters that take place within the church walls. The frequency, level, or intensity of oral prayer petitions taking place within a corporate gathering has no validating or authenticating influence upon what God describes as His *house*. What truly defines a *house of prayer* is the level of obedience that occurs regarding what God has commanded or required. As a matter of fact, the kind of obedience that God requires extends much deeper and further than outward religious conformity; it must permeate the heart so that the greed, selfishness, and corruption of the flesh do not exist. When this level of obedience is absent from our prayers, we become thieves and robbers seeking to obtain from God something we have no biblical right to. Our prayers become self-focused because of the greed and selfishness within our own hearts.

Let me interject here to point out that *all* of the house or temple was to be called a *house of prayer*, not just a particular part. No part of the house existed independently of the rest. (We will discuss this principle in greater detail in the chapter titled "Myths and Misconceptions.") This particular temple, known as Herod's Temple, had numerous chambers, courts, and rooms connected to it. As we have already explained, Jesus never had personal access to the most significant of these, since He was not a priest in any earthly religious system. Like most of the Israelite population, Jesus could enter no further than the courts surrounding the main temple (or temple proper). The *Court of the Gentiles* where Jesus is believed to have made His pronouncement was considered by both priest and people to be the least sacred or spiritual part of the temple, with no organized or structured religious activity whatsoever. Nevertheless, in Jesus' estimation, He expected the same level of devotion and obedience in the least part of the temple as He would expect from the main sanctuary where the priests ministered. The standard and level of obedience required remained consistent and applied equally to every part (or member), from the greatest to the least (or from the pulpit to the pew).

In other words, there is a single standard that God expects to be applied to every individual member. The corporate standard is the same as the individual standard. There is no difference. This type of prayer being defined and level of obedience being required is not only for pastors and leaders—it is for *everyone*! God expects everyone (not only specific groups or leaders) to pray both individually and corporately. And for prayer to be biblical and effective it must be accompanied by, built, and founded upon the principle of obedience. True, biblical prayer can never function independently from the required obedience God designed to accompany and empower it. This cohesive union or interconnection between prayer and obedience is a product of faith.

KEY PRINCIPLES

1. There is a deep and profound connection between prayer and obedience.

2. Prayer is much more than an oral declaration or request; it is a lifestyle.

3. From God's perspective, prayer has very little to do with what we actually say and everything to do with how we live and what we do.

4. We cannot gain access to God's house of prayer without meeting the prerequisite of obedience.

5. When we show disobedience or a blatant disregard for God's righteous requirements, we are no longer a legal or legitimate member of God's household (of prayer). Instead, we become thieves and robbers who are trying to gain illegitimate access to the resources of heaven without having any right to them.

6. Prayer is associated with a house because both have form and structure.

7. Prayer cannot exist or be effective independently from the foundation God intended for it to be built upon—*obedience*.

8. The kind of obedience that God requires extends much deeper and further than outward religious conformity; it must permeate the heart so that the greed, selfishness, and corruption of the flesh do not exist.

9. God expects everyone (not only specific groups or leaders) to pray both individually and corporately.

ENDNOTES

1. The vendors would have been required to pay a fee to peddle their trade on temple property, and everything sold in the temple would have inevitably reverted back to the priests or to their benefit.
2. We become enablers when we willfully participate in a religious system that is deviant and corrupt. Every time we give money for so-called "prayer cloths," "miracle water," or "breakthrough" prayer, we are effectively being complicit and supportive of error.
3. The blind and the lame were usually beggars due to the fact that they could not work on account of their physical conditions.

CHAPTER 3

FAITH AND OBEDIENCE

A statement that is often-repeated, especially in Christian circles, says, "There is power in prayer." This very popular idiom is misleading, however. If this was actually the case, Muslims would be the most powerful group of people on the earth. I have Muslim friends and relatives, so I know for a fact that in general Muslims are much more disciplined and devoted to their religious practices—especially when it comes to prayer—than the vast majority of believers and self-proclaimed "Christians." So if there is power in prayer alone, Muslims are the undisputed juggernauts.

It takes faith to make prayer potent (James 5:15). Prayer is not simply the utterance of words, requests, supplications, petitions, or desires. Whether religiously inclined or not, people pray this way all the time without ever having their prayers answered or effecting any change. So the utterance of mere words or petitions alone, no matter how desperate, does not guarantee results. Without faith our prayers are only wishful rants, powerless and incapable of producing anything but noise.

Faith, as many of us know, *"comes by hearing, and hearing by the word of God"* (Rom. 10:17 NKJV). So if faith only *comes* by hearing, and hearing by the Word of God, then faith can only be *exercised* by doing and being obedient to the Word of God! In other words, we can only *receive* faith by *hearing*, but we can only *exercise* faith by *doing*. Therefore faith is nullified without corresponding acts of obedience, and, by extension, so is prayer (James 2:14-20).

THE CORRECT FOUNDATION

True prayer is built upon a foundation of faith and obedience, not need or desire. There are billions of people in the earth with unmet needs and countless desires that will remain unfulfilled despite their many desperate cries to God for help. Prayer is unanswered due to the fact that we have neglected to build accurately and upon a correct foundation.

TRUE PRAYER IS BUILT UPON A FOUNDATION OF FAITH AND OBEDIENCE, NOT NEED OR DESIRE.

God is not moved by needs—that is not what moves God. It's not that He doesn't care. But when our prayer is built upon a poor foundation, it becomes impotent and ineffective. It doesn't matter how long or how hard we pray; if biblical faith and obedience are absent, it's like trying to start a car without an engine—it just won't work. God in His mercy may sometimes choose to deliver us in spite of our inaccuracies and our ignorance, but this becomes the exception and not the norm.

> *"Everyone then who hears these words of mine and does them will be like a wise man who built his house on the rock. And the rain fell, and the floods came, and the winds blew and beat on that house, but it did not fall, because it had been founded on the rock. And everyone who hears these words of mine and does not do them will be like a foolish man who built his house on the sand. And the rain fell, and the floods came, and the winds blew and beat against that house, and it fell, and great was the fall of it."*
> (Matthew 7:24-27 ESV)

42

You will notice that the word *house* is mentioned several times throughout this passage. It is not the exact Greek word used in Matthew 21:13; however, it is a female derivative of the exact male noun translated *house* and can be applied in a similar dimension. This means that the *house of prayer* principle quoted by Jesus from the prophets Isaiah and Jeremiah and the principle being described here are indirectly related. Therefore, whatever houses of prayer we are seeking to build, whether individually or corporately—meaning whether in our personal prayer lives or during public worship gatherings as a Kingdom community—they must be subjected to the same fundamental principles described in this text.

FOR PRAYER TO BE EFFECTIVE AND FUNCTIONAL, WE MUST HAVE A READINESS TO HEAR COUPLED WITH A WILLINGNESS TO OBEY.

Houses must have a foundation, which effectively determines their strength and longevity when tested by the elements. Both the wise and the foolish will have their houses tested, but the key is in the foundation. Even though both the wise man and the foolish man *heard* the words being spoken by Jesus and both were tested, only the wise man was fortunate enough to have what he had built not fall into ruin. This is because he was willing to put into practice what he heard. The foolish man was not that fortunate, however, because even though he managed to hear everything the wise man heard, he was never obedient. His disobedience thus caused the demise of the house he had built.

This principle also applies to the issue of prayer as it relates to a house or community of Kingdom citizens and blood-bought saints (1 Pet.

2:5; Heb. 3:6). We understand that prayer cannot exist in a vacuum on its own without the proper foundation. It doesn't matter how good or compelling the structure looks on the outside—the fancy words, eloquent speech, scripture quotations, or passionate cries—when the foundation (which is usually hidden) is inaccurate, shifting, or unstable like sand.

The difference between sand and rock is quite interesting. While rock is a firm, solid matter made up of tiny individual particles (such as sand), sand consists of individual particles that have never been molded or forged together to form a whole (like a rock). They are loose, individual grains without any consistency, integrity, or wholeness. Sand shifts and flows with the wind, making it a very unreliable and unstable foundation. It is symbolic of a lack of integrity, character, and internal accuracy, and it speaks of a disconnection between what we say and what we do or who we really are.

Please note that even though the wise man built accurately and upon a good and reliable foundation, he was not immune to adversity. Storms of adversity come to everyone! His accurate foundation did not preclude or deliver him from the storms. The accuracy of his foundation enabled him to withstand the storms, not stop or prevent them. This is the principle of prayer.

For prayer to be effective and functional, we must have a readiness to hear (which produces faith) coupled with a willingness to obey (which is how we exercise faith).

> *Beloved, if our heart does not condemn us, we have confidence toward God. And whatever we ask we receive from Him, **because we keep His commandments and do those things that are pleasing in His sight**. And this is His commandment: that we should believe on the name of His Son Jesus Christ and love one another, as He gave us commandment* (1 John 3:21-23 NKJV; emphasis mine).

According to John, our prayers or requests to God are effectively answered due to the fact that we are obedient to God's commandments and do those things that are pleasing to Him rather than pursuing our own pleasures. This implies that prayer becomes both impotent and ineffective when we demonstrate a lack of obedience or develop lifestyles that pursue our own pleasures rather than God's. We should not expect to receive anything from God when we are operating from a place of disobedience.

DISOBEDIENCE NULLIFIES PRAYER

Prayer and obedience are inseparable; therefore, a lack of obedience—disobedience—nullifies prayer! This is a very profound and important principle—and it is the area where believers miss it the most. Before we attempt to ask God for anything, we should first check to make sure that we have done what He has required.

It is worth mentioning here that this refers not only to outward acts of obedience but to internal heart issues as well (Ps. 66:18), as we will examine further in the following chapter. In fact, internal obedience is the first area that John addresses in the text above because he understood that the issues of life flow out of the heart (Prov. 4:23). When the source of our lives is corrupt, it corrupts everything else, including our thoughts and behavior. So in addition to checking whether or not we have done what is required before we pray, we should also take the time to examine our own hearts lest we pray in vain.

For example, we can't hate our brother or harbor unforgiveness in our hearts toward someone and then pray for forgiveness or healing from disease. Our hatred or unforgiveness will nullify our prayers. First we must correct our heart posture and actions (or inactions) by repenting of and getting rid of the hate or unforgiveness, and then we can expect to receive mercy and healing.

The same applies to dishonoring one's parents. The first commandment with promise is that we honor our parents. In doing so we are promised long life (Ex. 20:12). When we disregard God's commandments and dishonor our parents, we open up a door for premature death, which may be effected by cancer, some other terminal disease, or a fatal accident.[1] Until we exercise repentance, and/or a change of behavior if our parents are still alive, no amount of prayer is going to free us from our afflictions.

On a more practical level, if you are a student, don't ask God to help you in your exams if you have not been faithful and diligent in your studies. God rewards diligence, not slothfulness (Prov. 10:4; 13:4). No amount of praying is going to deliver you from the consequences of your own wrong actions (or inaction).

Prayer requires obedience to operate. When obedience is neglected, prayer is nullified.

John also upholds and confirms the truth taught by Jesus that the commandments of God can be summarized and condensed into two specific areas. The first area is vertical and is demonstrated through a deep and radical love for God. The second is horizontal and addresses our relationships and practical expressions of love for each other (Matt. 22:35-40). Biblical obedience is committed to, and expressed through, both areas. Any area of lack creates a weakness or deficiency in our foundations.

KNOWING THE WILL OF GOD

*Now this is the confidence that we have in Him, that if we ask anything **according to His will**, He hears us* (1 John 5:14; emphasis mine).

Another important issue, which John identifies in the text above, is the issue of knowing and understanding God's will. We can't ask or pray according to God's will if we don't know what His will is. Therefore, we first need to know and understand what God's will is before we can accurately pray according to it. It is commonly stated, "Faith begins where the will of God is known." So if we're ignorant of God's will, we can't have faith, and without faith we won't have the corresponding acts of obedience to make prayer powerful and effective.

The obvious implication from the text is that God does not hear, or chooses to ignore, prayers or petitions that are not in harmony with His divine intent. God is not egotistical, but neither is He obligated to conform to our pitiful, lowly standards. His ways are higher than our ways just as His thoughts are higher than our thoughts because He operates from a higher heavenly dimension (Is. 55:9). Instead of trying to bring God down to our level, we are responsible for elevating ourselves to His. This starts by learning His ways (Ps. 25:4; Rom. 12:2; Eph. 2:4-6; 4:20-24).

THE KEY TO GOD HEARING US IS IN US HEARING GOD!

When we are ignorant of God's will and ways, we lack faith. And when faith is lacking—with the corresponding obedience—prayer becomes ineffective. Therefore, not only does disobedience nullify prayer, but so does ignorance because it nullifies the faith by which prayer is powerfully activated. We should not be surprised then that one of Paul's major concerns for the community of believers in various regions was addressing this particular issue:

"For I do not desire, brethren, that you should be ignorant of this mystery..." (Romans 11:25 NKJV).

"Now concerning spiritual gifts, brethren, I do not want you to be ignorant" (1 Corinthians 12:1 NKJV).

"That the God of our Lord Jesus Christ, the Father of glory, may give to you the spirit of wisdom and revelation in the knowledge of Him, the eyes of your understanding being enlightened; that you may know..." (Ephesians 1:17-18 NKJV).

"For this reason we also... do not cease to pray for you, and to ask that you may be filled with the knowledge of His will in all wisdom and spiritual understanding... increasing in the knowledge of God" (Colossians 1:9-10 NKJV).

"But I do not want you to be ignorant, brethren, concerning those who have fallen asleep, lest you sorrow as others who have no hope" (1 Thessalonians 4:13 NKJV).

Two of the most powerful prayers ever prayed by an apostle for a community of Kingdom citizens were prayed by Paul in this regard. Paul obviously did not want the people to remain ignorant, and neither does God. He has made every provision necessary for us to access His divine database; the problem is that we often neglect to. He has given us His Word, and allowing our minds to be renewed by His Word daily enables us to better discern His voice.

GIVING GOD'S WORD PREEMINENCE

Every one of us wants God to hear us, but seldom do we take the time to hear God. We have tried to put the cart before the horse: In all actuality, the key to God hearing us is in *us hearing God!* Our prayers will never go beyond our ability to hear and obey. The Word of God must be given preeminence in everything we do.

Unfortunately, this is where the majority of us fail. Many of the people I have met who claim to be "prayer warriors" and "intercessors" seem to be biblically illiterate, or at least semi-illiterate. This observation is often especially true among those who appear to place much higher value on the amount of time or hours spent in the verbal exercise of what is traditionally called prayer, while placing very little time or emphasis on the study of God's Word. Many of them also claim to be "prophetic" when in reality they're mostly pathetic. Our ability to accurately discern the voice of God will never exceed our knowledge and understanding of Scripture—the written Word. Our prayers will never be any more effective than the Word (foundation) they are built upon. Therefore our emphasis should always be placed upon the Word, both in increasing our understanding as well as in obedience.

God made a profound declaration through Hosea the prophet:

> *My people are destroyed for lack of knowledge;*
> *because you have rejected knowledge,*
> *I reject you from being a priest to me.*
> *And since you have forgotten the law of your God,*
> *I also will forget your children.* (Hosea 4:6 ESV)

The context of this passage is very interesting but often overlooked. Israel, God's chosen people who are a type and shadow of God's redeemed Kingdom Covenant Community (Church), is charged by God with having no truth (faithfulness, stability), no mercy (kindness, steadfast love), and no knowledge of God in their midst (v. 1). For the people who are supposed to be God's representatives in the earth and demonstrating His character, this is quite an indictment!

God identifies several areas where the Israelites demonstrated moral depravity, especially as related to their interpersonal relationships—areas that clearly violated the ten basic laws of the Covenant (the Ten Commandments). Then God relates the consequences this sinful behavior will have upon the people, their land (including air and sea), and their natural resources.

This is where things get interesting. Humans normally have a tendency to point fingers in the wrong direction when things go wrong.

Here God specifically charges the Israelites not to do so because He has already identified who is to blame.

The economy was failing due to a lack of resources, and death and lack were present. But contending with the devil would not help because he was not the cause. Blaming the government leaders would not help because they were not the cause. God places the blame squarely upon the priests, with the prophets being condemned to a lesser degree (vs. 4-5).

Bear in mind that the two ministries of the priest and the prophet were to be an embodiment of true intercession. The priests were *intercessors* because they were the mediators between man and God, or from man to God. The prophets also were *intercessors* because they were the mediators between God and man, or from God to man. However, a lack of prayer or intercession was not the cause of Israel's destruction; neither was it a lack of priests or prophets. The cause of Israel's troubles was a lack of knowledge.

Imagine a priesthood functioning and performing their religious duties according to the norm, offering prayers as incense and sacrifices before God on behalf of the people and themselves. Imagine the religious leaders gathering faithfully in the temple during religious festivals with great pomp and pageantry as they led the people in worship before God. Imagine the prophets prophesying great encouraging words with promises of future blessing and breakthrough despite the present lack. Yet despite the huge number of priests and numerous sacrifices, fastings, intercessions, and prayers being offered both corporately as well as privately, the nation was still being destroyed! Despite the ministry of numerous prophets and prophecies, they were still being consumed! With all their religious and pseudo-spiritual activity, they still didn't know God.

Does that remind you of churches and believers today? Have we not grown accustomed to believing that more prayer (in our traditional understanding) is the answer to our problems? Do we not try to contend with satan, demons, governments, and leaders over issues for which our own careless disregard for God's righteous laws and requirements are at fault?

The priests and the prophets were ultimately at fault because they were the ones responsible for first knowing and then teaching God's laws to the people. They had neglected to study and appropriate God's laws (His written Word) in their own lives, and they had forsaken the responsibility to teach God's laws to the people. They could no longer accurately articulate or demonstrate the heart and character of God through sound biblical teaching or through the precise internal architecture and configuration of holy lives. This caused such a distortion of God's original divine intent that the very operating system of the nation began to crash. The preponderance of "illegal operations" being performed brought further ignorance,[2] spiritual anarchy, and lack of divine governance, thus causing the people to self-destruct.

TRUE KNOWLEDGE OF GOD IS DEMONSTRATED BY LOVE, KINDNESS, AND COMPASSION TOWARD OUR FELLOW MAN.

Note that God rejects such an ignorant and illegitimate priesthood— one that is unwilling or unable to develop the diligence and discipline necessary to pursue divine knowledge and truth by regularly and consistently interfacing with the divine omniscience of God as expressed through His eternal Word. To put it simply, God will reject any ministry that neglects, rejects, or does not highly value His Word or apply it to everyday life.

Because Israel's leaders neglected or forgot the foundation, all of their ministry, prayer, intercession, and prophesying was in vain. The foundation will always be the most important part of the house. The

51

Word of God must always be the most important element in our lives. We can't neglect the foundation and the principle of erudition and expect to stand. If God would not accept the children of Israel's priestly prayers, sacrifices, offerings, or ministry because of their scriptural neglect, what makes us think He will accept ours?

If the house of Israel was destroyed due to a lack of knowledge, then the reverse is true also. The house of Israel—God's Covenant Kingdom Community, including God's house of prayer—will be built by knowledge (Prov. 24:3-4).

TRUE KNOWLEDGE EQUALS OBEDIENCE

It's worth noting here that our true knowledge of God is demonstrated in our love, kindness, and compassion toward our fellow man—our obedience. It's also worth noting that Israel, specifically the priesthood, was reprimanded not only for neglecting or forsaking knowledge but for forgetting or despising what they had already heard and been taught. Only a hypocrite and a fool would seek to increase in knowledge while ignoring his responsibility to be faithful to what he has already learned. The foolish man's house didn't fall due to a lack of knowledge but due to a lack of integrity and faithfulness regarding what he had heard (Matt. 7:26-27). Most of us are in a ditch and our prayers are ineffective not because of what we don't know, but because of what we have failed to put into practice.

A RECENT EXAMPLE

While I was writing this chapter I received a call from a woman requesting prayer. She began to relay to me how she lived in a certain housing development that sounded like a housing complex or gated community of some sort, with different units or condos sharing the same property. She had a neighbor who had a dog(s) who lived right next door to her, but the neighbor would not clean up after her dog when it was out in the yard or shared compound. The caller was offended by this because the smell was invading her airspace.

The caller had complained to the housing association as well as to the neighbor, and had requested that the neighbor purchase some sort of product to use in the areas that the dog had sullied. She told me that her neighbor rudely refused and slammed the door shut in her face. Strife now existed between the neighbors, and she wanted me to pray because she didn't have any peace.

My immediate response was, "This is not an issue that requires prayer—at least not from me—it requires obedience!" I told her that if she was expecting me to pray that her neighbor would be more understanding and acquiesce to her request, I couldn't do that. The Kingdom of God doesn't operate that way. We are never to pray prayers to try to manipulate or control the free will of others. Only satanic covens and those who practice witchcraft do so.

I informed her that the biblical response was not to try to enforce her "rights," but to lay aside her rights in a demonstration of love and long-suffering toward her neighbor. I reminded her of Jesus' command to love our enemies, which includes blessing and praying for them (Matt. 5:43-48). I also instructed her to take a step of faith and make peace with her neighbor rather than just have someone pray for the situation. I suggested that she bake the dog owner a cake or purchase her a present of some sort, so that she would see the love of God demonstrated through this woman instead of seeing her bitterness and resentment. By doing so she would melt the ice, accurately reflect the Kingdom, and most likely win a neighbor and eradicate strife.

The caller listened attentively as I explained this biblical application to her situation and agreed. She was able to see that God wanted to demonstrate His love through her to her neighbor and was willing to lay down her own rights. Once she was able to make that shift from what she carnally wanted to exercising the will of God in this situation by expressing His love and mercy to her neighbor, I was confident that we could now pray because we would be operating in the perfect will of God and our prayers would be in accordance with His divine purpose. I prayed that God would cause the light of His love to shine brighter and brighter through her life so that she would be an effective witness and ambassador of Christ within her community. Upon completion of this prayer we ended the call. I have yet to receive any feedback from this caller, but I am absolutely confident that if she followed through on her part of obedience that God heard and answered powerfully. It is impossible for this type of prayer to fail.

> *WE ARE NEVER TO PRAY PRAYERS TO TRY TO MANIPULATE OR CONTROL THE FREE WILL OF OTHERS. THIS IS A FORM OF WITCHCRAFT.*

The point of this story is to show the precedence of biblical understanding and obedience, as well as to point out how many of our perceived problems can be fixed if we would simply take the time to focus on the correct biblical response. It is not enough to keep rehearsing religious prayers. We can "bind" the devil and "loose" whatever we want, but nothing is going to change until we receive faith from His Word and learn to exercise it in obedience.

I know some preachers and "prayer warriors" who would have taken that woman's request and tried to bind the "spirit of strife" or "demon" working through the neighbor that was trying to hinder the peace of the caller. Some would have even gone so far as to pray that unless the neighbor changed her attitude, that judgment would fall upon her and/or her dog(s), or that she would be removed from the premises so that a more peaceful or godly neighbor could occupy her home. Not only are such prayers inaccurate and void of the love of God, but they're satanic in origin and have no part in the Kingdom of God. God never designed prayer for the purpose of inflicting punishment or judgment upon others. And, as stated before, any attempt—whether through prayer or any other means—to manipulate or control the free will of others is a form of witchcraft.

CULTIVATING EFFECTIVENESS IN PRAYER

An effective prayer life is not necessarily one that spends two to three hours or more each day petitioning and crying out before God (Matt. 6:7; 23:14). An effective prayer life is one that spends ample time in the Word, seeks to grow in understanding, and continually walks in faith and obedience according to the revealed will of God. Our very lives can become a prayer so that there is no disconnect between what we say and what we actually do. Then our 15 minutes of oral prayer will accomplish much more than the 15 hours of prayer by one who has a poor or inaccurate foundation.

WE MUST SEEK KNOWLEDGE WITH THE INTENT TO OBEY.

If you're accustomed to spending two to three hours a day in oral prayer, you should be spending double that time studying the Word. I'm not talking about study for the mere accumulation of knowledge, because all that produces is hypocrisy and pride (1 Cor. 8:1). The study I'm referring to here comes from a desire to know God, understand His ways, renew our minds, and transform our lives. It is allowing the seed of God's Word to enter deep within us to impregnate us so that we can reproduce Christ in the earth. The knowledge we are seeking here is not simply head knowledge. It's a deep experiential knowledge similar to the principle found in Genesis 4:1 when Adam *knew* Eve his wife, causing conception and birth. We seek knowledge with the intent to obey.

It doesn't matter how much time you spend trying to beautify or work on the structure through memorization of scriptures, fancy clichés, or eloquent speech. If your foundation is weak through disregard for God's Word, it will all come toppling down! It doesn't matter how good your aim is if you have no bullets in your gun. And if you do have bullets in your gun, you better learn how to aim.

When your focus is on growing in understanding and obedience, you will notice that you accomplish more with less. This doesn't necessarily mean that you spend less time with God, but your time with Him will be much more profitable and effective. You will be more focused on God reproducing Himself in you than on uploading a bunch of carnal requests to Him. You will learn to listen more and talk less. You will stop praying silly prayers. You will learn to operate within the boundaries of your spiritual authority. And most of all, you won't be blinded by selfishness or carnal pursuits.

When we operate from this dimension we become healed from our hypocrisy. No longer will we imprudently ask God to do what we have been given the power to do on our own. This means that when my brother or sister has a need, I don't just offer up vain prayers or petitions to God on behalf of him or his need when I have the power to fulfill it. Why pray for my brother who is believing for God to provide him with a vehicle to get to work when there are two or three cars parked in my garage? Wouldn't it make more sense for me to donate one of my cars? Is it possible that God blessed me with three cars for the very purpose of meeting the need in my brother's life?

Why pray for your sister to get her rent and electric bill paid when there are thousands of dollars nestling in your bank account for a "rainy day"? Does it matter to you that your sister is presently having a rainy day and needs your help? Why go to God when it is in your power to meet the need? How can we claim to have faith to see someone's need met when we have the means to meet it ourselves but we're unwilling to?

56

Wouldn't our faith be more accurately demonstrated or expressed through our willingness to help meet the need?

FAITH WORKS BY LOVE

Faith works by love, and prayer works by faith (Gal. 5:6). We can't have one without the other and still be considered accurate. Each of these alone is not correct technology (1 Cor. 13:1-3). One of the consistent themes found throughout this book is love and how this virtue relates to faith, obedience, and prayer. As we saw in Chapter 1, prayer was first introduced in Scripture, in an official capacity, as a means of helping others and demonstrating love. When Jabez prayed his now-famous prayer, he was motivated by love. Every time we examined an account of the principle of prayer and obedience being violated in Scripture, it was both vertical as well as horizontal: Vertical in the aspect of our relationship to God, and horizontal in the aspect of our relationships with each other.

We can't love God and hate our brother.

If anyone says, "I love God," and hates his brother, he is a liar; for he who does not love his brother whom he has seen cannot love God whom he has not seen. And this commandment we have from him: whoever loves God must also love his brother. (1 John 4:20-21 ESV)

Most believers would probably read this text and casually excuse themselves by thinking it does not apply to them simply because they do not harbor any feelings of hate or emotional resentment toward any brother or sister in the Kingdom. But that is not primarily what the text is teaching. John qualifies his message by giving us an example of how true love is manifested, and the example makes it clear that love goes beyond emotional sentiment or words.

*Beloved, let us love one another, for love is from God, and whoever loves has been born of God and knows God. Anyone who does not love does not know God, because God is love. In this the love of God was made manifest among us, that God sent his only Son into the world, so that we might live through him. In this is love, not that we have loved God but that he loved us and sent his Son to be the propitiation for our sins. **Beloved, if God so loved us, we also ought to love one another.** (1 John 4:7-11 ESV; emphasis mine)*

John's argument is simple: God is love and love is from God. Those of us who have been truly born of God will love like God loves. In fact, anyone who doesn't love has no knowledge of God at all. God is the ultimate example. He revealed true love to us not primarily by what He thought or said but by what He did. He gave the ultimate gift, the ultimate sacrifice—His only Son—not in response to our love, but to initiate and demonstrate His own. God gave His only Son who emptied Himself of everything in response to a need that humankind could not meet. We had no way of paying the debt of sin, so Jesus was given as the payment and propitiation for all. This is how God expects us to love!

The love that John is describing here is a willingness to act and make the necessary sacrifices—no matter how great—for our brother or sister. This is a love that is willing to dig deep and sacrifice, not just in response to the love he or she once showed to us or for a favor owed, but when he or she is either incapable or unwilling to show love to us in return. It is totally selfless! This implies that the hate John is referring to in verse 20 is not an emotional disposition but a heart or mentality of indifference. It is an unwillingness to act on our brother's behalf in his time of need. It is an unwillingness to inconvenience ourselves for our sister's benefit. This is the biblical definition of hate. I know…ouch!

It gets worse! According to John, to hate our brother—which is to deny him true love—is the equivalent of being a murderer, thus making us void of eternal life!

Everyone who hates his brother is a murderer, and you know that no murderer has eternal life abiding in him.

By this we know love, that he laid down his life for us, and we ought to lay down our lives for the brothers. But if anyone has the world's goods and sees his brother in need, yet closes his heart against him, how does God's love abide in him? Little children, let us not love in word or talk but in deed and in truth. (1 John 3:15-18 ESV)

Loving just in word or talk includes religious prayers or petitions without the correct corresponding actions. It is being unwilling to lay down our lives for our brother by substituting words or prayers for practical acts of compassion when it is within our power to do so in our brother's time of need. This type of inaction or indifference, by definition, is tantamount to killing or murdering our brother! This puts a whole new spin of understanding on the previous texts we examined from Hosea and Jeremiah. (Feel free to put a marker here and refer to those texts again.)

PRAYER DOES NOT EXCUSE US FROM STEPPING UP AND TAKING ACTION WHEN A NEED ARISES; IT DEMANDS IT!

Again God's love is held as the standard and ultimate example. God the Father gave the ultimate sacrifice in His Son, and Jesus gave the ultimate sacrifice in laying down His life for us all. This God-type of love conquers fear, which is the enemy of faith. It frees us so we are no longer immobilized by thoughts such as: *What will happen if we give this away? Will there be enough for us? What will we do if an emergency arises? Who is going to help us? How will we ever make this money back? What about our family and future?* These can be tormenting thoughts because fear has torment, *"but perfect love casts out fear"* (1 John 4:18).

Jesus Himself said that the authenticity of our faith would be demonstrated through our love one for another (John 13:35). Prayer does not excuse us from stepping up and taking action when a need arises; it demands it!

YOU BECOME THE BLESSING

An event that occurred while I was serving at a conference brought this truth home to me. I was approached by a middle-aged man while I was attending to the book tables. He told me that he had seen me the previous day making my way from the conference facility and attempting to cross the highway on foot. As he was sitting in his car in the parking lot, he felt moved to pray for me and asked God to bless me. God immediately responded by saying, "You bless him!"

As I was standing face to face with him listening to him recount this story, he suddenly reached into his pocket and pulled something out that I could not see. He looked me straight in my eyes and asked with great humility, "Can I bless you?"

Of course I responded by saying yes, at which time he gave me what he had in his hand—a hundred dollar bill! I expressed my deepest gratitude, but then after he had left I stood there silently, in deep contemplation regarding what had just occurred. I had been blessed by people before, but what he said to me regarding his prayer and God's response stuck with me for many days. I don't know how much of a sacrifice it was for him to do what he did. He was a visitor at a paid conference with lots of items to be purchased in the Exhibit Hall. He could have easily come up with a hundred different excuses to disobey

God and just stick to the religious thing of just saying a prayer, but he didn't.

I thought about the countless times I had asked God to bless someone and done nothing. It is unlikely that God did anything either because God only responds to faith. He acts when we act. It is when we do what we *can* do that God steps in and does what we *can't* do. The visitor taught me a valuable lesson that day that far exceeds the monetary gift I received. Faith works by love, and prayer is useless without it.

> *What good is it, my brothers, if someone says he has faith but does not have works? Can that faith save him? If a brother or sister is poorly clothed and lacking in daily food, and one of you says to them, "Go in peace, be warmed and filled," without giving them the things needed for the body, what good is that? So also faith by itself, if it does not have works, is dead.* (James 2:14-17 ESV)

The standard religious—albeit hypocritical—response when someone has a need is to pray. We have all done it. However, no amount of prayer or "faith" declarations of blessing are going to suffice without taking action. Our first response when there is a need should be to act, not pray. Don't ask God to bless; you be a blessing! You reach out to help and meet the need, unless doing so will ultimately hurt the person.[3]

THE CONCEPT OF COMMUNITY

This was the prevailing mentality and culture when the New Covenant Kingdom Community was first birthed in the Book of Acts.

> *And all who believed were together and had all things in common. And they were selling their possessions and belongings and distributing the proceeds to all, as any had need.* (Acts 2:44-45 ESV)

Now the full number of those who believed were of one heart and soul, and no one said that any of the things that belonged to him was his own, but they had everything in common. And with great power the apostles were giving their testimony to the resurrection of the Lord Jesus, and great grace was upon them all. There was not a needy person among them, for as many as were owners of lands or houses sold them and brought the proceeds of what was sold and laid it at the apostles' feet, and it was distributed to each as any had need. (Acts 4:32-35 ESV)

No matter how many times I have read these texts, I am continually assaulted with the level of love, community, and commitment that our early covenant brothers and sisters had toward each other. We live in a time and culture that seems so far removed from such a selfless expression that it appears almost ludicrous to suggest such a thing. Religious Christianity will ask, "How can I *pray* for you?" but true covenant Kingdom communities ask, "What can we *do* for you?" or "How can I *help* you?"

PRAYER CAN NEVER BE MADE A SUBSTITUTE FOR LOVE. LOVE IS NOT AN OPTION; IT IS A DIVINE REQUIREMENT!

These believers were so deliberate in their actions and willingness to give that they totally and radically rejected the human compulsion toward personal ownership, embracing instead a spirit of community where shared ownership and shared resource was the norm. Their faith was living and vibrant, thus moving them into radical expressions of love. They were able to completely eradicate lack in their community so that *"there was not a needy person among them."*

Please understand that community here doesn't equal entitlement. It would be very easy for the lazy, irresponsible, or greedy to view this community principle as an avenue or opportunity to depend or sustain themselves on the sweat or hard work of others. This type of attitude is a violation of the core principle of community. You don't enter into a community dynamic with a mindset of what you can obtain or get. This type of mindset is corrupt and becomes a cancer to the very community it is depending on to sustain it. True Kingdom community revolves around the principles of love and self-sacrifice. The culture inspires every member to ask, "What can I bring to the table and offer for the benefit of the whole (community)?" It is never self-seeking.

If someone in this first-century community found himself in a rut—like the majority of us do at least one time in our lives—he was given more than just a hand-out; he was given support until he was lifted out of his rut and strengthened to a place where he could help others. This is partly why the apostles became so involved in the distribution. They were responsible for making sure that every person with legitimate needs received support, while also making sure that no support went to any dishonest or greedy person seeking to exploit the system. And the people gave willingly.

I have seen people get up during a service and place money at the speaker's feet while he or she is delivering a message, usually as an act of appreciation or commendation regarding what is being shared. Perhaps you have seen the same thing. But that is not what was taking place in this scripture when the believers laid the proceeds from selling their possessions at the apostles' feet.

Firstly, this was a highly voluntary, yet deliberate act, not one spawned from an emotional high or psychological compulsion. It is one thing to give whatever we have on us at the moment, but it's another thing to deliberately assess and then liquidate our assets to give to someone else. If you've ever sold a car or a house, you will know what

I'm talking about. It takes great effort! You have to get an appraisal (probably preceded by an inspection), and there can be cleaning, fixing, and other preparation involved. Then you have to market the item to potential buyers. Next come the interviews, and so on.

Secondly, the scripture doesn't only say *"possessions,"* it specifically identified *houses* and *lands.* To understand and appreciate the gravity of this sacrifice, we have to understand the dynamics of that culture. A house or land carried an even greater value and significance to these people than it does today because it represented birthright, family inheritance, covenant, and promise (1 Kings 21:2-3). It was their greatest resource.

This act of giving, though voluntary, was as deliberate and as premeditated as it gets. It required a process of effort, after which the seller brought the proceeds to the apostles for distribution. This would imply that it wasn't some one-time event that took place during a major gathering or service. It would have required a process of days or weeks or longer, with the donors coming to the apostles during the course of each day and bringing their sacrificial gifts. They would have remained anonymous to the receivers of the proceeds because the apostles were the ones responsible for distributing the proceeds to the ones in need rather than the givers themselves. The apostles were trusted to have the wisdom and discernment to distribute these resources efficiently so that every need was met—and they were profoundly successful.[4]

Everyone felt indebted to everyone else and nobody received the glory for being a super philanthropist except God! But the main point of these texts is that when there was a need, instead of trying to pray and bind the spirit of lack or poverty in their brothers' lives or in their community as a whole, the believers demonstrated great effort in their sacrificial giving by being God's hands extended. Their faith, motivated by love, stirred them all to radical action so that lack was completely eliminated and eradicated from their midst.

Prayer can never be made a substitute for love. Love is not an option; it is a divine requirement!

KEY PRINCIPLES

1. It takes faith to make prayer potent.

2. Without faith our prayers are only wishful rants, powerless and incapable of producing anything but noise.

3. We can only *receive* faith by *hearing*, but we can only *exercise* faith by *doing*.

4. Faith is nullified without corresponding acts of obedience, and, by extension, so is prayer.

5. True prayer is built upon a foundation of faith and obedience, not need or desire.

6. God is not moved by needs.

7. It doesn't matter how long or how hard we pray; if biblical faith and obedience are absent, it's like trying to start a car without an engine—it just won't work.

8. For prayer to be effective and functional, we must have a readiness to hear (which produces faith) coupled with a willingness to obey (which is how we exercise faith).

9. Prayer and obedience are inseparable; therefore, a lack of obedience—disobedience—nullifies prayer!

10. Before we attempt to ask God for anything, we should first check to make sure that we have done what He has required.

11. No amount of praying is going to deliver you from the consequences of your own wrong actions (or inaction).

12. We can't ask or pray according to God's will if we don't know what His will is. Therefore, we first need to know and understand what God's will is before we can accurately pray according to it.

13. When we are ignorant of God's will and ways, we lack faith. And when faith is lacking—with the corresponding obedience—prayer becomes ineffective.

14. Our prayers will never be any more effective than the Word (foundation) they are built upon.

15. We are never to pray prayers to try to manipulate or control the free will of others.

16. An effective prayer life is one that spends ample time in the Word, seeks to grow in understanding, and continually walks in faith and obedience according to the revealed will of God.

17. Faith works by love, and prayer works by faith.

18. Prayer does not excuse us from stepping up and taking action when a need arises; it demands it!

19. Prayer can never be made a substitute for love. Love is not an option; it is a divine requirement!

ENDNOTES

1. It would be overly presumptuous to assume that *all* premature deaths are attributed to some type of sin or parental dishonor. However, the biblical implications make this a possibility that cannot be denied.
2. Ignorance begets ignorance.
3. Many people are in the rut they are in due to their own negligence or disobedience. This understanding does not give us a license to sit as judge or jury regarding whether or not a person's predicament is due to their own wrongdoing or fault, or whether or not they are deserving of help. God gives grace and mercy to us even when we are at fault, and so should we when it comes to helping others. However, there are times when we need to allow people to experience the pain of their own poor choices without seeking to bail them out, or they will never learn. If you keep giving handouts to a lazy or slothful person, they will continue to be lazy or slothful. If you keep bailing out a person who consistently mismanages their money, they will continue to mismanage it knowing that they have you as a cushion, and your gift will ultimately do more damage than good. There is a time for everything (Ecc. 3:1-8).

    A gift may bring temporary relief in the short-term, yet cause irreparable damage in the long-term. There must be wisdom in our giving. We must be careful that we do not give rise to a spirit of entitlement or empower ungodly attitudes, practices, or beliefs by our liberal giving.
4. Note that it required apostolic wisdom to properly distribute to those who genuinely needed assistance. We see the same principle again later on in chapter 6 when the Hellenistic widows were being neglected. The apostles recognized that giving oversight of the proper distribution of resources to those who were genuinely in need would place a huge demand on their time; therefore, they had seven other leaders (apparently Hellenists themselves) selected to assist in the oversight of provision for these neglected widows. The prerequisite was that they be

"full of the Holy Spirit and wisdom" (v. 3). Wisdom was a necessary requirement due to the natural human tendency of people to want to take advantage of the system. There will always be those who are selfish and lazy, seeking entitlement to live off of the hard work and effort of others. Spiritual discernment and wisdom were necessary to weed out those who were seeking to exploit the system for their own selfish benefit from those who were genuinely in need and required assistance.

CHAPTER 4

INTERNAL ARCHITECTURE

The Epistle of James happens to be chock-full of very profound and important principles regarding the Kingdom, especially as it relates to faith and prayer. James attributes the lack of answers and failure of prayer to inaccurate internal architecture.

> *Where do wars and fights come from among you? Do they not come from your desires for pleasure that war in your members? You lust and do not have. You murder and covet and cannot obtain. You fight and war. Yet you do not have because you do not ask. You ask and do not receive, because you ask amiss, that you may spend it on your pleasures.* (James 4:1-3 NKJV)

Scholars hold conflicting interpretations and arguments regarding this passage due to several factors, including the strong language that James uses regarding war, fighting, and murder in his original readers' midst. Considering the historical climate of the time and the presence of converted Zealots[1] among their company, some scholars think that there was literal warring and murdering among various factions. Rather than get into a detailed examination of the differing views, however, which are of little consequence to the actual truths being conveyed here by James, we will focus on the spiritual and the practical aspects or principles he addresses.

69

Whether literally or in principle, hostilities and fights were taking place among this company of believers. James employs very strong language to describe the level of quarreling, dissension, and strife that was occurring. However, the fighting and hostility were actually only the symptoms. Of principal importance is the cause, which James attributes to a lustful desire for personal pleasure.

This unbridled desire to *obtain* is what motivated and fueled their covetous and hateful actions, including murder. As we have already discovered, murder is the principle of hate or indifference toward our brother's practical needs. It's very hard to notice the needs of others when we're consumed with our own personal needs or lust to obtain. This self-centeredness or self-indulgence then works against us so that we are never satisfied and feel like we never have enough.

Just as war in the natural is often the result of greed or self-interest, the preoccupation with self is what causes conflict among the company of believers, whether directly or indirectly. We then fight and war in the flesh (mistakenly thinking that we are in the spirit) as we seek to obtain by force the things that we carnally desire.

James then makes a startling comment that the reason the people do not have is because they *do not ask*. This almost seems to nullify his previous comments, but then he qualifies his statement with the next one: *"You ask and do not receive because you ask amiss, that you may spend it on your pleasures."*

I actually like how the KJV translates the last part of that verse, *"...that ye may consume it upon your lusts."* This is much stronger and more applicable language. In other words, our prayers are misdirected and doomed to fail because our focus is skewed and/or corrupted by a lustful self-indulgence.

The word translated as *amiss* in the text above is translated from the Greek word *kakōs*, meaning "bad, evil, improper," or just plain "wrong."[2] It can also be applied in certain contexts to something that is diseased or sick. This is not just a case of sincerely uttered prayers emanating from well-intentioned hearts that just happen to miss the mark. What James is confronting here are prayers that are inherently wrong, evil, and corrupt because they stem from a diseased and perverse preoccupation with self.

Pleasures (*lusts* KJV) is translated from the Greek word **hēdonē**, meaning "delight, desire, enjoyment, gratification, physical (or sensual) pleasure."[3] This word is where we get our English word *hedonism*. In this context, *pleasures* communicates the idea of self-indulgence, personal gratification, and a preoccupation with one's personal needs or desires. When we become so blinded by or obsessed with ourselves, we can't see beyond us. We may talk about "the Kingdom of God," but we are really thinking about our own personal kingdoms, and we either neglect or totally ignore the needs of others as our own carnal desires take precedence.

> OUR PRAYERS ARE MISDIRECTED AND DOOMED TO FAIL WHEN OUR FOCUS IS SKEWED OR CORRUPTED BY A LUSTFUL SELF-INDULGENCE.

I want to clarify here that James is in no way endorsing these corrupt desires when he states that the people didn't have because they didn't ask. Not only would he have been contradicting his earlier statements, but he would have been undermining his following statements and his entire letter or epistle as a whole. Whatever it is that this company of believers didn't have has absolutely nothing to do with their carnal desires being unfulfilled. Rather, what these believers are lacking here and have been unable to apprehend due to a lack of correct prayer is accurate, authentic internal architecture being displayed through godly wisdom. This seems to me to be the only logical interpretation in light of

71

James' previous comments several verses prior (Jam. 3:13-18 with 1:5-8).

Instead of accurate, correct praying, these people's prayers were self-focused and corrupt, intent on fulfilling their own personal pleasure instead of God's perfect ideal. Their focus was more on accumulating than becoming, on obtaining than maturing, on selfishly satisfying personal lusts than on selflessly expressing godly love. They prayed plenty of prayers, but they were praying amiss! They were praying amiss because their internal architecture was inaccurate.

MODERN-DAY ISSUES

From preachers and pastors in church meetings and corporate religious gatherings to "regular" people during their personal times of "communion," this self-centeredness and hedonistic mentality is rampant! From pulpit to pew to personal prayer closet, the majority of prayers being offered up today fall into this category described by James. The majority of prayer requests I receive on a daily basis fall into this category. Our number one concern is our own carnal, physical, or sensual pleasures being fulfilled. We are consumed with personal gratification.

Silent (and sometimes not so silent) wars are waged by pastors and religious leaders against other churches or ministries that they see as competitors or as a threat. We verbally attack and murder each other to get ahead. Some of us take great pride in the size of our networks, denominations, churches, or ministries. Some of us boast of our influence and recognition through television and media. For others it may be how many followers we have on Facebook or Twitter. In the words of Paul, *"For all seek their own, not the things which are of Christ Jesus"* (Phil. 2:21 NKJV).

It's all about *me!* "I need a new car... I need a new house... I need a new job... I need a new iPad... I need a husband/wife..." We gather corporately and our focus remains upon us and our personal needs. We pray to God, "Bless our church... Multiply our members... Give us a bigger building... and increase our finances." Something is terribly wrong with this overemphasis upon ourselves, our churches, and our ministries while neglecting the more important matters of the Kingdom!

God's Kingdom is concerned with such things as the execution of God's justice or judgment in the earth and the practical demonstration of mercy and compassion to those who are in need. God desires to use us to extend His Kingdom beyond our local Kingdom communities and congregations to affect our various territories. To do so we must communicate an accurate message that establishes a firm foundation of faith and truth, thus producing the corresponding substance or evidence of godliness, obedience, and practical displays of love (Matt. 23:23).

GOD'S PROVISIONS ARE STRATEGICALLY LOCATED ALONG THE PATHWAY OF FAITHFUL OBEDIENCE. ~SPIRIT FILLED LIFE BIBLE~

This is not to say that God is not concerned about our personal needs, because He absolutely is. In fact, it is because of His genuine love and concern that He admonishes us not to worry or take thought concerning what we need. Did you get that? We're not even supposed to be focusing our thoughts upon our physical needs, much less our prayers! Attending to our needs is God's responsibility, and He is well aware of them; actively pursuing and intensely desiring His Kingdom is primarily ours (Matt. 6:25-34; Luke 12:22-31).

BUILDING OUR OWN KINGDOMS

Fairly recently I was asked, "What is so wrong about a church or ministry continually asking and petitioning God to meet a financial need or increase its finances? After all, how else can a church expect to see that need met if they cannot approach God about it?" I responded by saying that much of the financial shortfall or "need" experienced by churches/ministries today has nothing to do with God's Kingdom but is instead focused on their own.[4] We may ascribe much of what we are building to God, or attach the word *Kingdom* to what we are doing or saying, but most of it is fleshly, corrupt, and personal.

THE DIFFERENCE BETWEEN CHURCH AND KINGDOM

I have found that it is very easy to confuse *Church* with *Kingdom*. The "Church" or Community of believers is not the Kingdom, but it acts as the agent or representative of the Kingdom. We don't pray, "Let the church come!" but *"Let Your Kingdom come!"* (Matt. 6:10). We are not to proclaim the "gospel of the church"; we are to proclaim the *"gospel of the Kingdom"*! (Matt. 24:14). We are not called to seek or pursue the church but to seek and pursue the Kingdom (Matt. 6:33).

Building churches and ministries should never be our primary objective. They are a means to an end and not an end in themselves! The Kingdom of God should be our primary pursuit; however, it is beyond the scope of this book to discuss this issue in significant detail.

BIBLICAL PRECEDENT REGARDING FINANCIAL NEEDS

When it comes to a church or ministry praying for finances in order to help expand, maintain, or sustain itself, we would do well to consider the fact that this practice is not found in the Bible. From Genesis to Revelation—throughout all the numerous prayers recorded for our instruction and benefit from people throughout all walks of life—never once have I found a prayer in that regard.

For example, when Moses had a need for the labor and material to build the first tabernacle, he didn't call a corporate prayer gathering to cry out to God to meet the need. David did not call a prayer meeting when God put within his heart the desire to build Him a house and then gave him the blueprint for the building of the temple. Solomon didn't either, when it fell to his charge to build the actual temple, even when he still didn't have all the required resources. Neither Ezra nor Nehemiah prayed for finances in their attempts to restore the walls and temple. And we see no evidence of the apostles doing so when the Jerusalem community of Kingdom citizens was in dire need due to famine and drought.

Moses relied on the willingness of the people to give (Ex. 25:1-8; 35:4-29; 36:2-7). David financed his Kingdom enterprise—Solomon's Temple—through conquest, personal sacrifice, and the willing generosity of donors (1 Chron. 18:7-11; 22; 28-29:20). Solomon was able to overcome any lack or deficit by requesting wisdom from God, who also granted him favor so that he was able to obtain the timber needed from one of his father's allies in exchange for food (1 Kings 5:1-12). Ezra and Nehemiah were confident in the favor of government officials (Ezra 1; 7; 8:24-36; Neh. 2). And the apostles trusted God to provide through the selflessness and compassion of the saints in support of their brothers and sisters in Jerusalem during their time of need (Acts 11:27-30; Rom. 15:25-27; 1 Cor. 16:1-4; 2 Cor. 9:1-5). They understood that God's will, done God's way, will never lack God's supply (Matt. 6:26-34). In other words, God will never assign someone a task without first making sure that there is sufficient provision or resources to fulfill it. And according to one quote from the *Spirit Filled Life Bible*, "God's provisions are strategically located along the pathway of faithful obedience."

In each of these biblical examples, faith was demonstrated by taking action according to how God sovereignly directed each particular individual or leader. They remained focused upon the Kingdom task at hand and trusted God completely for favor and provision to fulfill it. To have petitioned God through prayer in such a context would have been an expression of unbelief rather than faith, demonstrating poor internal architecture.[5]

Because of their willingness to act in faith rather than pray in unbelief, every need was met and there was no lack. The internal posture of their hearts was clearly accurate because the way they prayed, or rather, didn't pray, revealed an unblemished desire to please God and fulfill His will rather than to seek to obtain. They were not seeking to build their own kingdoms.

JESUS' ACCURATE INTERNAL ARCHITECTURE—A GENUINE HEART OF THANKSGIVING—WAS THE KEY TO UNLOCKING DIVINE SUPERNATURAL PROVISION AND RESOURCE.

Jesus provides us with another compelling example. Jesus—the Head of His Kingdom Community of redeemed saints—was asked to pay a temple tax, which He was not obligated to pay but felt inclined to anyway so as not to cause offense. He didn't cry out to the Father in prayer to help Him meet this financial demand. Instead, His response was to send Peter fishing.[6] This is called *walking in faith*, as opposed to wailing in fear (Matt. 17:24-27).

A HEART OF THANKSGIVING

On two other occasions recorded in Scripture, Jesus encountered a need. The need was not personal but corporate, requiring food for a multitude of people who had been following Him. On both occasions Jesus prayed; however, His prayers were never framed as desperate petitions seeking to obtain something from the Father. Instead, He took account of what He had in His possession and *gave thanks* or *blessing* (which in the Greek carries a strong connotation of praise and thanksgiving) to God for what the Father had graciously provided (Matt. 14:13-21; 15:32-38).

Jesus' accurate internal architecture—a genuine heart of thanksgiving—was the key to unlocking divine supernatural provision and resource.[7] Selfishness and greed cannot coexist with a heart of gratitude and contentment expressed through the giving of thanks. When our prayers are issued from such a correct heart posture, we have a recognition of God's mercy and goodness. As such, the emphasis is on praising and thanking God for what He has already accomplished rather than upon obtaining what we are longing to receive. This type of selfless gratitude in prayer will accomplish much more to move heaven than selfish or self-centered petitions ever will.

SELF-CENTERED PRAYERS

Several years ago I attended a prayer meeting that was held just a day or two after a couple of major disasters had occurred overseas, during a time of great calamity and distress in various parts of the earth. Thousands of people had died, and multiplied tens of thousands were adversely affected, having lost loved ones and everything they owned and being forced to exist without a home or the basic necessities of life like food and fresh water.

Being aware of the self-centeredness of this group's prayer focus in the past, I wanted to see how they would respond when the occurrence of these calamitous events was so fresh in our minds. I remained quiet as I listened to the prayer requests being submitted by those in attendance: "Please pray for me that God would provide me with a car." "Please pray for my child's recital next week." "I need prayer for healing from…"[8] "Let's continue to pray for the ministry's finances."

After about 30 to 45 minutes of prayer that centered completely on their personal needs (or wants)—including those of the church/ministry they represented—the prayer time was ended. Not one sentimental prayer of mercy was uttered for the people in the affected regions! They didn't even pretend to care to save religious face. A car took precedence over hunger. A recital took precedence over the homeless and hurting. We were unable to look past ourselves to see the needs of others who desperately needed our help.

Mind you, as we have already discussed in the previous chapter, simply praying regarding these desperate international needs would not have been sufficient without faith and love being practically demonstrated through giving (perhaps through a relief organization like the Red Cross); however, that is beside the point. The point is that regardless of the suffering taking place on a global scale that should have jolted this group's attention away from themselves, they continued to be enveloped and preoccupied with their own personal needs or desires. Their carnal prayer focus was indicative of a much deeper issue—a corrupt internal architecture that was selfishly consumed with its own satisfaction and comfort.

It is no wonder James sternly refers to such self-centered prayers as being *bad* or *evil* (translated *amiss*) and then goes on to describe the perpetrators of such a corrupt and unholy religious act as an *"adulterous people"* (James 4:4 ESV). Such self-centered prayer is carnal and worldly, which is a perfect description of the true character of men's (all genders) hearts in the last day, especially among religious people.

LAST-DAY RELIGION

But know this, that in the last days perilous times will come: For men will be lovers of themselves, lovers of money, boasters, proud, blasphemers, disobedient to parents, unthankful, unholy, unloving, unforgiving, slanderers, without self-control, brutal, despisers of good, traitors, headstrong, haughty, lovers of pleasure rather than lovers of

God, having a form of godliness but denying its power. And from such people turn away! (2 Timothy 3:1-5 NKJV)

To properly expound upon this particular text of scripture would probably require an entire book of its own, but we will restrict our observation to the primary elements of the text that relate to the issue of internal architecture. Paul gives us a prophetic glimpse into the kind of corrupt architecture or configuration that will define men's hearts in the last day. And just in case you were to develop the false assumption that Paul is referring primarily to non-religious people or those we often refer to as being "in the world," he clarifies that the people he is referring to are very much religious, professing godliness, knowledgeable of Scripture, and yet are internally corrupt (vs. 5, 7). They are also apparently guiltless when it comes to what religion recognizes as being the "major" sins—fornication, adultery, murder, etc.

THE ACCURACY THAT GOD DESIRES IS NOT SHALLOW OR SUPERFICIAL; IT IS DEEP AND PENETRATING. HE DESIRES TRUTH IN THE INWARD PARTS.

You will notice that the issues defined by Paul are mostly *internal* rather than external, which is key to the text. In other words, these people only *outwardly* appear upright or godly; they are really *internally* corrupt. This is the reason Paul describes this time as being *perilous*. The times are perilous not because of external acts of rape, murder, terrorism, and/or violence, but because of a corrupt internal architecture in people's hearts, especially among those who are supposed to be the salt and light of the earth (Matt. 5:13-16). Such an externalized and pharisaical form of religion is so toxic and diametrically opposed to what is truly Kingdom that we are commanded to turn away from, shun, or avoid it at all cost, including all who practice it!

The first corrupt trait Paul mentions is being *lovers of themselves.* This narcissistic mentality is what fuels the perversion. Then he almost ends his list of corrupt characteristics with the term *"lovers of pleasure rather than lovers of God"* (v. 4). What is interesting about this term is that *lovers of pleasure* in the Greek (**philēdonos**) is a compound word constructed from **phílos** ("friend, loving") and **hēdonē**—the same word used by James regarding praying amiss—meaning a lover of pleasure or an obsession with self. Therefore, what Paul is describing here is the very same principle that James identified as the predominant reason for wrong prayers.

These are a religious people with only a form or external appearance of godliness, while denying the true power or effect of the gospel on the inner man. They were skilled in producing or portraying an outer image that was totally inconsistent with their inner reality.

I don't know how many times I have heard this verse quoted from various religious leaders and believers in a context where the *power—* **dúnamis**—being referred to is an externalized demonstration of supernatural power. It is used to promote the idea and belief that true godliness or religion should embrace and demonstrate the supernatural (i.e., signs, wonders, healings, and miracles) without rejecting or denying it. While this may be true to a certain extent when the principle is applied in a much broader context, it is not exactly what the text is teaching here.

The religious company being described in this text is not adverse to externalized religion or supernatural activity. This is proven by Paul's use of Jannes and Jambres (v. 8) as being similar comparisons to this corrupt religious people. Jannes and Jambres were the Egyptian magicians or sorcerers who opposed Moses by also demonstrating supernatural phenomena or "miracles." They were in no way opposed to the supernatural—they practiced it! However, the power they produced or performed did not originate from an accurate internal disposition.

Internally they were deficient, evil, and corrupt, yet they were still able to manifest miracles.

The power that Paul is describing here, however, is not an externalized one. The power that this religious company denies or resists is not external behavioral adjustments, worship expressions, or even supernatural power displays. The power that Paul is describing here, which the religious deny and resist, is the power that can penetrate their hearts and transform them internally. It is the power to transform the inside of the cup rather than just the outside (Matt. 23:26-28).

These last-days people are content with altering their behavior on the outside so that they appear righteous. To everyone but God they appear sinless and upright. They have never been caught in adultery or extra-marital affairs. They know how to talk the talk and to a large degree even walk the walk in front of other people. They pray, fast, and read their Bibles. In fact, they are always learning, which implies diligent study. They continually seek after knowledge, read books, and probably author a few of their own. They attend seminars or conferences and may even be the keynote speakers. Yet with all of their learning, they never come to the knowledge of the truth. They actually resist it! They are content with outward form and superficial knowledge, never allowing the Word of God to get deep enough inside them so that it transforms their hearts.

They may be able to powerfully manifest healing, prophecy, signs, wonders, and miracles, and may even teach or train others to do the same. Supernatural occurrences may take place in their meetings, with many followers. They may even be well-known and well respected, of good reputation for their moral uprightness or character, yet still be internally dysfunctional and corrupt. This was true of King Saul in the Old Testament and the Pharisees in Jesus' day. And this type of religious shallowness or superficiality is now commonplace in today's culture where "image is everything." God rejects this form of religion, and He commands us to do the same! (Matt. 7:21-23).

INTERNAL ACCURACY VS. EXTERNAL PERFORMANCE

It doesn't matter how good the shell of the house looks on the outside. If the interior architecture is not up to code, it can render the house uninhabitable. While the majority of us are easily impressed and enamored by what we see on the outside—the exterior design, material, and painting— the Chief Architect and Inspector looks past that to quickly scrutinize any internal violations.

> *But the LORD said to Samuel, "Do not look on his appearance or on the height of his stature, because I have rejected him. For the LORD sees not as man sees: man looks on the outward appearance, but the LORD looks on the heart."* (1 Samuel 16:7 ESV)

David is an excellent example of the kind of accurate internal architecture that God desires. He is described in Scripture as *"a man after His (God's) own heart"* (1 Sam. 13:14; Acts 13:22). In fact, he was chosen by God not because of his outward appearance—his brothers appeared much better—but because of his accurate internal architecture.

WE WILL NEVER HIT THE MARK IN OUR PRAYERS UNTIL WE HAVE ALLOWED THE HOLY SPIRIT TO TRANSFORM US FROM THE INSIDE OUT AND STRIP US OF EVERY HIDDEN THING THAT DEFILES.

The thing that really fascinates me about David is that his heart was generally always in a correct posture before God, even though he didn't always act correctly. He was guilty of some of the most heinous moral violations in Scripture, such as adultery and then the murder of one of his faithful and loyal men.[9] Yet because of his internal accuracy, David became the standard by which the kings of Israel and Judah were judged. After committing his errors, and despite his many faults and weaknesses as a man, father, husband, king, leader, and friend, God described David as being *perfect* before Him (1 Kings 11:4; 15:3 KJV). He was judged by his heart rather than by his actions.

Conversely, Saul was a man who from the start was described as being of a likable appearance (1 Sam. 9:1-2). Based on external behavior and morality alone, and compared to David, Saul was a saint! Saul never committed adultery or murdered anyone in cold blood. He didn't lie (arguably), he didn't steal, he didn't worship any idols, he didn't dishonor his parents. Most of the commandments he broke were ones given to him personally and/or privately, so few would have known whether or not he had been disobedient. As a result, he was loved and respected by all the people. Saul's emphasis throughout his life was on maintaining the proper appearance. To him, as to many today, image was everything (1 Sam. 13:8-13; 15:1-26).

Based on our values and culture today, we would heap honor upon Saul while mercilessly rejecting David. God did the opposite! He never condoned David's sin; however, He placed a much higher premium and value on David's heart and internal disposition.

David himself was always quick to repent, with true repentance. Saul, on the other hand, was rejected in spite of his appearance, his reputation, his accomplishments, and his favor among men. He was rejected because he was deficient in accurate internal architecture, preferring an outward form of godliness that sought the applause of people rather than the deep, penetrating accuracy that brings the approval of God. One was a man after God's own heart while the other was a man after his own—a lover of pleasure rather than a lover of God!

The accuracy that God desires is not shallow or superficial; it is deep and penetrating. He desires truth in the inward parts (Ps. 51:6). It doesn't matter what people think of us. What does God think of us? Have we allowed ourselves to be totally and profoundly consumed by His passion and love? We will never hit the mark in our prayers until we have allowed the Holy Spirit to transform us from the inside out and strip us of every hidden thing that defiles and corrupts. We have to die to our own selfish desires and predispositions. We have to be more committed to the power of God working *in* us rather than merely focusing or settling on it working *through* us.

Judas was able to allow the miracle-working power of God to work through him without ever letting it work deeply within his heart to cure him of his own selfishness, misplaced priorities, and lustful indulgence. His incorrect internal architecture remained unchanged and untouched. The emphasis should always be upon what is happening on the inside (Luke 10:20).

God's standard of perfection is much different from ours. It is a perfection that is defined not by outward performance or external behavioral modifications but by the internal accuracy and posture of one's heart. This is not to say that God does not desire correct behavior, only that He desires something much deeper. Form is useless without substance. What use is a cup if the outside is clean and the inside remains contaminated? Everyone who drinks from the cup is going to be contaminated also. What use is a body without the life-giving spirit? Eventually it will stink and become toxic. What use is a lightbulb if the internal fuse is not intact? It will never be able to give any light.

Form only has meaning when there is internal substance. Our good works and good performance mean nothing unless they emanate from a correct internal disposition. Anyone can do the right thing with the wrong motives. True correctness is when internal accuracy produces correct behavior. The heart is the source and issue of life; therefore, it is impossible to be internally accurate and not produce external evidence of such accuracy through a holy lifestyle, including holy prayers (Prov. 4:23).

KEY PRINCIPLES

1. Our prayers are misdirected and doomed to fail when our focus is skewed and/or corrupted by a lustful self-indulgence.
2. Jesus' accurate internal architecture—a genuine heart of thanksgiving—was the key to unlocking divine supernatural provision and resource.
3. A carnal prayer focus is indicative of a corrupt internal architecture.
4. The accuracy that God desires is not shallow or superficial; it is deep and penetrating. He desires truth in the inward parts.
5. True correctness is when internal accuracy produces correct behavior.

ENDNOTES

1. A *zealot* was someone intent on preserving Judaism by uncompromisingly rejecting foreign occupation or rule, even if it meant suffering, dying, or killing to promote their patriotic cause. As such, they were recognized as overzealous religious fanatics who would resort to violence and murder, if necessary, to accomplish their goals.

2. *The Complete Word Study Dictionary: New Testament*, ed. Spiros Zodhiates Th.D. (Chattanooga, TN: AMG International, 1993), 2560; *Thayer's Greek-English Lexicon of the New Testament*, G2560 [e-Sword].

3. *The Complete Word Study Dictionary: New Testament*, ed. Spiros Zodhiates Th.D. (Chattanooga, TN: AMG International, 1993), 2237.

4. Admittedly, having seemingly unmet physical "needs" does not necessarily imply that one is out of the will of God or building one's own kingdom any more than the wicked or corrupt being able to easily finance their effort serves to validate what they are doing.

5. Oral prayer can become an expression of unbelief rather than faith when we choose to substitute petitions for practical obedience or when we continue to petition God for something He has already fulfilled even if it hasn't been physically manifested yet.

6. The activity of fishing here is indicative of work. By sending Peter fishing, which was his primary skill, trade, and source of income (Jesus didn't send him to till the land to find money), Jesus was teaching us a principle that divine provision often comes through our faithfulness to work in the area where He has gifted or placed us. This can also mean performing the natural tasks He has given us to do. He often uses (and blesses) what we have in our "hand"—our skills, natural giftings, strengths, or abilities.

7. This was not some casual religious exercise of saying "grace" before meals or praying to "bless" your food. Jesus was expressing a genuine heart of thanksgiving before the Father as a natural reflection of His internal posture. In addition, this was an exercise of faith being

expressed through selfless love and compassion. Jesus was willing to place the needs of the people above His own. By taking what they had (for their own nourishment) to meet the needs of the multitude *first*, their own needs were bountifully met.

8. This was the only legitimate prayer request of the bunch. In any biblical or human context, every other prayer request would be considered carnal and unacceptable before God.

9. Bathsheba's husband, Uriah, was one of David's thirty mighty men— an elite company of valiant warriors who were very faithful and loyal to David—and had probably been with David since the beginning when he fled from Saul and hid in the cave of Adullam (1 Sam. 22:1-2; 2 Sam. 23:39; 1 Chron. 11:41). By plotting Uriah's murder, David also became responsible for the deaths of the other soldiers who died with Uriah that day (2 Sam. 11:14-27).

CHAPTER 5

DIVINE REQUIREMENTS: CONFRONTING THE ISSUES

The prophet Isaiah, who confronted many grave and significant religious issues during his time, makes a powerful prophetic proclamation that critically exposes, identifies, and condemns the key issues or deficiencies that we have discussed up to this point. He then proceeds to make known God's divine requirements regarding prayer and fasting.

The context of what is written in this portion of the Book of Isaiah refers specifically to fasting. However, we can apply it in this context to prayer also because both exercises were performed simultaneously and prayer is clearly being implied as well. I am quoting the entire chapter here so that you are able to get the full context and content of God's message. I encourage you to take time and slowly read the entire text.

> "Cry aloud, spare not; Lift up your voice like a trumpet; Tell My people their transgression, And the house of Jacob their sins. Yet they seek Me daily, And delight to know My ways, As a nation that did righteousness, And did not forsake the ordinance of their God. They ask of Me the ordinances of justice; They take delight in approaching God. 'Why have we fasted,' they say, 'and You have not seen? Why have we afflicted our souls, and You take no notice?'

"In fact, in the day of your fast you find pleasure, And exploit all your laborers. Indeed you fast for strife and debate, And to strike with the fist of wickedness. You will not fast as you do this day, To make your voice heard on high. Is it a fast that I have chosen, A day for a man to afflict his soul? Is it to bow down his head like a bulrush, And to spread out sackcloth and ashes? Would you call this a fast, And an acceptable day to the Lord?

"Is this not the fast that I have chosen: To loose the bonds of wickedness, To undo the heavy burdens, To let the oppressed go free, And that you break every yoke? Is it not to share your bread with the hungry, And that you bring to your house the poor who are cast out; When you see the naked, that you cover him, And not hide yourself from your own flesh? Then your light shall break forth like the morning, Your healing shall spring forth speedily, And your righteousness shall go before you; The glory of the Lord shall be your rear guard. Then you shall call, and the Lord will answer; You shall cry, and He will say, 'Here I am.'

"If you take away the yoke from your midst, The pointing of the finger, and speaking wickedness, If you extend your soul to the hungry And satisfy the afflicted soul, Then your light shall dawn in the darkness, And your darkness shall be as the noonday. The Lord will guide you continually, And satisfy your soul in drought, And strengthen your bones; You shall be like a watered garden, And like a spring of water, whose waters do not fail. Those from among you Shall build the old waste places; You shall raise up the foundations of many generations; And you shall be called the Repairer of the Breach, The Restorer of Streets to Dwell In.

"If you turn away your foot from the Sabbath, From doing your pleasure on My holy day, And call the Sabbath a delight, The holy day of the Lord honorable, And shall honor Him, not doing your own ways, Nor finding your own pleasure, Nor speaking your own words, Then you shall delight yourself in the Lord; And I will cause you to ride on the high hills of the earth, And feed you with the heritage of Jacob your father. The mouth of the Lord has spoken." (Isaiah 58:1-14 NKJV)

Notice the seriousness and intensity of God's charge against His people in verse 1. He commands the prophet Isaiah to lift his voice and rebuke the people for their hypocrisy without restraint (*"spare not"*). This is not just a simple exhortation. God is soundly rebuking them for their sin, and He wants the prophet to communicate the full intensity of the rebuke without watering it down with diplomacy, tactfulness, or any false sense of tolerance. The reproof must be loud and clear so that it captures the people's attention.

WE MUST BE WILLING TO RECOGNIZE AND ACKNOWLEDGE THAT OUR PRAYERS ARE IMPOTENT AND FRUITLESS WITHOUT TRYING TO MAKE UP RELIGIOUS EXCUSES.

We can gather from verse 2 that these are a religious people similar to the ones we discovered in the previous text (2 Tim. 3:1-5). They are deeply and zealously religious, faithfully seeking after God daily—whether through prayer, fasting, worship, sacrifice, or corporate gatherings. To describe them in terms of modern Christianity, they read or study their Bibles, attend Bible schools, seminars, and conferences, or stay glued to Christian television. They know more truth than they can practice. Many of them rarely ever miss a church service or prayer meeting. They've attended every conference and read every book they can find on prayer and intercession. They cry out for justice and that God would end abortion in America. They look like they're holy, talk like they're holy, and act like they're holy, but they are really no better than the Pharisees of Jesus' day (Luke 18:11-12).

After a period of review, the people begin to recognize the futility of their prayers and sacrifice (fasting). They begin to make inquiry toward God regarding the lack of answers and their continual disappointment. After doing all that they have done, and following every principle of prayer and intercession that they have learned, why has the "breakthrough" they so often sought continued to elude them?

To their credit, they ask the right questions. Unlike many today, the people of Isaiah's day are not content to continue in the delusion that their prayers are succeeding. They are willing to recognize and acknowledge that their prayers are impotent and fruitless without trying to make up religious excuses. Something is wrong and they know it.

God responds to this inquiry by revealing the key issues of corruption and violation of God's original intent and purpose regarding prayer and fasting. The problem has nothing to do with style, methods, formulas, techniques, strategy, agreement, or identifying and targeting the demons or spiritual principalities at work.

WHAT CAUSES PRAYER TO FAIL

Satan is referred to in Scripture as *"the accuser of our brethren,"* but I have found that many brethren are often guilty of accusing satan of things he is not directly responsible for (Rev. 12:10). According to God, any failure in the people's prayer was their own doing, or was a result of the following issues:

A. *Self-gratification and personal pleasure*

Though outwardly "correct" and religious, the nature of this group's internal architecture was corrupt, elevating personal pleasure above self-denial (v. 3). Most of the Church's current emphasis today is on what God can do for us, or rather, on what God can do for *me!* This is a clear violation of the doctrine of the Kingdom of God as taught by Jesus. Jesus' command to His followers and disciples was to take up their crosses and follow Him, not to take up a cause that pertains unto themselves, their needs, or their desires. Self-denial is the true mark of the Kingdom of God, while self-indulgence is what defines the kingdom of satan (Gen. 3:1-6; Matt. 4:1-10; 16:24; Luke 6:20; John 8:44).

This self-indulgence practiced by the children of Israel, with its reluctance to embrace self-denial, is made even more apparent by the people's attempt to make sure that they suffered as little hardship or loss as possible during their time of fasting. They continued to be driven by greed and the accumulation of wealth, even oppressing those who worked for them in order to achieve more and not suffer any loss during their time of "consecration." In other words, while they fasted and abstained from physical labor themselves, they exacted the lost labor with interest from their employees by working them in an oppressive manner. Their fasting or outward acts of self-denial were only superficial at best.

This type of superficiality is no different from what the Church by and large practices today through the convenient invention of various types of "fasts." The word *fast* literally means "to abstain from food"…period! Thus in the morning when we wake up, we usually have *breakfast*—meaning "to break the fast"—because there was no intake of food into our bodies while we slept (unless we woke up for a snack).

However, somewhere along the line someone read the first and tenth chapters of Daniel and developed the misconception that Daniel was introducing a new type of fast—where one abstains only from wine, pleasant food, or delicacies. This is obviously much easier on the body than abstaining from all food. This erroneous misconception has now become somewhat of a doctrine in most of the Church. Examine the text again and you will see that this is not at all what it is teaching. What many of us have wrongly labeled a "fast" was actually a specific abstemious vegetarian diet that Daniel adhered to and which proved to be superior to the Babylonian system of cuisine and nutrition (Dan. 1:8-15). While nothing is wrong with the practice, and while the tenth chapter of Daniel clearly indicates that Daniel was denying and humbling himself before God, neither of the texts in question describe Daniel's actions as a fast.[1]

There is no such thing as a "meat fast," "sweet fast," "bread fast," or any other similar type of contrived "fast." Either you are fasting or you're not. Either you are abstaining from food or you're not. Calling it anything else is unbiblical and cannot be supported with Scripture. This means that you can't "fast" television, the Internet, or Facebook, because they do not constitute food. If you choose to abstain from these things, you should by all means go ahead and do so, since it can be very beneficial; but do not call it a fast.

> *THERE IS NO SUCH THING AS A "MEAT FAST," "SWEET FAST," "BREAD FAST," OR ANY OTHER SIMILAR TYPE OF CONTRIVED "FAST." EITHER YOU ARE FASTING OR YOU'RE NOT.*

The folly and hypocrisy of this practice is revealed in how we trade one indulgence for another. One woman told me several times that she was on a forty-day fast, and she even posted this on Facebook and Twitter. Upon questioning her, I found out that she was on a "Daniel fast" and only abstaining from meats; however, she never made that part public. Her desire to make her "fast" public and post it on social networking sites revealed not self-denial, but a desire to be recognized as someone devoted, disciplined, and/or spiritual. She was seeking to bolster her image. What she demonstrated by her actions was self-indulgence.

Similarly, I've had numerous people tell me that they were "fasting" this or that, only to find that their indulgences were redirected elsewhere. The person "fasting" meats was pigging out on a veggie pizza or veggie burger. The person "fasting" television was spending more time on the Internet. And the person "fasting" bread was stuffed on salads. Where was the affliction? Where was the self-deprivation? Where was the intense pain of hunger? When we claim to fast and deny ourselves one thing while filling our stomachs or appetites on something else, is that really a fast? Is that really the best we can offer God?

I received a prayer request from an intercessor and her team requesting my assistance in praying for a major conference their church/ministry was about to host. Their ministry had asked for members to volunteer to go on a "Daniel fast" for three weeks (21 days). But the focus of their petition was that "the conference be a huge success with great attendance and finances." The emphasis was upon themselves (their church/ministry): filling the seats of their auditorium, receiving a great intake of finances for their ministry through systems of extraction and generous offerings, and having a "successful" conference that would make everyone happy and cause many to want to return the next year. Man's agenda superseded God's agenda in an example of self-gratification in action.

Once again the prayer was inaccurate and the "fasting" was superficial, with no true abandonment of selfish or carnal indulgences in the practical aspect of food or in the internal dimension of their hearts. This is hardly an isolated example. In the modern church we have become very skilled and proficient at performing religious rituals while still pursuing and finding personal pleasure. Whether it be publicly announcing our fasts or times of prayer and consecration to others, posting our prayer and fasting on social networking websites like

Facebook and Twitter, satisfying our appetites with other substitutes, or promoting our own selfish desires or agendas above God's, the underlying motif is self. Like the Pharisees, we already have our reward (Matt. 6:5-6).

B. *Strife, contention, and a lack of genuine compassion or love*

The people Isaiah addressed were so self-absorbed that nothing took precedence above their own happiness or rights. They were without a firm anchor of love and compassion or an accurate Kingdom mentality where one willingly lays aside his or her rights for the benefit of another (Matt. 5:23-25, 38-48). They were a people without any form of restraint or constraint, selfishly enforcing their rights and pursuing their own happiness to another's hurt, thus creating strife and contention (v. 4).

It's interesting that the text uses the clause *"you fast for strife and debate,"* instead of saying *"you fast in strife and debate."* This is significant because the issue wasn't necessarily that they were fasting during times of personal or relational conflict, ignoring interpersonal relationships while still inclined to perform religious ritual. This would be unacceptable in itself, but the accusation here is much more serious.

As in the Epistle of James, the fighting and feuding here was the result of a carnal wisdom that was expressed through self-seeking and a lust for personal pleasure (Jam. 3:13-4:4). Therefore, the people's prayers and fasting were emanating from a corrupt source. Rather than addressing this source, however, they took it a step further. They took the sanctified disciplines of prayer and fasting and turned them into instruments or weapons for the advancement of their own carnal desires.

The best practical example I could find of this in Scripture was in regard to Naboth's vineyard. King Ahab wanted to purchase Naboth's vineyard, but Naboth refused, for good reason. Ahab then returned home sulking and depressed, refusing to eat. When his wife, Jezebel, inquired of him regarding his unusually sullen demeanor, she was told the story of what had transpired between Ahab and Naboth. In an attempt to correct this situation and satisfy her husband's lusts, she relied on the unlawful execution of her power. She had the elders of Israel proclaim a fast, hired two false witnesses to accuse Naboth publicly, and then had him executed. The purpose of the fast was not to humble or accurately posture the people before God but to procure for Ahab what was not rightfully his through treachery and murder (1 Kings 21:1-16).

Today, some would call this practice *charismatic witchcraft*—an oxymoron of sorts—but this behavior has occurred for centuries, long before the Charismatic movement. Like the children of Israel, many today employ prayer and fasting as a means of unlawfully obtaining what they want or striving with their brothers/sisters. Some seek God for bigger ministries, churches, buildings, finances, or anointings while being driven by a spirit of pride and competition. Some strike others down with the *fist of wickedness* in the name of God and prayer, hoping to procure that which they lust for or desire. I have heard of people who have prayed and fasted that God would give them someone else's husband or wife, hoping that the present spouse would meet an untimely death. Some use prayer as a weapon of warfare *against* people, asking God to judge them, remove them, kill them, change their behavior, or afflict them, especially in situations where they felt they were personally wronged.

THERE IS NOT ONE OCCASION IN SCRIPTURE WHERE ANY PATRIARCH, PROPHET OR SAINT EVER PRAYED THAT GOD WOULD STOP OR PREVENT THE PERSECUTION THEY WERE FACING.

I was quite appalled when I was told about a Christian teleconference hosted by two prophets. One of the prophets allegedly got a "sensing" that someone on the call line was praying against them. He proceeded to pray himself by cursing and calling down judgment upon the person. This is not only unbiblical, it is satanic! Jesus commanded us to *bless* those who curse us, and He was referring to any evil or negative declaration or invocation pronounced against us (Luke 6:27-28).[2]

An email was forwarded to me some time ago from a student at a prestigious university in the United States. Without going into too much detail, this man and his wife were experiencing some opposition from various groups for their stand in trying to facilitate the advancement of the Kingdom of God on campus. He sent an email requesting prayer for him and his wife and against any sabotage or backlash perpetuated by a certain opposing group against them.

A number of things about this prayer request concerned me. Firstly, I wasn't sure what his intentions were—they may have been honorable—but I could never endorse praying *against* anyone, whether an individual or a group. This is **not** how Scripture teaches us to pray. Secondly, fear of opposition or "backlash" was an internal deficiency that they needed to correct and approach God about personally, not a legitimate cause for requesting prayer. And thirdly, my concern was that this couple had been given a grand opportunity to be a partaker of Christ's sufferings, but they were too concerned about their own personal comfort and security to recognize or embrace the blessing of it (Matt. 5:10-12).

Jesus never prayed or uttered a negative word against His persecutors, and neither did His disciples.[3] When Peter and John were arrested and threatened by the religious council, they didn't run back to the community (company of believers) in fear requesting prayer. They reported what had taken place, and the Kingdom community came together, praying to God for boldness and a greater demonstration of God's Kingdom power. They didn't pray *against* those opposing them or seek to invoke God's judgment against them (Acts 4:1-30).

There is not one occasion in Scripture where any patriarch, prophet, or saint ever prayed to God that He would stop or prevent the persecution they were facing for righteousness. The reason is because such behavior would be tantamount to rebuking the blessing of God from their lives. And if we do this, we are refusing to identify with Christ's sufferings (Matt. 5:10-12; Luke 6:22-23; Acts 5:41; Rom. 8:16-17; Philip. 1:27-29; 2 Tim. 2:11-13; 1 Pet. 3:14-17; 4:12-14; Rev. 2:10).

C. Ritualistic religious compliance without accurate internal configuration

The people to whom Isaiah prophesied had correct external actions, but they were being governed and motivated by an incorrect internal principle (v. 5). Even though they had the correct outward form, they were lacking in true or genuine humility, repentance, faith, and obedience emanating from a deeper level. To anyone looking at them from the outside, they appeared passionately devoted to God, committed to His ways, and conformed to His purpose. They were everything we would expect a good Christian disciple to be—disciplined in prayer and fasting, faithful to attend religious gatherings, passionate in worship, etc. When they fasted, they abstained from food completely, not cutting corners like many do today. They appeared zealous toward God and uncompromisingly righteous.

However, from God's perspective, they were no different from the religious company we examined in Second Timothy 3:1-5. These people only had a form of godliness, without the internal substance necessary to truly validate it. True righteousness, faith, and obedience stem from a much deeper place than mere external performance or behavior.

The Pharisees, as we have alluded to before, were notorious for practicing an externalized form of religion built upon a technology of cleaning the outside of the cup while the inside was left untouched, corrupted, and defiled (Matt. 23:25-28). They would not commit literal acts of murder, but they would harbor unrighteous anger toward others or attack (insult) them verbally, which in God's eyes amounted to the same thing (Matt. 5:21-22). They would never be caught in adultery or fornication, yet they would entertain lustful thoughts and make allowances for divorce and remarriage, amounting to the same thing

(Matt. 5:27-32). They fasted more than anyone else (Matt. 9:14; Luke 18:11-12), prayed longer than anyone else (Matt. 23:14), and were experts when it came to the knowledge of Scripture (Matt. 23:6-8; Luke 5:17). But they only gave the appearance of being righteous and obedient when in fact they were not.

Jesus warns His listeners to beware of this type of perverse technology (Matt. 16:6), which is what Paul echoes when he tells the Ephesian believers to shun and avoid it (2 Tim. 3:5). Jesus also makes it clear that there can be no real access into the Kingdom of Heaven unless our righteousness *"exceeds the righteousness of the scribes and Pharisees,"* having a much greater depth of internal accuracy and correctness than mere outward acts of religion (Matt. 5:20).

Before we proceed into the next chapter, I would recommend taking some time to reflect upon these core issues that hinder prayer some more. Chances are at least one of these issues is currently at work in your life. We must all examine ourselves and allow God to deal with any area of self-deception regarding our true motives and internal architecture. As we change our thinking and confess these issues before God, we can then proceed to understand and apprehend the higher standard which God has required.

KEY PRINCIPLES

1. Self-denial is the true mark of the Kingdom of God, while self-indulgence is what defines the kingdom of satan.

2. Prayer and fasting should never be used as a means of unlawfully obtaining what we want or striving with our brothers and sisters.

3. Prayer should never be used as a weapon of warfare *against* people, asking God to judge them, remove them, kill them, change their behavior, or afflict them, especially in situations where we feel we have been personally wronged.

4. It is incorrect to pray that God would stop or prevent the persecution we are facing for righteousness.

5. True righteousness, faith, and obedience stem from a much deeper place than mere external performance or behavior.

ENDNOTES

1. The act of mourning in the ancient East could often be accompanied by fasting, as evidenced from Scripture (1 Sam. 31:11-13; 2 Sam. 1:11-12; 3:31-35). However, it is unlikely that Daniel fasted unless the description of specific foods abstained from in this instance was meant to inform us that Daniel had lessened his abstemious dieting restrictions from chapter 1 and was up till then fully partaking of the Babylonian cuisine. Whether these foods were symbolic of all foods or were simply meant to suggest that Daniel had reverted to his earlier diet as he attempted to seek God is not clear. Whatever the case, complete and total abstinence from food is undeniably both the culture and connotation of fasting among the ancient people in Scripture.

2. The word *curse* in Scripture is often incorrectly interpreted by many of us in the Western world as referring to "cussing" or obscene language. However, the word is primarily an antonym to *bless* (speak well of or pronounce blessing upon) and refers to speaking, wishing, or pursuing evil against someone in order to seek his or her ruin.

3. On one particular occasion, when the disciples were still in a place of immaturity, James and John sought to follow in the footsteps of the prophet Elijah by calling down fire from heaven against the Samaritans who had rejected—which is the first form of persecution—Jesus and His apostolic company's ministry. Jesus soundly rebuked them for this response. They were operating in a wrong spirit. Jesus then reminded them that His purpose was not to destroy men's lives but to save (Luke 9:51-56).

CHAPTER 6

DIVINE REQUIREMENTS: CORRECTING THE ISSUES

In the previous chapter we examined the key issues of religious corruption that had crippled or neutralized the effectiveness of Israel's prayer and fasting initiatives. The Book of Isaiah, chapter 58, is still the text under discussion. You may want to leave a bookmark where the entire text was quoted in the previous chapter so that you may easily refer to it as we continue our discussion. We have already discussed the first five verses of the chapter and will herein proceed with verse number 6.

After making it clear that God was totally dissatisfied with the Israelites' empty religious forms and practices, which emanated from an inaccurate internal disposition, the prophet begins to enumerate what God's true intentions are. This means that a new and updated reformation position is being promoted and established in Israel, built upon new insight and technology regarding prayer and fasting. The standard is being raised. The bar is being lifted higher as God's expectations are being made known. The line is being drawn. The nation could either repent and upgrade their current internal disposition and practices or they could continue in their religious tradition, void of any true spiritual substance. They could completely disregard what is being said and reject the prophet as being overly critical and presumptuous. After all, at no previous time had God ever explicitly stated that He expected more from them during a fast.

Similarly, God's divine intent and righteous requirements regarding prayer and fasting must become the basis of a new and higher standard for God's Kingdom citizens. The bar is once again being raised. God's prophets are once again crying out for reformation. As it was in Isaiah's day, so it is in ours, and the principles are the same. These correct principles by which we must now operate, delivered by God through the hand of Isaiah, are as follows:

THE PRINCIPLE OF LIBERATION

A. *Liberation*

> *"To loose the bonds of wickedness...undo heavy burdens...let the oppressed go free and... break every yoke"* (Isaiah 58:6).

This verse describes a militant push and deliberate forceful advance against every system of human oppression—whether spiritual or social— that seeks to impose itself against the just and righteous standards of the Kingdom of Heaven. It describes a mentality that motivates and accurately focuses the spiritual activities of prayer and fasting as we are stirred by the suffering and oppression of others. But it also produces correct practical actions or initiatives, whether individually or corporately, within the various spheres of our existence as we seek to eradicate these spiritual or social ills.

You will notice that what is described here appears very similar to what Jesus proclaimed—also quoted from the Book of Isaiah—as the fulfillment of His primary mission:

> *And the scroll of the prophet Isaiah was given to him. He unrolled the scroll and found the place where it was written,*

"The Spirit of the Lord is upon me,
because he has anointed me
to proclaim good news to the poor.
He has sent me to proclaim liberty to the captives
and recovering of sight to the blind,
to set at liberty those who are oppressed,
to proclaim the year of the Lord's favor."
(Luke 4:17-19 ESV)

Everything Jesus did in His life was toward this end. But Jesus never accomplished any of this by simply remaining in His prayer closet crying out to God. He didn't just accurately communicate with the Father and then proceed to live a life of self-indulgence. Everything He prayed or proclaimed was accompanied by corresponding acts and a lifestyle of obedience. He was constantly waging war against oppression, whether that oppression came in the form of religion, disease, or demonic influence. His emphasis was on practically helping the poor rather than upon building His own reputation or mighty ministry (Matt. 19:21; John 13:29). He was always concerned about the needs of others (Matt. 14:14-19; 15:32-37).

TO LOOSE THE BONDS OF WICKEDNESS WILL NOT ONLY REQUIRE ACCURATE PRAYER, BUT ACCURATE ACTIONS.

Because Jesus is our model, it is not sufficient for us to simply correct our prayer focus and repent for making our petitions largely about us or our personal needs. We must experience a complete heart transformation and change of direction in our lives as a whole. We have to seek practical ways to get involved and attack wickedness, poverty, and oppression within our own individual spheres, and then corporately as a Kingdom community. And we can't just wait for oppression to come knocking on our doors. We have to militantly pursue it and seek it out so that we can destroy it. Our prayers must be accurate, but they must be accompanied with corresponding acts of obedience. Our prayers must become a lifestyle, and then our lifestyle will become our prayers.

Instead of the focus being upon ourselves, it should be placed upon others less fortunate than us—and there are always others less fortunate than us.

To loose the bonds of wickedness will not require only accurate prayer, but accurate actions, and these actions will be undertaken primarily by those who proclaim themselves to be Kingdom citizens.

You can sign petitions and boycott companies or agencies as much as you want to—there's not necessarily anything wrong with that. You may even choose to avail yourself of all your democratic rights. However, these type of actions alone are not going to overcome the swell of evil.

For example, it concerns me when I see Christians choosing to stick red tape on their mouths to proclaim life or marching upon Capitol Hill, supposedly to defend the rights of the unborn, while skirting the root issues of abortion. The real issue in abortion is not the right of a woman or mother to choose whether or not to give birth; likewise, it is not about who sits in government or the judiciary. The underlying issue is sin that is rooted in lust. And we have no right to confront sin in others until we have confronted the sin in our own lives first (James 1:14-15; Luke 6:42).

More than three quarters of all abortions come from unwed mothers (as much as 83% according to the National Abortion Federation's statistics listed on their website).[1] This means that the primary issue is fornication, or sex outside of marriage. If we can correct the fornication and sexual sin, we will hardly have any issue with abortion. But to do so, we need to look in the mirror first. Sadly, the same sexual sins and deviances practiced in the world are found in the Church. When the same younger and older people who choose to indulge themselves and push the limits as far back as they can go without getting exposed or caught then boldly lift their voices, tape their mouths, display bumper stickers, and march in protest against abortion, we have a problem of hypocrisy. We can't break any yoke or loose any bonds of wickedness in anyone else—much less in a nation—until those yokes or bonds have been dealt with in our own personal lives and community of believers first (1 Pet. 4:17).

Trying to confront issues such as abortion while ignoring their root causes will produce little to no results. It's like complaining about roaches when you keep your house filthy, or trying to fix the heater when you left the window open on a cold night, or trying to treat lung cancer without first addressing the cigarette or nicotine addiction that caused it. This is not to say that we should not oppose abortion or be pro-life, but that we should approach the issue more biblically, honestly, and intelligently, considering ourselves first.

Fornication and adultery are destructive both to the individuals involved as well as to their nation as a whole. This is why God implemented drastic measures in the Old Testament to prevent and contain these sins (Deut. 22:13-30). What good is it trying to convince unbelievers to value the lives of the unborn when they do not even know how to value their own lives? We must stop focusing on correcting the external symptoms of sin and learn to address the root cause of it. By treating the cause we will inevitably eliminate the adverse symptoms.

THE PRINCIPLE OF COMPASSION

B. Compassion

"To share your bread with the hungry, and... bring to your house the poor who are cast out. When you see the naked, that you cover him, and not hide yourself from your own

flesh... extend your soul to the hungry and satisfy the afflicted soul" (Isaiah 58:7, 10).

This passage describes a heart and mentality of love, mercy, and compassion that is exercised deliberately and practically toward those who are in need. This mindset is not content to pray a wishful prayer while shutting up its bowels of compassion to share its bread with the hungry. It is not afraid to inconvenience itself for the sake of the poor or homeless. It is willing to cover the nakedness of others both spiritually and practically. It is not blind or self-absorbed so that it fails to recognize the needs of others; it does not turn away its head in pretense that it didn't see or try to evade the responsibility of helping others by relying on someone else to do so.

ONE SHOULD NOT SEE A BROTHER OR SISTER IN DIRE NEED AND THEN RESPOND WITH A RELIGIOUS, PRAYERFUL DECLARATION OF PEACE AND PROVISION WITHOUT TAKING THE NECESSARY STEPS TO PRACTICALLY MEET THAT NEED.

Having this heart and mentality means extending ourselves to others even when we feel stretched enough as it is with our own challenges and responsibilities. It means self-less love in action—the kind of love demonstrated by the Father and by Jesus. This is the kind of love we are called to emulate and without which we are disqualified as true sons and daughters of the Kingdom (1 John 3:14-23; 4:7-11, 20-21).

From what is being described here, we see that the emphasis is upon others from an internal dimension of genuinely seeking after another's welfare. But this internal posture is also devoid of hypocrisy in that it does everything within its power to meet the need. It doesn't just ignore the practical implications, or just depend or rely upon God or someone else to meet the need. Unlike the hypocrite described by James, the emphasis here is not just upon praying but upon the principles of faith, love, and compassion in taking proper action by doing. One should not see a brother or sister in dire need and then respond with a religious, prayerful declaration of peace and provision without taking the necessary steps to practically meet that need (Jam. 2:15-16).

WHEN CONFRONTED BY A NEED WE PERSONALLY KNOW WE HAVE THE RESOURCE TO MEET, THE CORRECT RESPONSE IS TO MEET THE NEED, NOT PRAY AND ASK GOD TO DO IT FOR US!

After I wrote the first draft of this section, a situation was brought to my attention where a young man who was an immigrant from another nation had to return to his home nation for various reasons after having lived in the U.S. for several years. He had been a Bible school student who had been very active at the local church where he fellowshipped. He was now back home in his country of birth without a job, money, or a place to stay due to circumstances mostly beyond his control. This brother was responsible and hardworking, but he faced a situation where he needed help from others in order to get back on his feet. After posting about his current predicament on a social networking website where he was connected to a large number of Christian friends and church members, several responded with encouraging words and promises of prayer. But his need remained unmet.

Finally, one particular friend spoke up and condemned the religious nonsense by quoting from the same text in James, pointing out that prayer alone was not going to put a roof over his friend's head or food in his stomach. Someone needed to step up and practically do something, which the friend then did. Others followed and the need was met.

I expect it was much easier for many of those who learned about this young man's need to hide behind prayer and brush the need aside because he was in another country. One would have to inconvenience oneself and make a deliberate act to get his contact or banking information to wire him some money. One would probably need to look up the conversion rate for that particular nation. It would require some forethought and planning, similar to that taken by the early Covenant Kingdom Community of believers (Acts 2:44-45), as we discussed in Chapter 3.

The point is that love requires sacrifice—and most of us don't want to be inconvenienced. Christians today love to use prayer as a substitute for obedience or practical acts of compassion, thus rendering their prayers ineffective and powerless. But only a foolish hypocrite would ask God to do what he has been given the power to do himself. True prayer and fasting demand practical demonstrations of love and compassion; they do not excuse us from them!

When we are confronted by a need that we personally know we have the resource to meet on our own, the correct response is to meet the need, not pray and ask God to do it for us! Even if we don't have what is necessary to fully meet the need, each of us is still obligated to do what we can so the need is partially met *before* we pray, unless we're asking God to work a miracle and multiply what we have to give.

How can we say we're praying for a young single mother of two children who is struggling to put food on the table during the Thanksgiving season when we've got hundreds or thousands of dollars saved up in our bank account to go on a shopping spree the Friday after

Thanksgiving?[2] What good is our prayer? I have story after story where I have seen this kind of hypocrisy displayed by Christians and religious leaders alike. It would take an entire book to relate every story to you. Many of you reading this are probably being assaulted with memories of similar kinds of hypocritical displays. God is requiring more!

FALSE COMPASSION

Let me interject that what is being described here is not false compassion. Many large companies and organizations frequently donate large sums of money to various charities, but they don't do so out of genuine compassion. They give because it is more profitable and advantageous for them to do so, especially when tax time comes around or when they are seeking to bolster their public image. Genuine compassion is not about handing someone money just to get rid of them or because you're weak-minded and just hate saying no. It isn't even about easing your conscience so you can sleep better at night. And it certainly isn't about encouraging or empowering laziness, slothfulness, or a spirit of entitlement because giving in such a context ultimately causes greater harm than good. True compassion is always demonstrated from a correct heart posture. Even Paul alluded to the fact that people can demonstrate great acts of philanthropy, generosity, and personal sacrifice while being void of genuine love (1 Cor. 13:3). Correct action or behavior alone may satisfy the religious, but it never satisfies God. He requires more! Our actions must emanate from a heart of love.

COMPASSION IS A KINGDOM PRIORITY

During times of calamity the citizens of the Kingdom should be leading the charge to provide relief through giving and practical acts of compassion. Instead of depending on government funding to eliminate poverty in a city or community, the Kingdom of God should be brought to bear upon the need through the love and compassion of the saints.

111

Instead of investing in bigger, more luxurious buildings with game rooms, movie rooms, our own personal Starbucks, or any other extravagance we deem necessary for comfortable Christianity, we should be attending to the things that have always been a priority to God and His Kingdom. These include the needs of the poor, the fatherless (orphans), widows, and strangers (foreigners) [Ps. 82:3-4; Zech. 7:8-13; Matt. 19:21].

PRAYER ONLY WORKS BY FAITH, AND FAITH ONLY WORKS BY LOVE.

It's interesting to me that the few times when Jesus commanded someone to give (other than in a general sense in response to someone who asks—Matt. 5:42), it was never to Himself or even to the temple treasury. (This was probably because He knew the priests would misappropriate or squander the gift like many do today.) He never tried to build Himself a new synagogue or temple, purchase a new ship for apostolic missions, or extract offerings in order to procure a herd of donkeys for Himself and His entourage of apostles. I'm sure many people willingly and voluntarily gave to support Jesus and His ministry, but His focus was always upon meeting the needs of the poor. And He commanded everyone following after Him to *follow* His perfect and complete example by doing the same (Matt. 19:21; Mark10:21; Luke 6:38; 9:1-14; 11:41; 12:33).

THE FUTILITY OF PRAYER WITHOUT COMPASSION

We can fast and pray all we want to when a need arises, calamity strikes, or a people are impoverished, but without corresponding acts of compassion, such a response is a demonstration of hate and unbelief rather than true love or faith. The person or people in need require more than our pious religious activity or vain repetitious prayers; they require love and compassion in any way we can give it. However, this doesn't necessarily mean that we should just blindly give away our substance to every need that presents itself, because there are times when giving or helping some people will ultimately result in hurting them even more. But we should be conscious of the fact that we are God's hands extended and that God requires much more from us than just religious prayers. Prayer only works by faith, and faith only works by love (Gal. 5:6).

Don't forget that the audience Isaiah is addressing here was not a bunch of estranged heathens but an established religious company who were veterans in the practice of prayer and fasting. The fact that God had to take the time to identify and explain these divine requirements through His prophet implies that these requirements were not presently being met. In other words, despite all of their religious activity, and their fasting and praying faithfully and diligently, wickedness continued to prevail. Burdens continued to exist, oppression continued unabated, yokes were never broken or destroyed, the hungry were not being fed, and the poor, naked, homeless, and destitute received no relief. These people's empty prayers were incapable of turning the tide of evil or of effecting any change in the lives of the poor, hungry, and hurting. Their neighborhoods, communities, and nation had not been positively affected to any significant degree. Their religion was as impotent and as useless as the kind demonstrated in the story of the Good Samaritan, where both the Levite and the priest ignored the man's desperate need and passed by on the other side.

THE STORY OF THE GOOD SAMARITAN

And behold, a lawyer stood up to put him to the test, saying, "Teacher, what shall I do to inherit eternal life?" He said to him, "What is written in the Law? How do you read it?" And he answered, "You shall love the Lord your God with all your heart and with all your soul and with all your strength and with all your mind, and your neighbor as yourself." And he said to him, "You have answered correctly; do this, and you will live."

But he, desiring to justify himself, said to Jesus, "And who is my neighbor?" Jesus replied, "A man was going down from Jerusalem to Jericho, and he fell among robbers, who stripped him and beat him and departed, leaving him half dead. Now by chance a priest was going down that road, and when he saw him he passed by on the other side. So likewise a Levite, when he came to the place and saw him, passed by on the other side. But a Samaritan, as he journeyed, came to where he was, and when he saw him, he had compassion. He went to him and bound up his wounds, pouring on oil and wine. Then he set him on his own animal and brought him to an inn and took care of him. And the next day he took out two denarii and gave them to the innkeeper, saying, 'Take care of him, and whatever more you spend, I will repay you when I come back.' Which of these three, do you think, proved to be a neighbor to the man who fell among the robbers?" He said, "The one who showed him mercy." And Jesus said to him, "You go, and do likewise."
(Luke 10:25-37 ESV)

Note that the story or parable of the Good Samaritan came about in response to a religious theologian's attempt to test Jesus and justify himself regarding his own righteousness. His question, *"And who is my neighbor?"* in response to the command to love our neighbor reveals a selfish and self-righteous disposition to narrowly limit or define who is worthy of love based upon a false personal and/or religious value system. To his corrupt understanding, the word *neighbor* probably meant personal friend, family, or colleague—those "worthy" of love. In other words, he was only committed to helping others in whom he had a personal interest and from whom he could obtain favor or reward. This is akin to cronyism or nepotism, a mentality that was prevalent among the Pharisees and lawyers (religious scholars/theologians) back then, just as it is in many churches today.

After sharing the story about the Samaritan, Jesus counters with a question of His own. However, the question Jesus asks is framed differently from the "expert in theology." By asking, *"Which of these... proved to be a neighbor...?"* instead of *"And who is my neighbor?"* the emphasis is shifted from the worthiness of the person who is to receive love (self-interest) to the responsibility of accurately giving or expressing love (self-less compassion). In other words, true Kingdom technology is focused upon being a *neighbor* while earthly religion is preoccupied with being *neighbored.*

EXPOSING RELIGIOUS HYPOCRISY AND NEGLECT

Not surprisingly, one of the key issues Jesus confronted the Pharisees and lawyers on regarding their "outside-of-the-cup" technology was their internal architecture of greed and wickedness.

While Jesus was speaking, a Pharisee asked him to dine with him, so he went in and reclined at table. The Pharisee was astonished to see that he did not first wash before dinner. And the Lord said to him, "Now you Pharisees cleanse the outside of the cup and of the dish, but inside you are full of greed and wickedness. You fools! Did not he who made the outside make the inside also? But give as alms those things that are within, and behold, everything is clean for you.

"But woe to you Pharisees! For you tithe mint and rue and every herb, and neglect justice and the love of God. These

you ought to have done, without neglecting the others." (Luke 11:37-42 ESV)

These religious leaders would faithfully tithe down to the last penny, yet neglect *"justice and the love of God,"* the very issues being addressed by Isaiah in regard to the people's vain fasting. How can someone be faithful to tithing or "sowing seed" to their local church and still be considered wicked and greedy? By neglecting justice, mercy, and the love of God. When we demonstrate love only to those in our cliques or personal circles of self-interest while neglecting or ignoring the stranger or those without the ability to repay—the poor, widow, orphan, foreigner, or destitute—we are not walking in true love. Thus God brands us as foolish, wicked, and greedy (Matt. 5:46).

THE MENTALITY OF HELPING OTHERS BASED UPON OUR OWN SELF-INTEREST OR WHAT WE HOPE TO GET OUT OF IT IS CORRUPT.

Note also that paying tithes or giving to our local churches does not absolve us of our responsibility to help others. How can we claim to love and honor God, whom we can't see, while despising and forsaking the people in need—His own creation created in His image—whom we can see (1 John 4:20)?

SHEEP AND GOAT NATIONS

There has been a lot of talk and discussion regarding "sheep nations" and "goat nations" in recent years. We would do well to note, however, that the biblically qualifying mark of a sheep nation is not its religious tolerance, number of churches or size of churches, national prayer gatherings, Christian leadership, or acceptance of Judeo-Christian-based principles. The identifying characteristic of a sheep nation is found in its practical acts of love, mercy, kindness, and compassion toward those who are hungry, thirsty, destitute, afflicted, imprisoned, and oppressed.

"When the Son of Man comes in his glory, and all the angels with him, then he will sit on his glorious throne. Before him will be gathered all the nations, and he will separate people one from another as a shepherd separates the sheep from the goats. And he will place the sheep on his right, but the goats on the left. Then the King will say to those on his right, 'Come, you who are blessed by my Father, inherit the kingdom prepared for you from the foundation of the world. For I was hungry and you gave me food, I was thirsty and you gave me drink, I was a stranger and you welcomed me, I was naked and you clothed me, I was sick and you visited me, I was in prison and you came to me.' Then the righteous will answer him, saying, 'Lord, when did we see you hungry and feed you, or thirsty and give you drink? And when did we see you a stranger and welcome you, or naked and clothe you? And when did we see you sick or in prison and visit you?' And the King will answer them, 'Truly, I say to you, as you did it to one of the least of these my brothers, you did it to me.'

"Then he will say to those on his left, 'Depart from me, you cursed, into the eternal fire prepared for the devil and his angels. For I was hungry and you gave me no food, I was thirsty and you gave me no drink, I was a stranger and you did not welcome me, naked and you did not clothe me, sick and in prison and you did not visit me.' Then they also will answer, saying, 'Lord, when did we see you hungry or thirsty

117

*or a stranger or naked or sick or in prison, and did not
minister to you?' Then he will answer them, saying, 'Truly, I
say to you, as you did not do it to one of the **least** of these,
you did not do it to me.' And these will go away into eternal
punishment, but the righteous into eternal life."*
(Matthew 25:31-46 ESV)

Notice Jesus' use of the term *least* in this passage. It is translated
from the Greek word ***eláchistos***, meaning least in rank, dignity, or
importance.[3] The people Jesus is describing here are those many would
consider to be "bottom of the barrel." They are the neediest and have no
natural prestige, power, or prominence, therefore making them the least
likely to receive help or favor based upon any natural human inclination
or expectation of them being able to reciprocate in like manner. This
means that the ones who were rejected and condemned by Jesus may
have been quite generous and "compassionate" to those within their
higher circle or able to return the favor. However, they showed no
compassion to those of lesser value or importance, or those who were
unable to repay, like in the story of the Good Samaritan.

The mentality of helping others based upon our own self-interest or
what we hope to get out of it is corrupt. We do not give out of an
expectation of what we hope to get back in return. Neither do we give
out of a carnal desire for personal recognition. This is a violation of
Kingdom principle (Matt. 6:3-4). It is clear that the righteous in this
passage were not performing their acts of compassion based upon what
they hoped to receive from people or even in an attempt to merit God's
favor. If they had been doing it out of a "sowing and reaping" reward
mentality they would not have been so surprised by Jesus'
commendation to them regarding what they did for Him. The wicked
were also surprised by their condemnation, but this should be expected
since they probably only showed compassion to those in their own upper
circles (where it would have been quite easy or natural for them to do

so), or to those who were able to return the favor. Therefore, their expectation was always on earthly reward.

The point here is that biblical compassion should be a (super)natural occurrence in our lives. It should come "naturally," from a correct internal disposition (of Christ-like love), not only to close friends and family, but to anyone in need. Our arms should be extended to embrace and minister to those beyond our immediate circles, to the very least (like the people living in a shelter, the poor family in the neighborhood, or the half-naked person lying on the street). And our compassion doesn't always have to be demonstrated through the giving of material substance; it can also be expressed through the giving of our time (as in visiting the sick and imprisoned).

THE PRINCIPLE OF SANCTIFICATION

C. Sanctification

> *"Take away the yoke from your midst, the pointing of the finger and speaking wickedness... turn away your foot from the Sabbath, from doing your pleasure on My holy day... honor Him, not doing your own ways, nor finding your own pleasure, nor speaking your own words"* (Isaiah 58:9, 13).

The obvious principle being communicated here is one of obedience and true repentance. While the Israelites' prayers and fastings were plentiful, they had no genuine connection to God that brought a revelation of His holiness or recognition of their own internal deficiencies. Their blindness continued unabated, fueled by their own self-indulgence. The emphasis was always upon getting God to serve them instead of them serving God in righteousness and truth. What they demanded from God took precedence over what God demanded from them. Their personal kingdoms overshadowed His own.

God became nothing more to them than a heavenly "sugar daddy" ready to indulge their fleshly desires. They cared nothing for covenant. When they called on the name of God frequently and repetitiously, it was not because everything revolved around Him, because to their thinking everything really revolved around them. They lacked the true intimacy with the Father and the internal heart posture that was desirous to please Him and fulfill His demands. Their hearts were untouched and completely disconnected from Him. With all of their praying they still didn't know Him. This type of prayer, though common even in religious Christianity, is a travesty.

IF YOUR TIME SPENT IN PRAYER TO GOD DOESN'T CHANGE YOU TO BECOME MORE LIKE HIM, DON'T EXPECT YOUR PRAYER TO CHANGE ANYONE OR ANYTHING ELSE!

The truth of the matter is that time spent in prayer doesn't always necessarily translate into time spent with God! These people were diligent in prayer (and fasting), probably spending hours at a time. The Pharisees were also diligent in prayer, spending countless hours crying out "before God." Many religious people pray; however, often all they are really doing is fulfilling a religious exercise without any genuine connection to God. These people were estranged from God. They may have been passionate in their prayers; they may even have shed tears. But regardless of the time spent, scriptures quoted, spiritual warfare strategies implemented, "prophetic" acts performed, decrees or declarations made, God was not in it and He was not listening (Ps. 66:18).

Real prayer should produce intimacy with God—the One we are praying to[4]—and should result in a greater knowledge and understanding of who God is, which should in turn lead to a transformation of our personal lives. If your time spent in prayer to God doesn't change you to become more like Him, don't expect your prayer to change anyone or anything else! Your prayer must affect you first, and it starts with genuine repentance and a desire to fulfill the requirements of God. As we stated earlier in this writing, prayer is nullified through disobedience. We must allow God's sanctification process to penetrate the deceitfulness of our own hearts if we are to be effective in prayer.

The hours we spend in prayer on a daily basis or during corporate gatherings may impress our family, friends or religious leaders, but they don't impress God. This may come as a surprise to some of you reading this, but long prayers don't impress satan or the forces of darkness either. One ounce of faith and obedience has far greater potency than a ton of religious prayers.

EVERY FORM OF INEQUITY, INJUSTICE, AND OPPRESSION IN OUR CHURCHES OR KINGDOM COMMUNITIES IS A HINDRANCE TO PRAYER.

It's important to note that the issues of disobedience and unrepentance being identified here are not what the Church today would consider as major or game-changing. Religion has a way of minimizing or diminishing things that are really very important to God while magnifying things that aren't. We might think that only fornication, adultery, murder, and other blatantly immoral acts would be the undermining issues being identified, but they weren't. Instead we find less salient issues: the existence of a yoke, indicative of various forms of injustice or oppression being perpetuated by these religious people; accusation, gossip, or slander *("pointing of the finger")*; deceit, flattery, boasting, or cursing [including any form of evil speech] *("speaking wickedness")*; and pursuit of personal pleasure, dishonoring God, and an independent or un-submissive spirit that does and says what it pleases or what feels good at the time without regard for what God requires.

Every form of inequity, injustice, and oppression in our churches or Kingdom communities is a hindrance to prayer. It doesn't matter how much we may try to justify it or cover it up; it has to be dealt with. Every issue described above has the ability to undermine all of our efforts and create a barrier between us and God.

I know many women (and a few men) who claim to be "intercessors." At the same time, I know many church/ministry leaders who choose to engage or participate in gossip quite frequently. Some even use prayer as a guise for spreading harmful gossip and accusations to others as they pass their poison around to friends, leaders, and/or other unsuspecting "intercessors." The tongue is a temptation for all of us. We boast of our ministries, our numbers, our exploits, our encounters, even exaggerating certain details to make the stories more sensational to our hearers. We speak and invoke curses, employing witchcraft and seeking judgment upon those created in God's image without a righteous cause. We pursue our own pleasure and self-interest, dishonoring God and feigning ignorance to His righteous requirements. We're blinded by religious tradition as we attempt to call on His name. Most of Christianity today is in pursuit of another personal "blessing" or "breakthrough" as we delight in pursuing our own personal pleasures above God's, yet we expect our prayers to be heard.

Many of us will gluttonously indulge ourselves during the holiday season in December. Then we assume a religious posture of prayer and fasting in January because it is convenient for us to shed the unwanted pounds we gained through our own lack of restraint or self-indulgence.

God will not accept this type of sacrifice because it is a violation of the core principles and technology of prayer.

TRUE REPENTANCE

God is requiring sanctification and true repentance, and true repentance requires a change of mind, a change of heart, a change of direction, and a change of behavior. It is not enough to just cry out to God and say we're sorry. It is not enough to just go through the motions of repentance without producing the fruit of it.

One of the misconceptions, I believe, that has helped to empower the false, delusional form of repentance that has become so popular in religious Christianity today is rooted in our original born-again experience. We were taught that repeating or reciting a "sinner's prayer" of repentance would grant us access into God's Kingdom and procure our salvation. However, this is an unbiblical assumption. Nowhere in Scripture do we ever find an example of the apostles or believers introducing anyone to Christ by having them repeat a certain prayer. The only biblical formula for appropriating the gift of eternal life (salvation) is genuine faith and confession.

> *Because, if you confess with your mouth that Jesus is Lord and believe in your heart that God raised him from the dead, you will be saved. For with the heart one believes and is justified, and with the mouth one confesses and is saved.* (Romans 10:9-10 ESV)

Salvation is activated by believing in your heart (genuine faith) and confessing (not personal sin, but the Lordship of Jesus). This is not a prayer in the traditional sense. Rather it's a divine principle where faith enters the heart—the core of our being and the source of our lives—as a seed and germinates, resulting in a corresponding confession or witness. In other words, once your heart is transformed by the incorruptible seed, everything else in your life follows because the heart is the source of all life. When God has your heart, He has all of you!

Praying a "sinner's prayer" or confessing your sins before God is not what saved you and not what God requires.[5] You were saved the moment God acquired your heart through a recognition of Christ's finished work and your desperate need for salvation, and this was confirmed and established by an accurate (verbal) confession. Ignoring this principle is like teaching your parrot to repeat the sinner's prayer and then expecting it to be saved. God has always been after our hearts, not our empty religious prayers or confessions, and it is the same with repentance.

The children of Israel succumbed to the same delusion and deception by bowing their heads in fasting and spreading sackcloth and ashes as an outward sign of humility and repentance (Is. 58:5). I'm sure they went through all the motions of "confessing" their known sins before God while beseeching Him for mercy and forgiveness. They may even have wept as they prostrated themselves, creating a false image of penitence while their hearts remained untouched, their minds remained unchanged, and their lives remained unaltered. There was no depth or substance to their religious counterfeit for repentance—it was all superficial! They were practicing the religious thing to do in order to escape judgment, avert crisis, or secure blessing.

IF MY PEOPLE...

The Church by and large has employed this very tactic by mobilizing local and national prayer gatherings during times of crisis or calamity to cry out to God in "repentance" according to the often-quoted (or misquoted) text from Second Chronicles.

> *"If My people who are called by My name will humble themselves, and pray and seek My face, and turn from their wicked ways, then I will hear from heaven, and will forgive their sin and heal their land."* (2 Chronicles 7:14 NKJV)

ASSUMED UNDERSTANDING BASED UPON RELIGIOUS TRADITION IS THE BREEDING GROUND FOR ERROR.

The usual tendency for most Christians is to take a scripture verse outside of its original context and then proceed to (mis)quote or (mis)apply it in a way neither the original author nor the Holy Spirit ever intended.[6] In this instance the original and wider context is not necessary for a correct understanding; however, we must realize that when it comes to Scripture, assumed understanding based upon religious tradition is the breeding ground for error.

Several clearly stated conditions to this prophecy are outlined in the text, and only one of them relates to prayer in the traditional sense. In our religious circles today, we usually emphasize the praying part, with superficial forms of repentance, when that is clearly not what the Lord requires. The conditions or requirements are:

- Humility (accurate internal dimension)
- Prayer (accurate technology according to God's standards)
- True Worship (singularly seeking God's face rather than our own self-interest)
- Repentance (not cries for mercy, but an actual turning away from wickedness where there is a change of direction and a change of behavior)

Unless **all** of these conditions are met, we cannot expect God to hear from heaven, forgive our sin, and heal our land. We can't just pick the parts we like, perform them the way we like, and then expect God to acquiesce to our requests. This would fall under the category of *"doing* *your own ways"* (Is. 58:13). Partial obedience is equivalent to no obedience at all.

Later on in Second Chronicles God promises to destroy the people if they turn away from Him or forsake His statutes and commandments. God was not requiring their religious prayers, admission of guilt, or desperate cries for help; He was requiring their hearts be given to Him in complete and absolute obedience (1 Kings 8:30-50; 9:1-9; 2 Chron. 7:12-22).

THE TECHNOLOGY OF PHINEHAS

While Israel lived in Shittim, the people began to whore with the daughters of Moab. These invited the people to the sacrifices of their gods, and the people ate and bowed down to their gods. So Israel yoked himself to Baal of Peor. And the anger of the Lord was kindled against Israel. And the Lord said to Moses, "Take all the chiefs of the people and hang them in the sun before the Lord, that the fierce anger of the Lord may turn away from Israel." And Moses said to the judges of Israel, "Each of you kill those of his men who have yoked themselves to Baal of Peor." And behold, one of the people of Israel came and brought a Midianite woman to his family, in the sight of Moses and in the sight of the whole congregation of the people of Israel, while they were weeping in the entrance of the tent of meeting. When Phinehas the son of Eleazar, son of Aaron the priest, saw it, he rose and left the congregation and took a spear in his hand and went after the man of Israel into the chamber and pierced both of them, the man of Israel and the woman through her belly. Thus the plague on the people of Israel was stopped. Nevertheless, those who died by the plague were twenty-four thousand. And the Lord said to Moses, "Phinehas the son of Eleazar, son of Aaron the priest, has

turned back my wrath from the people of Israel, in that he
was jealous with my jealousy among them, so that I did not
consume the people of Israel in my jealousy. Therefore say,
'Behold, I give to him my covenant of peace, and it shall be
to him and to his descendants after him the covenant of a
perpetual priesthood, because he was jealous for his God
and made atonement for the people of Israel.'"
(Numbers 25:1-13, ESV)

This biblical account taken from the book of Numbers regarding the noble actions of Phinehas, the grandson of Aaron, serves to further reinforce the principle of sanctification or repentance. While the children of Israel continued to abide at Shittim (also known as the Acacia Grove), they began adopting the corrupt worship practices of their nearest neighbor, Moab. The lustful obsession of elevating personal gratification or pleasure above the divine requirements of God causes them to commit sexual whoredom with the daughters of Moab. In effect, by the people embracing this corrupt value system and worship culture from Moab, they had become yoked or joined to the false god, Baal.[7]

By this time, God's anger is hot against Israel for their apostasy and a plague breaks out upon the nation. He commands Moses to execute His righteous judgment against the offending leaders by public hangings or executions.[8] Moses, for whatever reason, then turns and commands the judges to kill every offending person within their jurisdiction who had joined himself unto Baal; however, there is no record of either Moses or the judges doing what they had been commanded to do. Instead, what we find is the entire congregation of Israel, including Moses, gathered together at the door of the tabernacle weeping before God in what appeared to be genuine contrition and repentance.

In the middle of their praying and weeping a defiant leader emerges with a Midianite woman, in plain sight of the entire congregation and Moses, but they apparently continue with their religious activity and do nothing. This is when Phinehas is introduced into the scene. When

Phinehas sees what is happening he decides to take action, whether or not he is actually authorized to do so. I imagine he probably paused for a moment to assess what was happening and allow Moses and the appointed leaders or judges time to react. When no action was forthcoming and the people continued in their vain religious expressions of repentance, Phinehas felt compelled to stand up for God's honor. He rose up from among the congregation, grabbed a spear or javelin in his hand, and went after the leader who would dare to profane the name of God in the midst of His congregation. Apparently, by this time the man and the woman were already in a tent and in the middle of full sexual intercourse. Phinehas took the spear and thrust it through the both of them, entering through the man's back and the woman's belly. Only then was the plague stopped.

ONE MAN IS ABLE TO ACCOMPLISH MUCH MORE THROUGH A SINGLE RIGHTEOUS ACT OF OBEDIENCE THAN AN ENTIRE UNIFIED CONGREGATION EVER COULD THROUGH RELIGIOUS PRAYER ALONE.

The key here is that it took more than a unified, corporate, religious display of repentance with prayer and weeping to appease God and bring an end to the plague He had unleashed upon them. It was not until Phinehas rose up and executed God's righteous judgments or requirements that God took notice. In fact, God took absolutely no notice of the congregation's pseudo repentance, despite all of their weeping. However, the actions of Phinehas had such a profound effect upon God that not only did He end the plague because His wrath was appeased, but He established an everlasting covenant with Phinehas and his future descendants regarding the priesthood (Ps. 106:28-31). Phinehas didn't capture God's heart and full attention as a result of his prayer or priestly religious activities; he was able to capture God's heart and full attention as a result of his obedience and willingness to execute God's righteous judgments. One man was able to accomplish much more through a single righteous act of obedience than an entire unified congregation could through religious prayer alone. We can pray, fast, weep, prayer walk, and cry out to God until we literally expire from this earth, but until we give the required obedience we will have done it all in vain.

THE EFFICACY OF PRAYER

When God's righteous requirements are met and the principles discussed above are practiced, the efficacy of prayer (and fasting) is astounding:

- *Your light shall break forth like the morning* (v. 8)—joy, prosperity, favor, breakthrough.
- *Your healing shall spring forth speedily* (v. 8)—health, wholeness, restoration.
- *Your righteousness shall go before you* (v. 8)—powerful testimony or witness, Kingdom advance.
- *The glory of the Lord shall be your rear guard* (v. 8)—no longer will we have to chase after revival or manifestations of God's glory because God's glory will follow us.
- *You shall call and the Lord will answer* (v. 9)—answered prayer, miracles, supernatural manifestations.
- *You shall cry and He will say, "Here I am"* (v. 9)—salvation, presence of God in our midst.
- *Your light shall dawn in the darkness* (v. 10)—faith and victory in the midst of crisis.[9]
- *Your darkness shall be as the noonday* (v. 10)—peace in the midst of the storm.

- *The Lord will guide you continually* (v. 11)—divine guidance or direction so that we never stumble in ignorance.
- *And satisfy your soul in drought* (v. 11)—provision in the midst of scarcity.
- *And strengthen your bones* (v. 11)—strength, provision, internal fortification.
- *You shall be like a watered garden* (v. 11)—flourishing and fruitfulness.
- *And like a spring of water whose waters do not fail* (v. 11)—endless spiritual resource, abundance.
- *You shall build the old waste places* (v. 12)—wisdom, strength, and resource to build; instauration, restoration.
- *You shall raise up the foundations of many generations* (v. 12)—restoration, restitution, spiritual legacy; ability to establish accurate foundations that succeeding generations can stand on.
- *You shall be called the repairer of the breach, the restorer of streets to dwell in* (v. 12)—new identity, assignment, and destiny; reformation, restoration, reparation.
- *You shall delight yourself in the Lord* (v. 14)—newfound joy and pleasure in serving God.
- *I will cause you to ride on the high hills of the earth* (v. 14)—promotion, power, authority, a higher spiritual dimension.
- *And feed you with the heritage of Jacob your father* (v. 14)—provision; possession of earthly and spiritual inheritance.

When the principles of liberation, compassion, and sanctification become embedded in our personal and/or corporate lives and prayer initiatives, there will be no limit to our prayers' effectiveness. We will experience a boomerang effect of great spiritual and earthly blessing when we put the interests of God and our fellow man above our own.

KEY PRINCIPLES

1. Jesus never accomplished anything by simply remaining in His prayer closet crying out to God.
2. Our prayers must be accurate, but they must be accompanied with corresponding acts of obedience.
3. Our prayers must become a lifestyle, and then our lifestyle will become our prayers.
4. To loose the bonds of wickedness will not require only accurate prayer, but accurate actions, and these actions will be undertaken primarily by those who proclaim themselves to be Kingdom citizens.
5. True prayer and fasting demand practical demonstrations of love and compassion; they do not excuse us from them!
6. True compassion is always demonstrated from a correct heart posture.
7. Prayer is a futile exercise without compassion.
8. Paying tithes or giving to our local churches does not absolve us of our responsibility to help others.
9. The identifying characteristic of a sheep nation is found in its practical acts of love, mercy, kindness, and compassion toward those who are hungry, thirsty, destitute, afflicted, imprisoned, and oppressed.
10. The mentality of helping others based upon our own self-interest or what we hope to get out of it is corrupt.
11. Time spent in prayer doesn't always necessarily translate into time spent with God.
12. Real prayer should produce intimacy with God.

13. If your time spent in prayer to God doesn't change you to become more like Him, don't expect your prayer to change anyone or anything else.

14. The hours we spend in prayer on a daily basis or during corporate gatherings may impress our family, friends or religious leaders, but they don't impress God.

15. One ounce of faith and obedience has far greater potency than a ton of religious prayers.

16. Every form of inequity, injustice, and oppression in our churches or Kingdom communities is a hindrance to prayer.

17. Praying a "sinner's prayer" or confessing your sins before God is not what saved you and not what God requires.

18. You were saved the moment God acquired your heart through a recognition of Christ's finished work and your desperate need for salvation, and this was confirmed and established by an accurate (verbal) confession.

ENDNOTES

1. Susan Dudley, PhD, "Women Who Have Abortions," (Washington, DC: National Abortion Federation, 2003); available from http://www.prochoice.org/about_abortion/facts/women_who.html; Internet; accessed 31 July 2012.

2. Thanksgiving is an American holiday that is usually celebrated on the fourth Thursday in November. The Friday after Thanksgiving, known as "Black Friday," is recognized for being the biggest shopping day of the year in the U.S., as it leads up to Christmas.

3. *The Complete Word Study Dictionary: New Testament*, ed. Spiros Zodhiates Th.D. (Chattanooga, TN: AMG International, 1993), 1646.

4. Prayer also produces intimacy with the person(s) you are praying for, as well as the person(s) you are praying with.

5. The principle of confessing sins has been inaccurately applied to unregenerate sinners. This principle was actually given to born-again believers who were already walking with Jesus on occasion of a heresy where some denied having any sin (1 John 1:8-10).

6. The Holy Spirit is the true Author of all Scripture and, therefore, has the right to put an entirely new twist upon a scripture or apply it in a way that does not apparently "fit" the original usage or context. However, this Author's prerogative taken by the Holy Spirit occurs rarely, with very few instances found in Scripture, and was exercised only through apostolic wisdom and insight.

7. This is the first time that Baal is officially introduced in Scripture, but from this point on until the destruction of both kingdoms (Israel and Judah), he is revealed as a major antagonist to accurate Kingdom architecture and true worship. The false god, Baal, and its entirely corrupt system of worship are synonymous in Scripture with a mentality of personal (or sexual) pleasure or self-indulgence. In other words, any preoccupation with self, material blessing, carnal "needs," or personal satisfaction is a form of Baal worship and, therefore,

antithetical to God's Kingdom. And every sexual sin is a form of Baal worship.

8. Note that God holds the leaders responsible for the nation's or community's sins due to their permissive inaction, lack of proper governance, or poor examples. Note also that God's divine requirement in this instance was not prayer, fasting or weeping, but radical obedience and the execution of God's justice.

9. God never promises us that we shall escape or never experience crisis, only that we shall never be overcome by it.

CHAPTER 7

THE SPIRIT OF ERROR

Therefore I exhort first of all that supplications, prayers, intercessions, and giving of thanks be made for all men, for kings and all who are in authority, that we may lead a quiet and peaceable life in all godliness and reverence. For this is good and acceptable in the sight of God our Savior, who desires all men to be saved and to come to the knowledge of the truth. (1 Timothy 2:1-4 NKJV)

The occasion and context of the passage of scripture quoted above is very interesting. Paul, who is recognized by most biblical scholars to be the author of this apostolic epistle, is writing, among other reasons, to encourage his spiritual son, Timothy. Timothy was facing the extremely difficult task of dealing with various doctrinal errors and practices taking place at the covenant Kingdom community (church) at Ephesus.

This Ephesian Kingdom community, as you may recall, was birthed through Paul during his third missionary journey. Upon arriving in Ephesus, Paul was introduced to a group of disciples (twelve men) who were followers of John the Baptist's teachings, but who had not yet been introduced to the gospel of Jesus Christ or the person of the Holy Spirit. Upon discovering this, Paul proceeded to upgrade them in present truth, baptize them in the name of Jesus, and lay hands on them for the impartation of the Holy Spirit with the evidence of speaking in other tongues. Not only do they speak with tongues, but they prophesy as well (Acts 19:1-7).

This is a Spirit-filled, tongue-talking, prophesying community of Kingdom citizens that had been in existence for almost a decade as of Paul's writing to Timothy. They have apostles, prophets, evangelists, pastors, and teachers operating and functioning within their midst (Eph. 4:11). However, despite all of the rich spiritual resources and five-fold ministry leadership available, and despite having a significant number of years in existence to be considered no longer green or juvenile, they are still being assaulted by doctrinal error and incorrect religious practices.

As I urged you when I was going to Macedonia, remain at Ephesus so that you may charge certain persons not to teach any different doctrine, nor to devote themselves to myths and endless genealogies, which promote speculations rather than the stewardship from God that is by faith. The aim of our charge is love that issues from a pure heart and a good conscience and a sincere faith. Certain persons, by swerving from these, have wandered away into vain discussion, desiring to be teachers of the law, without understanding either what they are saying or the things about which they make confident assertions. (1 Timothy 1:3-7 ESV)

...holding faith and a good conscience. By rejecting this, some have made shipwreck of their faith, among whom are Hymenaeus and Alexander, whom I have handed over to Satan that they may learn not to blaspheme.
(1 Timothy 1:19-20 ESV)

According to Paul, this error currently plaguing the Ephesian community is the result of deep internal deficiencies on the part of those desiring to be teachers. They are lacking in *"love that issues from a pure heart, a good conscience, and a sincere (un-hypocritical) faith"*—all issues related to internal architecture, and which have become a recurring theme in the technology of prayer.

By departing from these core principles and values, these teachers have wandered into error. There is nothing necessarily wrong with their desiring to be teachers, but their desires issue from corrupt motives (probably self-promotion) and an incorrect internal disposition. They desire to be deep, profound, and clever, yet they are completely clueless, blind, and ignorant regarding what they taught or affirmed. The error they promote has evolved into greater error, warranting serious action by Paul against two of the primary offenders—Hymenaeus and Alexander— due to its blasphemous nature.

> *THE DEGREE THAT THERE IS DEFILEMENT WITHIN US WILL BE THE DEGREE THAT THERE IS DEFILEMENT OR ERROR IN OUR TEACHING AND MINISTRY.*

Error doesn't always originate from poor biblical understanding; it can originate from an incorrect internal posture—an impure heart, a defiled conscience, and hypocritical faith. When our hearts or consciences are defiled, everything else gets defiled, including the revelation we claim to receive from God. The degree that there is defilement within us will be the degree that there is defilement or error in our teaching and ministry, which is why God always focuses on our hearts rather than our actions (Prov. 4:23; 1 Sam. 16:7).

With this particular context of error and defilement in mind, Paul proceeds to discuss prayer, connecting his thoughts with the word *therefore*. In other words, everything discussed by Paul in First Timothy chapter 1 regarding the doctrinal errors plaguing the Ephesian community and the cause of these errors directly pertains to his exhortation in chapter 2 instructing the Ephesian believers to pray for *all* men (people).

Several different aspects of prayer are identified in this exhortation (1 Tim. 2:1-4):

- *Supplication* – petition; to make known a particular need.
- *Prayer* – prayer addressed to God; an expression of worship.
- *Intercession* – interview or conversation; to entreat; petition made on behalf of oneself or another.
- *Thanksgiving* – expression of gratitude and thankfulness to God.

Rather than attempt to get too technical with the various synonymous terms Paul chooses to employ in his exhortation for prayer,[1] I want to point out that none of these terms carry any negative connotation. The primary preposition *for* found in the sentence, which emphasizes this point, carries a positive connotation. It can also be translated *on behalf of*, as it has been in several earlier translations such as the LITV, WNT, and EMTV.[2] The importance of this point will be developed further shortly.

With the doctrinal errors and incorrect religious practices taking place within this Ephesian community of Kingdom citizens, Paul's *first* course of action is to correct the deficiencies in their personal and corporate prayer initiatives. Since our prayers very often are a reflection of what is going on in our hearts, it stands to reason that the error and corruption already prevalent in the community found its expression through a distortion of their prayers or prayer focus.

It appears that a spirit of exclusivity and/or narcissism has taken hold of their hearts so that their prayers—both individually as well as corporately—have become focused upon themselves and their immediate community without a genuine love or concern for the wider community beyond them. They are self-consumed, focusing upon their own ministry, leaders, needs, network, people, etc., while promoting what appears to be a legalistic doctrine (probably a form of Judaism) that has been making their witness weak and ineffective.

Any individual, church, or ministry whose prayer initiatives are focused exclusively upon themselves and their personal vision is an individual, church, or ministry operating in error! The Kingdom of God does not revolve around any one man, church, ministry, organization, people, or group. We will be no help to anyone until we lift our gaze beyond ourselves. Prayer should be offered up to God for *all* men (people).

CIVIL GOVERNMENT AND LEADERSHIP

Paul then continues to elaborate on this point by identifying two key people-groups that should be given particular emphasis when it comes to prayer: earthly or civil government and all those who operate within a position of authority. His purpose for placing emphasis on civil government and earthly leaders is not for attacking them with vicious prayers like those denounced by the prophet Isaiah (Isa. 58:4); neither is it for the purpose of opposing them or their legislation, as biblically offensive or inaccurate as they may be. And it is not for the purpose of asking God to judge these leaders or remove them from power.

We mentioned before that there is nothing in Paul's instruction for prayer that carries any negative connotation. Supplications are *for*, not against! Prayers are offered up *for*, not against! Intercessions are made *on behalf of*, not against![3] Thanksgiving and gratitude are given *for*, not complaining and griping expressed against!

In fact, when we examine the text and the verbiage Paul uses to describe the purpose of these prayers for civil government and leadership, we discover that the goal is not to change them or the situation or circumstances, but to change the ones praying instead.

> "...that *we may lead a **quiet** and **peaceable** life in all **godliness** and **reverence**."*

139

The word *quiet* in this text is translated from the Greek word *éremos*, meaning "composed, quiet, and tranquil."[4] It describes an inner quality and disposition that is not affected by what is going on externally around it. The word *peaceable* is similar. It is translated from the Greek word *hēsúchios*, meaning "still, quiet, and undisturbed from without."[5] *Godliness* and *reverence* carry the same connotation regarding an inner disposition or quality. They describe an inward reality that is not determined by outward circumstances.

ANY INDIVIDUAL, CHURCH, OR MINISTRY WHOSE PRAYER INITIATIVES ARE FOCUSED EXCLUSIVELY UPON THEMSELVES AND THEIR PERSONAL VISION IS AN INDIVIDUAL, CHURCH, OR MINISTRY OPERATING IN ERROR!

This is not to say that we should never experience righteous anger or indignation over the destructive course our nation's leaders choose to stubbornly embark upon with the nation in tow, or that we should just casually accept or support policies we know were designed to undercut or undermine Judeo-Christian values or Kingdom principles. Instead it is to say that our response should be one of prayer issuing from a heart of love, respect, and honor **on behalf of** those God chose to establish in positions of leadership. By praying accurately and correctly *for* them, instead of reacting viciously and violently against them and their policies while hoping for their removal or demise, we engage a principle that establishes our hearts in tranquility and peace, dispels our anger or frustration, and promotes true godliness and reverence.

This principle is extremely important because it runs counter to what is practiced by most of Christendom today. I am horrified by the dishonor that we give to earthly leaders who are either non-religious or hold to a different value system than our own.

RELIGIOUS ISSUES RELATED TO OUR CURRENT AMERICAN PRESIDENCY

Our current president here in the United States, Barack Obama, receives nowhere close to the support of his predecessor, George W. Bush, from the evangelical religious community because he is not recognized as being "Christian."[6] Very few will genuinely pray for him, the protection of him and his family, or his success in government. By the actions of much of the American evangelical church community, we would think that there was a hidden clause somewhere in the scripture text that made it read, "for *godly* kings and all *Christian* leaders who are in authority," but there isn't! There are absolutely no preconditions!

Prior to the November 2012 elections I was approached by a young prophet who was inquiring of me whether or not I felt that President Barack Obama would be reelected to office. When I responded that several of my peers received visions that he would be and that I had no reason to doubt them, he immediately began to rebuke this outcome and pleaded with me to pray *against* it, claiming he (the president) was wicked and needed to be removed! All I could do was shake my head and walk away.

I know people who call themselves "intercessors" who make it their duty to pray against our current president and his policies, and who petition God to raise up someone else in his place. I have heard just about every foul word used by Christian and non-Christian alike against our duly elected leadership. I have seen less than flattering posts—to put it mildly—being made on Facebook and Twitter as Christians I know make fun of him and insult him. I have seen religious leaders mobilize prayer and support among nearly all denominations of Christianity against him and his government. After listening to the propaganda from some of these religious groups or organizations, one could easily believe that God was a Republican and President Obama was the anti-Christ!

If you are under the assumption at this point that the author is either pro-Democrat or pro-Obama, you are wrong on both counts. What we are communicating here is not partisan politics or the endorsement of any one candidate or leader above the other. In the context of the technology being discussed at present, it matters not who you voted for during the general elections or if you even voted at all.[7] The principle being expounded upon here supersedes and transcends all persons (regardless of their religious persuasion), politics, or parties. It transcends all race, popularity status, or culture. And it applies to any leader in government, whether he or she is Jewish, Christian, Muslim, atheist, agnostic, righteous, or wicked. The minute a person becomes sworn in after due democratic process (assuming the nation is a democracy), all prior loyalties or party allegiances are nullified, and he is deserving of our honor, respect, and cooperation (Rom. 13:1-7). This approach is far more accurate, constructive, and beneficial to the nation than the usual evil tendency of using our influence, energy, resources, or partisanship in an attempt to undermine the appointed leader's initiatives in order to see him fail. We are cursing our leaders when we seek to procure their failure or their demise.

GIVEN BY DIVINE COMMAND

In case you somehow missed it, this wasn't some casual advice or optional suggestion given by the apostle Paul to the Ephesian covenant community or to God's global Kingdom Community as a whole. This is a divine command issued from heaven with apostolic authority that is as binding today as it was upon the original audience in Ephesus.

We must no longer continue to use prayer as a weapon to wound and kill instead of to bless and build. It is a violation of the Kingdom of God and of sound doctrine.

There are even some recognized prophets here in America who not only practice this evil but who teach and encourage others to do the same. But the principle of the Kingdom is not that we overcome evil with greater evil—i.e. witchcraft prayers—but that we overcome evil with good (Rom. 12:21).

BLESSING AND CURSING

But no human being can tame the tongue. It is a restless evil, full of deadly poison. With it we bless our Lord and Father, and with it we curse people who are made in the likeness of God. From the same mouth come blessing and cursing. My brothers, these things ought not to be so.
(James 3:8-10 ESV)

How can we bless God with our mouths and then turn around and use them to curse (speak evil of) people who were made in God's image? Every time you open your mouth to declare something negative or evil against someone you are cursing him or her. In the words of James, *"These things ought not to be so"*!

EMPEROR NERO

It's interesting to note that the civil leadership in power during the time of Paul's writing of this epistle in First Timothy was the wicked emperor Nero. Nero was the same leader responsible for murdering numerous Christians by having them ripped apart by dogs, nailed to crosses, and burnt alive in his garden.[8] He was as anti-Kingdom and as anti-Judeo-Christian values as they come, wickedly insane, and believed by many to be the antichrist. He was the epitome of wicked leadership. Yet despite all of this, Paul exhorts the Kingdom citizens at Ephesus to pray *for* him, not petition God for his removal or death. In doing so, the believers would find quietness, stillness, rest, peace, godliness, and reverence within their souls despite the intense persecution and turmoil taking place around them—peace in the midst of the storm and victory in the midst of the crisis (Is. 58:10)!

NEGATIVE PRAYER UNDERMINES THE GOSPEL

According to Paul, this is the only type of response that God will call *"good and acceptable"* in His sight—when we pray *for* earthly leaders instead of against them—because He desires all people (humankind) to be saved and come to the knowledge of the truth. This suggests that an inaccurate response—one that makes prayer a weapon of evil, judgment, or vengeance—is capable of not only hindering or hampering the salvation of mankind, but it can also give an inaccurate representation of God and His Kingdom, which blinds people to the knowledge of the truth. This applies not only to prayer but to every word that proceeds out of our mouths.

GOD PLACES LEADERS IN POWER ACCORDING TO HIS DIVINE PURPOSE, NOT ACCORDING TO OUR RELIGIOUS PREFERENCE.

Our harsh, critical, degrading words issuing from hearts void of true honor and respect toward those God has appointed to positions of leadership have undermined our message and the gospel of the Kingdom. This is not about exercising our democratic rights to freedom of expression or freedom of speech. Freedom is not the right to do what you want; it is the power and responsibility to do what you should! Besides, democracy is not Kingdom! God's Kingdom is made up of absolutes, and we don't get to vote or gripe about them or the King.

I don't know of any church or religious community where the members are allowed to publicly criticize or pray against the established leadership. A person would be labeled a rebel (or worse) and possibly excommunicated from fellowship for doing so. So what does that say about religious leaders who condemn such behavior when performed against them, but who turn around and condone or even encourage such behavior when it is performed against God-appointed civil government?

We will never be able to reach these leaders until we change our attitudes and behavior by giving them due honor and respect. Our hearts have to change toward them before any of them will be willing to listen to anything we have to say.

HONOR: THE KEY TO KINGDOM ADVANCE

Nebuchadnezzar and other succeeding kings of Babylon experienced powerful divine encounters through the prayer and ministry of Daniel because Daniel heeded Jeremiah's instructions to submit to the king of Babylon and to pray for his (kingdom's) welfare and peace (Jer. 27:4-8; 29:1-7). The result was that God's Kingdom was advanced in Babylon despite the antichrist system being promoted and practiced there. Daniel and his three friends became a powerful witness because they honored the king, seeking his welfare without ever seeking his demise. Even during times of persecution when they had to make a stand for righteousness, they did so respectfully, never cursing or criticizing the king or his public policies. They didn't do so because the king was likeable, feared God, or was favorable to their Jewish heritage, culture, or values. This man was responsible for robbing, destroying, and profaning God's temple, murdering and afflicting their people, separating them (and many others) from their families, and placing them in captivity and bondage. Yet they never allowed these things to determine or sway their response toward him as king (Dan. 1-7).

The same could be said of Joseph in the midst of an oppressive and idolatrous nation called Egypt. While Joseph slaved in Potiphar's house and fulfilled his sentence in prison, he never prayed judgment upon the nation, criticized the justice system for imprisoning an innocent man, or condemned Pharaoh as the one ultimately responsible for the atrocities perpetuated by the nation of Egypt. As gifted as both Joseph and Daniel were in the interpretation of dreams, they would have never been promoted to positions of leadership for effecting Kingdom purposes if either of them had proven to be antagonistic to the civil authority's leadership or regime.

God places leaders in power according to His divine purpose, not according to our religious preference. We would do well to remember this principle when we pray, lest we find ourselves fighting against God. When it comes to the Kingdom of God, its advancement is not determined by who sits in seats of civil or governmental authority. Its advancement is determined by our accurate response to pray for and honor our leaders regardless.

Of course, this doesn't mean that prophets cannot confront or criticize leaders—whether civil or otherwise—regarding areas of sin or disobedience, because there are numerous examples in Scripture that testify otherwise. The root issue being dealt with here is error of the heart. God's prophets are especially required to deliver His messages or rebukes from an accurate internal posture, giving honor to God first and the leader second when such honor is due.

THE PURIFYING EFFECT OF PRAYER

When Paul instructed the Ephesian Kingdom community to pray with supplications, prayers, intercessions, and giving of thanks for all men, including kings and civil leaders, it seems that he had a two-fold purpose in mind. Not only was Paul seeking to correct any deficiencies in their personal and corporate prayer initiatives, but he was also seeking to correct the internal deficiencies in their internal architecture as well. By praying in this prescribed manner, focusing their petitions with a heart of gratitude beyond themselves, internal transformation would occur. The old saying that "by creating an act, you create a habit; by creating a habit, you create a character; by creating a character, you create a destiny" definitely comes into focus. Gradually their selfless prayer would have caused an internal shift into Kingdom alignment. Gradually this upgraded prayer focus would have purged the error from their hearts, curing them of any anger, bitterness, or resentment they might have had toward the wicked emperor Nero or any other member of civil government.

THE ADVANCEMENT OF THE KINGDOM OF GOD IS NEVER DETERMINED BY WHO OCCUPIES THE HIGHEST CIVIL OR GOVERNMENTAL POSITIONS. ITS ADVANCEMENT IS DETERMINED BY OUR ACCURATE RESPONSE TO PRAY FOR AND HONOR OUR LEADERS REGARDLESS.

In other words, Paul didn't tell the believers to get their hearts right and then pray. He was basically saying that praying in such a fashion was the correct response to reversing the prevailing internal error identified in the first chapter. By praying correctly, the internal error would be neutralized. By employing a similar strategy and adopting a similar prayer initiative both individually as well as corporately, focusing our prayer beyond ourselves and especially on civil government and earthly leaders in an attitude of thanksgiving, we can be cured of our internal error also.

KEY PRINCIPLES

1. Error doesn't always originate from poor biblical understanding; it can originate from an incorrect internal posture—an impure heart, a defiled conscience, and hypocritical faith.

2. The degree that there is defilement within us will be the degree that there is defilement or error in our teaching and ministry.

3. Any individual, church, or ministry whose prayer initiatives are focused exclusively upon themselves and their personal vision is an individual, church, or ministry operating in error.

4. The Kingdom of God does not revolve around any one man, church, ministry, organization, people, or group.

5. Prayer should be offered up to God for *all* men (people).

6. Prayers are offered up *for*, not against! Intercessions are made *on behalf of*, not against! Thanksgiving and gratitude are given *for*, not complaining and griping expressed against!

7. Prayer was designed primarily to change us rather than our situations or circumstances.

8. Prayer was never designed as a weapon to wound and kill, but to bless and build.

9. Freedom is not the right to do what you want; it is the power and responsibility to do what you should.

10. God places leaders in power according to His divine purpose, not according to our religious preferences.

11. The advancement of the Kingdom of God is never determined by who occupies the highest civil or governmental positions. Its advancement is determined by our accurate response to pray for and honor our leaders regardless.

12. By praying correctly and focusing our petitions beyond ourselves in an attitude of thanksgiving, the internal error resident within us can be neutralized.

ENDNOTES

1. Most scholars believe that it was not Paul's intention to establish clear distinctions between these various aspects of prayer, but that the terms were used to create a cumulative effect for emphasis.

2. Literal Translation of the Holy Bible, Weymouth New Testament, and English Majority Text Version respectively.

3. Note that the only scriptural occurrence where intercessory prayer is used with the negative connotation of "against" is in Rom. 11:2 where Elijah is said to have appealed or interceded to God *against* Israel. "Against," in this context, doesn't mean speaking negative word curses or judgment over someone. Elijah was simply pointing out to God that Israel had rejected Him by killing His prophets and destroying His altars. By pointing out their sins to God he was interceding *against* them, which was appropriate in this context. However, God still did not condemn them, but expressed hope concerning a righteous remnant (Rom. 11:4).

4. *The Complete Word Study Dictionary: New Testament*, ed. Spiros Zodhiates Th.D. (Chattanooga, TN: AMG International, 1993), 2263.

5. Ibid., 2272.

6. While this statement may not necessarily be true in certain demographic religious circles, from a general or "big picture" perspective it is entirely accurate.

7. From a worldly standard or position, to have not voted gives us even less of a "right" to complain or criticize anyone at all. From a Kingdom point of view, we have absolutely no right, regardless!

8. Tacitus, *Annals* XV.44.

CHAPTER 8

MYTHS AND MISCONCEPTIONS

*I desire therefore that the men pray everywhere, lifting up
holy hands, without wrath and doubting.*
(1 Timothy 2:8 NKJV)

As Paul continues to address the error in the Ephesian covenant
community while instructing the believers to pray, he focuses
his attention on men—this is not the Greek word used elsewhere
to express humankind or people in general. Paul expresses his desire that
all the male believers participate in this prayer initiative *everywhere*,
without exception (v. 8). Of course, this was not an attempt by Paul to
make prayer the exclusive activity or responsibility of men, because we
know both from Scripture as well as Paul's personal teachings that
women participated in prayer also (1 Cor. 11:5; 1 Tim. 5:5).

Paul never goes on to explain his reasoning for singling out the men
in this instance with regard to prayer. It may be because any error that
had compromised the community's prayer initiatives at this point could
be traced back to the men (as the chief violators) or because he was
seeking to emphasize the men's responsibility in taking the lead in this
regard.

Some Bible interpreters are of the opinion that since Paul only
mentions men here, as distinct from women, he was *only* referring to
corporate expressions of prayer, or prayer being offered up during public
gatherings. At first glance it certainly could appear that the public

dimension was being described here, considering the fact that the believers' public worship may have been somewhat influenced by Jewish culture, which only required synagogue prayer of men. However, this assumption is incorrect for at least two reasons:

1. Paul explicitly uses the word *everywhere*, not "every place of worship," even though some scholars believe that the latter is what is being implied. The English word *everywhere* is translated from two Greek words meaning—get ready for this—*everywhere*! It is referring to every place and every location without exception, and the particular context in which it is used here does not diminish that fact. God's Word isn't that difficult to understand; we just choose to make it so.

2. Only a religious hypocrite would create a dichotomy between his or her private and public worship. Everything we do publicly should be a reflection of what we do privately, so it would be absurd to believe that Paul is espousing the notion of separating the two. If men are being singled out for praying publicly, then the expectation should be that they are also praying privately, just as women are expected to dress modestly at all times, not just during times of corporate or public worship gatherings (Matt. 6:5-6; 1 Tim. 2:9-10)!

Either way you choose to slice it, this text in First Timothy 2:8 calls into question several common practices and theological presuppositions of religious Christianity today, especially among those who claim to be "present truth." We will attempt to identify these as misconceptions.

FIRST RELIGIOUS MISCONCEPTION

Misconception #1: Women have a greater calling to and are better suited for prayer.

There is absolutely nothing in Scripture to support this myth. On the contrary, while addressing doctrinal error and incorrect religious practices occurring among the Ephesian Kingdom community, Paul clearly identifies men as the primary leaders in this regard. There need be no doubt at all that women prayed, as we have already pointed out, but Paul issues a distinct charge to men—all men—first. He commands them to pray everywhere!

MEN WERE NEVER INTENDED TO BE MERE SPECTATORS BUT LEADING PARTICIPATORS IN EVERY PRAYER INITIATIVE.

When we say that Paul issued a distinct charge to men *first*, it is because the following verse where he speaks to the women is connected by the phrase *"in like manner also"* (v. 9). This implies that every part of Paul's previous instruction to men to pray—including the requirement for holiness, purity, and accuracy of life and character *("lifting up holy hands")* and the removal of every form of evil desire, intent, strife, or contention that would make prayer a malevolent weapon of judgment, vengeance, or wickedness *("without wrath and doubting")*—applies to the women also.

Therefore, the charge to pray was really issued to both men and women, with the men being singled out and mentioned first because of their leading role in this regard. They were never intended to be mere spectators but leading participators in every prayer initiative.

If, as some believe, Paul was only referring to public gatherings where men were the dominant figures in prayer, we have to conclude that this was the prevailing culture then, and that it also should still be binding upon us today, since Paul's use of the word *everywhere* implies this was not culturally exclusive to Ephesus. Either way we choose to approach the text, we cannot escape the conclusion that men led or carried most of the responsibility for prayer, at least publicly, and perhaps both publicly and privately.

Fast-forward to Christianity today in the twenty-first century and you find just the opposite. Women do all or most of the praying while men take a backseat. In fact, some so-called "experts" even claim that women are better suited for prayer and intercession due to their emotional and psychological makeup. The fact that God chose men to lead in this role argues for the opposite. Except for widows, who often have a greater measure of time on their hands to dedicate to prayer, men should be the most committed, most dedicated, and most devoted to this biblical practice (1 Tim. 5:5).

If God requires the men to lead in this fashion, it is because He has good reason. Making excuses or minimizing the man's role, whether publicly or within the family context, because of a lack of enthusiasm or commitment on his part is counterproductive to God's purposes. The minute we establish and become complacent with substitutes, we, in effect, bar him from ever recognizing or fulfilling his role. We also deny others around him the true power, authority, and blessing that is inherent in the man fulfilling said role.[1]

Just as the woman was created with a womb that cannot be substituted by anything or any (male) man, so too the man was created with unique capabilities that cannot be substituted. If we want to see God's global Kingdom Community matured to the full measure and stature of Jesus so that we hasten His return, it will require men rising up to fulfill their God-given roles. We thank God for the women and their zeal and faithfulness in answering the call to prayer, but it is time for the men to emerge and lead the charge. Men everywhere must answer the call to pray! Leaders must activate men into their positions. It will take great effort from all parties involved to superimpose God's culture against a modern culture that is so far removed from that which God prescribed, but the results will be worth the effort.

SECOND RELIGIOUS MISCONCEPTION

Misconception #2*: Prayer is the responsibility of a select few.*

Once again, Scripture teaches quite the opposite. When Paul charges the men to pray everywhere, he obviously intends the same charge to apply to the women also, even if it is to a lesser degree. This means that every single man and woman, without exception, has a responsibility to pray and not to depend on a select few to do it for them.

> *Is anyone among you suffering? Let him pray. Is anyone cheerful? Let him sing praise.* (James 5:13 ESV)

This is a fascinating text because it gives very clear instruction and includes very powerful and practical Kingdom principles. James is inquiring of his audience as to whether or not any of them are *"suffering."* This is not the type of suffering that is the result of sickness or physical infirmity. The word for *suffering* here is translated from the Greek word **kakopathéō**, meaning "something ill or evil, to be afflicted, suffer trouble, or undergo hardships."[2]

Every one of us will experience hardship or trouble at some time or other during our lives, but the way we respond to it is James' primary concern. The first response for many Christians today is to call someone else for prayer—preferably some recognized ministry, prophet, pastor, prayer group, or "intercessor." But according to James, when anyone is suffering hardship or affliction, he (or she) should be the one to pray (for himself)! Just as the expectation of James 5:13 is that the cheerful person would express his joyful merriment in songs of praise, the expectation should be that the person suffering hardship would pour his heart out in prayer to God. It would be ridiculous for the cheerful person to expect someone else to sing or express his merriment for him, and it is just as ridiculous for the afflicted person to expect someone else to do the praying.

155

I have had people call for prayer for just about every personal inconvenience or hardship you can think of. Most of this inaccuracy is due to the poor teaching and dependency syndrome that religious Christianity has inculcated into the minds of its followers. This practice not only violates the apostolic teaching of Scripture, but it also contradicts one of the foundational principles of the Protestant Reformation led by Martin Luther in the 1500's—the priesthood of *all* believers (1 Tim. 2:5; 1 Pet. 2:5-9)!

ANY TRUTH OR PRINCIPLE TAKEN TO THE EXTREME—BEYOND THE ORIGINAL BOUNDARIES AND PARAMETERS OF SCRIPTURE—QUICKLY DEGENERATES INTO ERROR.

In Luther's day, prior to the Reformation, the people depended on the priests, monks, bishops, cardinals, or pope to go before God on their behalf because they were biblically illiterate and had no confidence in their own prayers. They were taught to embrace this dependency and to rely on their spiritual leaders, as many Christians do today. Luther strongly rejected this dependence as unbiblical and taught instead the truth of our direct access to God. If this dependence was unacceptable then when the majority of the people didn't have access to the Scriptures (even if they had access to a Bible, most would not have been able to understand it since it was only available in Latin), it should be even more repugnant and reprehensible now during a time when the Scriptures are easily accessible (in any language and in many versions) and biblical ignorance is inexcusable.

Debunking the Prayer of Agreement

A woman called me some time ago to receive prayer for something very trivial. It was a minor inconvenience. When I brought this text taken from the Book of James to her attention and encouraged her to pray for herself, she became very offended and proceeded to bring to my attention the scripture that states, *"If two of you agree on earth concerning anything that they ask, it will be done for them by My Father in heaven"* (Matt. 18:19).

This "prayer of agreement," as it is often called, is another major religious misconception about prayer. It is worthy of being addressed as one of our major points of discussion; however, since it distracts from our main text and the story, we will only address it briefly.

The error, again, is due to both ignorance and the poor but common practice of trying to interpret a text outside of its context. Some have even developed a "theology" that we need to "touch and agree" (hold hands) in prayer for better results, because the KJV translation of Matthew 18:19 uses the words *"as touching"* instead of *"concerning."* This is obviously not what the text is teaching.

Unity and agreement are powerful spiritual principles; however, their importance can be greatly exaggerated when it comes to prayer, especially when there is a blatant disregard for other key foundational principles. Any truth or principle taken to the extreme—beyond the original boundaries and parameters of Scripture—quickly degenerates into error.

UNITY OR AGREEMENT IN ERROR SIMPLY MAKES FOR UNIFIED OR GREATER ERROR; IT DOES NOT GUARANTEE EFFECTIVENESS IN PRAYER.

The Muslims are very united in their prayers, as are followers of many other religions. The Pharisees were a very unified and connected network of religious leaders who were very committed to the practice of prayer also, yet how many of us would claim that their prayers were powerfully effective?

The Israelites were God's covenant people, yet there were many times when God chose to ignore their corporate cries and petitions despite their unified and connected efforts (Judg. 10:10-14; Mic. 3:4; Zech. 7:5-13). And what about Elijah and the prophets of Baal? Four hundred and fifty unified prophets of Baal cried out to their god and cut themselves, yet they received no answer. Elijah, on the other hand, stood alone and prayed to God, and He answered by fire (1 Kings 18:1-40). Unity or agreement in error simply makes for unified or greater error; it does not guarantee effectiveness in prayer.

As I attempted to explain this principle to the caller, I calmly informed her that she was making the common mistake of quoting this text out of its original context. Matthew 18:19 was never intended to be a recipe or formula for personal, or rather, self-seeking prayer requests. In the context of Matthew 18, the prayer of agreement specifically refers to matters relating to preserving the integrity or correct internal architecture of God's Kingdom community, not deliverance from hardship or the meeting of personal needs.[3]

If this "prayer of agreement" was supposed to be used indiscriminately in such a manner, then James would have certainly encouraged it in the instance of someone suffering. James did not say to seek prayer from someone else or a partner in agreement. He said *"let him* (or her) *pray"*!

Sometimes it's simply our own spiritual slothfulness or laziness that makes us incapable of praying or approaching God for ourselves. In some instances it is because we have chosen to be isolated and disconnected from a place of true Kingdom community, thus leaving us lacking in faith, open and vulnerable to be assaulted by the enemy, and desperate for prayer from a mighty man or woman of God to deliver us from our afflictions.

Most of the churches or ministries who encourage this type of dependency are either doing it out of greed (because often people have been manipulated to believe that they need to plant a monetary seed with their request as a way of moving God to answer),[4] out of a false religious sense of duty, or out of a selfish desire to grow in popularity (it has become popular for various ministries and churches to have "prayer lines" to cater to these requests, which in turn helps their popularity ratings among the general religious populous who consider this service an expression of love, which it actually isn't).[5] This is not much different from what Martin Luther had to deal with during the period of the Reformation.

Praying for Wisdom

This same principle applies to those lacking or desiring wisdom. I have lost count of the number of times I have been asked by believers—some of whom were spiritual leaders—to ask God to grant them wisdom. This sounds like a very spiritual, noble, and godly request, and in fact it is. However, it is an inaccurate request for the simple reason that it contradicts the biblical standard of taking personal responsibility in prayer. Why should I ask God to grant you wisdom when you have been given the right and responsibility to do so yourself?

> *If any of you lacks wisdom, let him ask God, who gives generously to all without reproach, and it will be given him. But let him ask in faith, with no doubting, for the one who doubts is like a wave of the sea that is driven and tossed by the wind. For that person must not suppose that he will receive anything from the Lord; he is a double-minded man, unstable in all his ways. (James 1:5-8 ESV)*

> *GOD DOES NOT GRANT SPECIAL*
> *ACCESS TO HIS THRONE TO CERTAIN*
> *SPIRITUAL LEADERS OR*
> *"INTERCESSORS."*

The apostle James is very explicit in stating that if you lack wisdom, then you should be the one to ask God![6] Don't ask me or anyone else to ask God for you! Of course the wisdom being referred to here pertains to trials or tests, but that point is irrelevant. God is clearly desirous of giving us wisdom, and the text confirms that He is also very generous and un-reproachful. If you don't have the faith or confidence that God will hear you, what makes you think you have the required faith that God will answer me? It is your responsibility to approach God boldly and with faith. Each one of us as a Kingdom citizen has equal access to God. God does not grant special access to His throne to certain spiritual leaders or "intercessors."

THIRD RELIGIOUS MISCONCEPTION

Misconception #3: *The purpose of prayer is for averting personal crises.*

Paul's apostolic command to pray was clearly never intended to be used as a fire insurance or fire prevention policy, either personally or corporately. It was not occasioned by the existing evil government or by an overly optimistic desire to see the social, political, or economic climate of the nation radically changed. The purpose, in this instance, was for effecting positive change primarily within the believers themselves so that they became more accurate and effective witnesses for Kingdom advance (1 Tim. 2:3-8).

Similarly, James does not say that one should only pray during times of crisis (Jam. 5:13). I find it very hard to believe that James is even suggesting that we should pray about the crisis. His only instruction is to pray, without indicating specifically what the afflicted person should be praying about. Fortunately for us there are other places in Scripture, including the entire epistle of James, where we can receive valuable insight regarding how we should pray.

Watch and Pray

When Jesus came to the garden of Gethsemane and instructed His disciples to watch with Him and pray, it was during a time of deep internal affliction, agony, and impending evil. A great darkness and tribulation was almost upon them. Yet Jesus makes it clear that His instruction to watch and pray is not for the purpose of averting the impending crisis, but to ensure that their minds and internal heart postures are in an accurate state, able to withstand temptation and respond accurately during the time of trouble (Matt. 26:36-41).

Had Peter (and the other disciples) watched and prayed like his Master had commanded, he probably would not have fallen into the temptation of physically assaulting the officer sent to take Jesus into custody. He also probably would not have denied Jesus three times. His response during the time of crisis was inaccurate because his internal heart posture was not adequately prepared through personal prayer. Peter's hasty reaction of striking angrily with the sword and cutting off the ear of the high priest's servant is representative of the personal assaults many modern-day Christians perpetuate verbally—whether through witchcraft prayers or otherwise—upon the ears of those who have offended or disappointed us (Matt. 26:51; John 18:10).

Scripture even takes the time to identify the name of this servant whose ear Peter cut off, which is rare for insignificant characters in Scripture unless the person's name carries some special significance. His name was *Malchus*. Interestingly, this name means "king" or "ruler"— the very type of person religious Christians love to attack or criticize with their words, especially when the said ruler is perceived as anti-Christ, anti-Christian, or anti-religious! Striking others, whether physically or verbally, is an ungodly and worldly practice that undermines the true message of the Kingdom and hinders its advance.

Do Not Be Anxious

Consider also Paul's instruction to the covenant Kingdom community located at Philippi:

> *Be anxious for nothing, but in everything by prayer and supplication, with thanksgiving, let your requests be made known to God; and the peace of God, which surpasses all understanding, will guard your hearts and minds through Christ Jesus.* (Philippians 4:6-7 NKJV)

The command not to be anxious for anything is a prohibition against the self-centered tendency to be worried or concerned about our own personal needs, wants, or desires. You will notice that Paul once again employs three of the four terms used for prayer in First Timothy 2:1 as the remedy or countermeasure for this evil anxiety. Prayer (all types) with thanksgiving is considered the cure that is able to transform our anxiety into peace, with the implication being that we are to pray to God directly rather than to advertise our prayer requests to others. Again, each of us is responsible for presenting our own requests to God personally and directly when we are in need of God's peace to counteract our anxiety.

It's worth noting also that our requests are not to be self-centered. Paul said *"in everything,"* not "for everything"—there's a difference! Regardless of what situation we may find ourselves in, we are to pray and give thanks, because it releases God's peace—our true need! Contrary to what we may have previously thought we needed on account of what we were going through, this is where the true deficiency lies (John 14:27; 16:33; Rom. 14:17; Gal. 5:22).

Paul never promises an outward change in our situation or circumstances but an inner change and transformation within us. We shall have peace—an inner condition of tranquility and rest—and our hearts and minds will be protected from the corruption and defilement that leads us into error (1 Tim. 1:5-6, 19).

Prayer Should Change Us First

Taking these scriptural examples or principles into consideration— including Paul's instruction to the Ephesian covenant community to pray for the then-existing wicked leaders of their time, commanding the men (and by extension the women) to pray everywhere with the requirement of holiness and the absence of resentful anger or critical dissent, especially toward the unrighteous rulers in authority— it would appear that the principle is the same: Prayer is for the purpose of changing us rather than our situations. This does not mean that God is not interested in changing our current conditions, only that He is interested in changing us first.

PRAYER IS FOR THE PURPOSE OF CHANGING US RATHER THAN OUR SITUATIONS.

With this understanding in mind, James affirms the right and responsibility of every saint or Kingdom citizen to pray without depending on someone else to do it for him or her, especially during times of crisis. In fact, according to James, the only time we have a legitimate biblical right to request prayer support for a personal need, or in response to a personal crisis, is when we are *sick* (meaning physically weak, infirmed, or feeble), and even then there are conditions attached.[7]

Physical Healing

> *Is anyone among you sick? Let him call for the elders of the*
> *church, and let them pray over him, anointing him with oil in*
> *the name of the Lord. And the prayer of faith will save the*
> *one who is sick, and the Lord will raise him up. And if he has*
> *committed sins, he will be forgiven.* (James 5:14-15 ESV)

The context of this passage implies that the sick or bedridden person in need of healing is an actively integrated member of a Kingdom community where there are functioning elders. This implies that the sick member has been engaged and connected. It does not allow for the man (or woman) to be isolated or disconnected and then pick up his phone to call some prominent or successful healing ministry or notable miracle worker with whom he has no relationship. The infirmed person must call for his own elders, and these elders (plural)—implying either the entirety or at least two of the governing leadership body—are to respond by visiting the sick member to pray for him in person. It is not sufficient to just put the sick member's name on the corporate community's prayer list, to enlist "intercessors," or to have the leadership pray for healing over the phone. The principle requires the leadership to demonstrate the loving hearts of true shepherds by visiting the sick member's bedside even if it requires rearranging their busy schedules (Ezek. 34:1-16).

Let me interject here that the context of the passage, as well as the Greek words used, seem to indicate that this is either a terminal illness or, at the least, some type of infirmity that causes the person to be confined to his bed, unable to seek out the elders personally himself. This is not a matter of a simple headache, common cold, or anything else of a trivial nature. You don't call for the elders to visit you just because you have a sore throat.

The elders, having responded to the request initiated by the sick member, will then gather around the sick person's bedside, corporately pray and anoint the sick person with oil, and the *"prayer of faith"* is supposed to bring healing and restore him or her to wholeness.

This is the way that God designed for physical healing to be administered within a Kingdom community in situations where the sick member is unable to corporately gather due to the severity of the illness. The responsibility in this regard is twofold: 1) The sick member must initiate the request for the elders without just assuming that they will somehow be "led by the Spirit" and appear. And 2) The elders are to promptly respond to the request by visiting the sick member's bedside for prayer without trying to delegate this responsibility to someone else such as the prayer team. Of course, the expectation should be that these elders are anointed, divinely appointed, and full of faith and power.

What we often refer to today as miracles are simply spiritual principles that we do not understand. We need to stop trusting in our own human wisdom and start depending more on His. When we start doing things God's way we will receive God's promised results!

In the next verse it would almost appear that James is proceeding to contradict some of what he just said:

Therefore, confess your sins to one another and pray for one another, that you may be healed. The prayer of a righteous person has great power as it is working. (James 5:16 ESV)

Of course we know that James is not contradicting his previous statements here at all. The principle of obtaining healing through faith prayer when you are sick is still the subject being discussed and emphasized. In the previous verse, the sick person was confined to a sickbed and unable to physically go to the elders or corporately gather with the other saints. This should only represent the infrequent few. These bedridden believers are to call for the elders to come to them. For the rest of us, or the vast majority who are not bedridden, God has ordained our access point for healing to be within the Kingdom community itself, where healing is administered through covenant relationships, confession, and prayer.[8] This makes our responsibility to be integrated and connected with each other that much more important, especially as sickness and disease seem to be even more rampant as the day of the Lord approaches (Heb. 10:25).

> *WHAT WE OFTEN REFER TO TODAY AS MIRACLES ARE SIMPLY SPIRITUAL PRINCIPLES THAT WE DO NOT UNDERSTAND.*

You will notice that it is the prayer of a *"righteous person"* that has great power, or as the NKJV renders it: *"The effective, fervent prayer of a righteous man avails much."* This term refers to every righteous member within the covenant community, not a select group of "intercessors" or even the senior leadership. The same healing is effected by the individual members as is achieved by the corporate eldership! The only requirement is righteousness.

FOURTH RELIGIOUS MISCONCEPTION

Misconception #4*: Only a specific group of people are called to a ministry of intercession.*

Although this very popular myth is closely connected to Misconception #2, it is definitely worth mentioning as a point of its own since it is so widely practiced even among many "apostolic" and "prophetic" churches today. It has become somewhat of a "sacred cow" doctrine that is zealously protected by its proponents. Numerous books, conferences, and teachings promote the idea that there is such a particular ministry—distinct from that which is expected from every born-again saint—where only a select group of people (mostly women) are called to function.

The Temple Principle

You will recall that earlier on in this writing we discussed Herod's Temple and its structure in light of Jesus' declaration, *"My house shall be called a house of prayer"* (Matt. 21:13). We noted that when Jesus made this statement He did so from one of the outermost courts usually referred to as the *Court of the Gentiles*—an area in the temple dedicated to non-Jews, which was never recognized for prayer gatherings or any other type of structured or organized religious activity by the Jews.

When Jesus quoted the prophets regarding prayer and God's house, effectively applying the text to the situation at the temple, He was clearly not referring to the Court of the Gentiles alone, since it was never known or regarded for prayer in any aspect. He said *"My house"*—not "this (or any) part or portion of My house"—*"shall be called a house of prayer"*! The entire temple as a whole—inclusive of every part, including the outer Court of the Gentiles—was being highlighted in His statement. The principle is that every part, every portion, and every member is included in God's requirement for prayer.

Therefore, to say that only certain, select members are called to a ministry of prayer or intercession is a violation of the very principle that Jesus proclaimed. If the temple, which represents God's covenant people, was dedicated completely to prayer (meaning no part was exempt), then the principle must remain consistent in the reality as well (1 Cor. 3:16-17; 6:19; 2 Cor. 6:16).

Lack of Scriptural Evidence for Any Special Ministry of Intercession

Absolutely nowhere in the biblical record do we find such a special ministry as intercession, with the word *ministry* here being employed in reference to a particular area of service for God to which one has to be specifically called. Nowhere in the New Testament will you find any indication of a specific group of people, chosen and called from within the community of born-again believers, to minister specifically or especially in prayer or intercession. This is for good reason: God never intended for any aspect of prayer to be the ministry or responsibility of a select few.

The New Testament informs us about certain groups of people in regard to prayer: We know that widows (older women whose husbands had passed away and whose children were presumably grown) were expected to display a greater dedication to the discipline of prayer due to the fact that they had no other responsibilities or distractions, such as work or family (Luke 2:36-37; 1 Tim. 5:5). We know that the apostles gave themselves continually to prayer along with the ministry of the Word (Acts. 1:12-14; 6:1-4). We know that the prophets and teachers prayed and ministered before God (Acts 13:1-3). And we know that the saints or covenant community of born-again believers—inclusive of every member—continued steadfastly in prayer also (Acts 12:5; Rom. 12:12; Eph. 6:18; Col. 4:2). But these verses give no reference to any specific group or team of "intercessors."

In fact, even the very words *intercession* and *intercessor*—words very rarely used in Scripture—have been given entirely new meanings and related functions by certain segments of Christianity today. For instance, the word *intercession* in Scripture is translated from a Greek word that basically means "petition." This word does not carry all of the elaborately fabricated connotations that many ascribe to it today as some type of woeful, intense, and laborious spiritual exercise often accompanied with "travail." *The Bible Exposition Commentary* shares some valuable insight concerning this word:

> *Intercessions* is best translated "petitions." This same word is translated "prayer" in 1 Tim. 4:5, where it refers to blessing the food we eat. (It is rather obvious that we do not intercede for our food in the usual sense of that word.) The basic meaning is "to draw near to a person and converse

confidently with him." It suggests that we enjoy fellowship with God so that we have confidence in Him as we pray.[9]

The word *intercession* can therefore be applied to prayer in general, without all of the hoopla that generally accompanies it. It does not necessarily imply high-level spiritual warfare, emotionally desperate pleas, or even a relentless seeking. There is, however, a principle of *intercession* that has very little to do with the traditional religious understanding or practical exercise of prayer. This will be discussed in the following chapter.

The word *intercessor* in the Hebrew carries a variety of meanings, the most applicable being "one who meets or makes contact with God for the purpose of entreating Him." Again, neither the word *intercession* nor the word *intercessor* communicates a type of prayer or ministry that is in any way superior, separate, or exclusive to what is generally expected from every believer.

THE RESPONSIBILITY TO WATCH AND PRAY IS A DIVINE REQUIREMENT EXPECTED OF EVERY KINGDOM CITIZEN AND KINGDOM COMMUNITY.

Some have used the existence of specially appointed watchmen in the Old Testament, who were primarily responsible for keeping watch, to attempt to make an argument in support of the practice of intercession today. However, the most biblically accurate substance for this typology is the prophets (2 Kings 9:17-18; Is. 62:6; Ezek. 3:17; 33:1-7; Hos. 9:8; Hab. 2:1). Furthermore, even though prophets—who act as watchmen— are very closely associated with all aspects of prayer in Scripture by virtue of their very calling and function, the responsibility to *watch and pray* is not theirs alone. It is a divine requirement of every Kingdom citizen and Kingdom community (Mark 13:33-37; Luke 21:36; Col. 4:2; 1 Pet. 4:7).

The result of the widespread acceptance of this myth is that many saints have surrendered their God-given responsibility to a group of "professionals." The idea is that these prayer experts have made themselves available and are now responsible for carrying the load and shouldering the burden that was intended to be shared by every member of the community, including the leadership.

Church Leaders Are Responsible to Intercede

Some leaders are too "busy," lazy, or intoxicated by their own self-indulgence to pray, so they establish an intercessory prayer team to do it for them. Leaders have been charged with an even greater responsibility in this area, so when leaders are lax or resign themselves to shifting their responsibility to others, they inevitably reproduce the same distorted mentality in their followers (Is. 56:10-11; Matt. 26:40-41; 1 Thess. 5:6; 2 Tim. 4:5; Rev. 3:3).

The false premise that some are called to pay (give), some are called to pray (intercede), and some are called to preach (declare the good news of the gospel) hinders the spiritual development of the saints, the maturation of God's Covenant Community, and the advancement of the Kingdom of God here on earth. The truth of the matter is that we are *all* called to do each of the above.

Honoring the Faithful Few

Special honor should be given to those who have willingly and selflessly surrendered themselves to the service of prayer and intercession. Very often unseen, unappreciated, and unrecognized, these faithful few—particularly women—have been shouldering or carrying a heavy burden that God never intended for them to carry alone. They have waited, they have watched, they have warred, and they have pursued God relentlessly, while the rest of us—particularly the men—continue with our "busy" lives. This is a travesty!

Of course there will always be individuals who have a greater affinity or who experience a greater passion toward prayer or intercession than other believers, just as some have a greater inclination toward giving. They may feel better qualified, experience a greater urgency, or even conclude prayer is their primary calling. But this does not justify the formation of an elite class of intercessors who are responsible for all the praying. Having certain people lead in prayer is one thing, but having them do all (or even most) of the praying is another.

The Dangers of Making Intercession Only the Ministry of a Select Few

When we promote the idea that any form of prayer is the ministry or responsibility of a select few, we are abandoning one of the foundational principles of the Kingdom, the priesthood of all believers. This misconception distorts the covenant view whereby we each have equal access, right, and responsibility to approach God on behalf of ourselves, our families, our communities, our leaders, our nations, and the world. It creates a dependency syndrome that says, "The intercessors will handle it"; encourages laziness by the other members; and creates an ungodly dichotomy or division that God never intended for His Bride.

In addition, this false concept often leads to a spirit of pride or elitism, especially among the immature. It can also open up a doorway for manipulation, control, and gossip among the "intercessors."

I have seen firsthand how witches and ravenous "wolves" have infiltrated churches, assimilated themselves into the intercessory prayer teams, and then used that influence to manipulate the leadership. On one occasion a single woman who claimed to be a prophetess and intercessor became actively involved in the church's intercessory team. She appeared to be very gifted and passionate in her prayer and was also very faithful in her attendance to services and prayer meetings. It wasn't very long before she was promoted to "chief intercessor" by the leadership.

Her relationship with the leadership grew until she was able to exert significant influence in their decisions. They trusted her counsel. In addition, she was given greater responsibility and became an instructor in the ministry's Bible school. After a couple of years or at least several months, it was discovered that she was actually a witch (I am not certain how they actually made that discovery, but the leadership was also alerted through a vision one of the members had). To make matters worse, it was also discovered that she had seduced several of the men into sexual sin during the tenure of her ministry. This would never have happened if the entire church body, including the leadership, had been watching and praying. As it stands, they trusted the fox to guard the chicken coop and paid dearly for it.

> *WHEN WE PROMOTE THE IDEA THAT ANY FORM OF PRAYER IS THE MINISTRY OR RESPONSIBILITY OF A SELECT FEW, WE ARE ABANDONING FOUNDATIONAL KINGDOM PRINCIPLES.*

When the entire Kingdom community recognizes and accepts their responsibility to pray—including the leadership—it eliminates that hierarchical tier most often pursued by those with diabolical motives, places everyone on an equal level, and creates a safety net of numerous checks and balances as everyone is watching and seeking God.

New Testament Protocol Regarding Prayer and Intercession

Neither Jesus, the apostles, nor any of the early Kingdom Community leaders ever acknowledged or identified such an elite class of people with regard to prayer. On the contrary, when two of the key apostolic leaders were arrested and threatened—namely Peter and

John—the entire corporate Kingdom community prayed, not an elite group of intercessors.

> *As soon as they were freed, Peter and John returned to the other believers and told them what the leading priests and elders had said. When they heard the report, **all the believers lifted their voices together in prayer to God**: "O Sovereign Lord, Creator of heaven and earth, the sea, and everything in them—you spoke long ago by the Holy Spirit through our ancestor David, your servant, saying,*
>
> *'Why were the nations so angry?*
> *Why did they waste their time with futile plans?*
> *The kings of the earth prepared for battle;*
> *the rulers gathered together*
> *against the LORD*
> *and against his Messiah.'*
>
> *"In fact, this has happened here in this very city! For Herod Antipas, Pontius Pilate the governor, the Gentiles, and the people of Israel were all united against Jesus, your holy servant, whom you anointed. But everything they did was determined beforehand according to your will. And now, O Lord, hear their threats, and give us, your servants, great boldness in preaching your word. Stretch out your hand with healing power; may miraculous signs and wonders be done through the name of your holy servant Jesus."*
>
> *After this prayer, the meeting place shook, and they were all filled with the Holy Spirit. Then they preached the word of God with boldness.* (Acts 4:23-31 NLT; emphasis mine)

We can glean some very important principles from this corporate prayer initiative, several of which have been discussed before: Nothing in this prayer is vindictively antagonistic against the religious rulers who had threatened Peter and John—the believers made no attempt to attack or counterattack those who opposed them with prayer. Nor did they attempt to persuade God to stop or avert the crisis. They did not overemphasize the kingdom of darkness, demons, or satan in the usual, delusional sense of "binding" and "loosing" the spiritual enemy that was opposing their advance, as we see some do today. These prayers reveal an accurate biblical perspective regarding the situation and a clear measure of sight, which allowed the believers to remain anchored to the truth. They recognized the sovereignty of God, as well as their own human responsibility, and the need for His grace to overcome. But our greatest point of emphasis here is that these believers did not call a group of specialized intercessors. All the believers prayed—and so powerful was their prayer that the entire meeting place shook (v. 31)!

This is not an attempt to be facetious, but I've been in numerous prayer meetings with those who claim to be specially called intercessors, and the only thing found shaking at the end of the prayer was my head in disbelief! We will never experience or surpass the type of potency in prayer we read about in Acts until the entire Kingdom community gets involved.

When Peter was imprisoned again, with the intent to have him executed, constant prayer was offered to God for him by the entire church or corporate Kingdom community, not a select group of "intercessors."

> *About that time Herod the king laid violent hands on some who belonged to the church. He killed James the brother of John with the sword, and when he saw that it pleased the Jews, he proceeded to arrest Peter also. This was during the days of Unleavened Bread. And when he had seized him, he put him in prison, delivering him over to four squads of*

*soldiers to guard him, intending after the Passover to bring him out to the people. So Peter was kept in prison, but **earnest prayer for him was made to God by the church.*** (Acts 12:1-5 ESV; emphasis mine)

Once again we find that it is the corporate body of born-again believers who pray, not a specialized group of spiritual warfare advocates or elite intercessors. And once again the results are profound: Heavenly angels are dispatched to deliver Peter out of prison through a series of miraculous occurrences (Acts 12:5-10).

WE WILL NEVER EXPERIENCE OR SURPASS THE TYPE OF POTENCY IN PRAYER WE READ ABOUT IN ACTS UNTIL THE ENTIRE KINGDOM COMMUNITY GETS INVOLVED.

Similarly, when Paul addresses the subject of spiritual warfare and encourages his readers at Ephesus to pray *"always with all prayer and supplication in the Spirit, being watchful,"* he is not addressing a select group of "watchman intercessors" but the corporate Kingdom community, including every individual member (Eph. 6:10-18).

And finally, when Paul is in need of prayer support in the fulfillment of his apostolic commission,[10] he doesn't establish a group of personal intercessors; he makes known his request to the entire Kingdom community as a whole (Rom. 15:30-33; Eph. 6:18-20; Phil. 1:19-20; Col. 4:2-4; 1 Thess. 5:25; 2 Thess. 3:1-2; Heb. 13:18). How strikingly different from that which is both preached and practiced today!

175

FIFTH RELIGIOUS MISCONCEPTION

Misconception #5: Israel should be our primary prayer focus.

The nation of Israel has always been very near and dear to the heart of God. It is impossible for anyone taking an open and honest view of Scripture or biblical history to deny this fact. After all, it was through Israel that both the written Word (the Scriptures) and the Living Word (Jesus) came. They are a people specially called and chosen by God, and His intimate involvement with them can be traced all the way back to Abraham. The Jews are God's covenant people and the apple of His eye (Deut. 7:7-9; Zech. 2:8).

Notwithstanding, the nation of Israel is not to be our primary emphasis, whether in prayer or in any other regard. Our focus is to be placed solely and completely upon the Kingdom of God *first*, recognizing the fact that even though Israel was a type and shadow of God's eternal Kingdom, the natural nation of Israel is not the true measure or substance (Matt. 6:10, 33; 1 Cor. 15:24-28).

The apostle Paul reiterates this principle when he instructs the Kingdom community at Ephesus to pray. His clear command is that every type of prayer be made or offered up on behalf of *all men*, and the intent is equally clear: *"For this is good and acceptable in the sight of God our Savior, who desires **all men** to be saved and to come to the knowledge of the truth"* (1 Tim. 2:1, 3-4; emphasis mine).

This particular instruction, delivered to a non-Jew (Timothy) and intended for a non-Jewish community (the Ephesian covenant community), argues against any form of exclusivist or elitist mentality regarding Israel and the Jews, especially with regard to prayer. Paul reminds his audience that what is *"good and acceptable"* to God is not prayer offered up primarily or exclusively for themselves or for Israel, but prayer made on behalf of *all men*, because He desires *all men* to be saved.

God Loves the World

God didn't send His Son to earth just so that He could redeem or ransom Israel. The Gentile nations—which include every one of us who are non-Jews (according to the flesh)—were never an afterthought in the redemptive plan of God. The text clearly states, *"For God so loved **the world** that He gave His only begotten Son,"* thus making Him a ransom for all (John 3:16; 1 Tim. 2:5-6).

Even though the gospel was sent or given to Israel first (Acts 3:26; Rom. 1:16), it is inaccurate to assume that the physical Jews carry a greater level of priority or a higher degree of importance with regard to God's Kingdom purposes. Jesus is not returning for an earthly Kingdom in Israel; He is returning for a spiritual Kingdom comprised of every tribe and nation with the whole earth as its territory (Matt. 21:43; Luke 13:29; 17:20-21; John 3:3-5; 18:36; 1 Cor. 15:50; Rev. 11:15).

I love and appreciate Israel as much as the next guy. But it becomes very upsetting and disconcerting to me when I hear various pro-Israel segments of religious Christianity promote a doctrine or emphasis that makes Israel the apex of God's divine purposes and the future of that nation the most critical aspect of our earthly assignment. Very often what is portrayed is inaccurate and insulting to other nations. This is especially true regarding the Arab world, with those of Arab descent often being depicted at best as being of lesser importance to God, or at worst as being mortal enemies to His Kingdom.

God loves the Arabs and Muslims just as much as He loves the Jews. But we have been ineffective in communicating God's love to this segment of humanity due in large part to the distorted gospel we have presented and the lack of genuine prayer issuing from a heart of love, compassion, and concern for their spiritual and physical welfare. It is true that many Arab nations and groups have set themselves against the political nations of Israel and the West—often with extreme violence— but from a Kingdom viewpoint the Arab people themselves are not the enemies of God, and neither should they be to us. Even if they were, we are still obligated to love and pray for them (Matt. 6:44).

Praying for the Peace of Jerusalem

David gave an exhortation in song regarding praying for the peace of Jerusalem (Ps. 122:6), but that does not make Israel our primary prayer emphasis today. If so, we could say the same about Jeremiah's prophecy regarding the Lord's intent that the Jewish captives pray to the Lord for the peace of Babylon (present-day Iran and Iraq) so that they in turn could have peace. David's original audience all worshipped or dwelt in Jerusalem, so it was expected that they should pray for the city and its leaders, just as the Israeli captives were expected to pray for their cities of residence while in captivity in a foreign land so that they, too, could prosper and experience peace (Ps. 122:6; Jer. 29:4-7).

Israel is worthy of our love and support, but any undue emphasis placed upon Israel becomes a distraction from our true Kingdom assignment and purpose. God's desire has not changed—He *"desires all men to be saved and to come to the knowledge of the truth."*

KEY PRINCIPLES

1. The charge to pray was really issued to both men and women, with the men being singled out and mentioned first because of their leading role in this regard. Men were never intended to be mere spectators but leading participators in every prayer initiative.
2. Just as the woman was created with a womb that cannot be substituted by anything or any (male) man, so too the man was created with unique capabilities that cannot be substituted.
3. Every one of us, whether male or female, without exception, has a responsibility to pray and not to depend on a select few to do it for us.
4. When anyone is suffering hardship or affliction, he (or she) should be the one to pray (for himself/herself).
5. Any truth or principle taken to the extreme—beyond the original boundaries and parameters of Scripture—quickly degenerates into error.
6. Unity or agreement in error simply makes for unified or greater error; it does not guarantee effectiveness in prayer.
7. The "prayer of agreement" specifically refers to matters relating to preserving the integrity and correct internal architecture of God's Kingdom community, not deliverance from hardship or the meeting of personal needs.
8. It is your responsibility to approach God boldly and with faith.
9. Each one of us as a Kingdom citizen has equal access to God. God does not grant special access to His throne to certain spiritual leaders or "intercessors."

10. The command not to be anxious for anything is a prohibition against the self-centered tendency to be worried or concerned about our own personal needs, wants, or desires.

11. Prayer (all types) with thanksgiving is considered the cure that is able to transform our anxiety into peace, with the implication being that we are to pray to God directly rather than to advertise our prayer requests to others.

12. Regardless of what situation we may find ourselves in, we are to pray and give thanks, because it releases God's peace—our true need!

13. Prayer is for the purpose of changing us rather than our situations.

14. The only time we have a legitimate biblical right to request prayer support for a personal need, or in response to a personal crisis, is when we are *sick* (meaning physically weak, infirmed, or feeble).

15. God has ordained our access point for healing to be within the Kingdom community itself, where healing is administered through covenant relationships, confession, and prayer.

16. Every part, every portion, and every member is included in God's requirement for prayer.

17. God never intended for any aspect of prayer to be the ministry or responsibility of a select few.

18. The nation of Israel is not to be our primary emphasis, whether in prayer or in any other regard.

ENDNOTES

1. Numbers 30 describes the authority inherently resident within a father or husband to overrule or nullify a woman's vow made unto God while under his authority. It underscores the principle that men carry a greater degree of rank and spiritual authority similar to the way it is exercised in the Godhead. Men and women were created equal as persons, but they are not equal in the rank and authority they possess.

2. *The Complete Word Study Dictionary: New Testament*, ed. Spiros Zodhiates Th.D. (Chattanooga, TN: AMG International, 1993), 2553; *Thayer's Greek-English Lexicon of the New Testament*, G2553 [e-Sword].

3. The Matthew 18:19 principle of agreement should be interpreted in the specific context it was given. Specifically, it applies to preserving the integrity and correct internal architecture of God's Kingdom community (this is **not** "church discipline" as is commonly interpreted), but in a wider context the principle simply echoes the foundational purpose of prayer examined in the first chapter—it is for the execution of God's divine purpose in the earth, not the acquisition of personal blessing or breakthrough, deliverance from personal hardship, or to have personal needs or desires met. The emphasis here is on what heaven desires!

   The word translated as any "thing" (*pragma*) in this verse is not a license for making any type of carnal petition or request in prayer and confirming it with agreement. In fact, the word *pragma* is often used in a limited sense to refer to judicial matters, which in this sense would apply to what heaven has authorized to be "bound" or "loosed" (prohibited or permitted; retained or remitted) in the community of believers. This was obviously a corporate transaction, which, in turn, required a corporate participation or response in prayer, thus the need for agreement. When this text is interpreted outside of the clear parameters provided by the context, we arrive at erroneous conclusions regarding prayer. There is no scripture that promotes the idea that God pays special attention to prayer when two or more are in agreement together. The Kingdom of God is not an earthly democracy that operates based upon the volume of responses or popular vote. In other words, it makes no difference to God whether one, two, two hundred, two thousand, or two million people pray regarding a matter. Faith (with the corresponding obedience) is what moves heaven to action, not the number of people praying. Jesus' prayers weren't effective because He had a large number of believers in agreement with Him; His prayers were effective because He lived and operated in complete faith and obedience to the Father's will.

4. This is not the same as the biblical principle of *honor* where it was considered dishonorable to approach God, a ruler, or a prophet without a gift (Ex. 23:15; 34:20; Judg. 3:17; 1 Sam. 9:6-8; 1 Kings 10:1-2). Every representative of God is deserving of honor, but it is a violation of this principle when gifts are given as a way of buying God's favor (Matt. 10:40-42).

5. Having a compassionate "help line" instead of a religious "prayer line" would be a more valid expression of love and much more effective for community transformation.

6. This is relating to wisdom on a personal level. On a corporate level, Paul placed great emphasis on praying for wisdom and understanding for the Kingdom communities (churches) with which he was apostolically related. As such, there should always be an emphasis by apostolic leadership on petitioning God for spiritual wisdom and sight for the entire body.

7. Technically speaking, this is not really a request for prayer; this is a request for the elders. Prayer is the avenue through which the elders exercise their faith in a corporate dimension to meet a physical need. The sick person is in need of healing, not prayer. Healing is the need and prayer is the avenue or vehicle through which this particular need is supernaturally met.

8. The matter regarding confession of sin to individual members reveals the connection that often exists between sin and sickness or disease.

9. *The Bible Exposition Commentary*. Copyright © 1989 by Chariot Victor Publishing, an imprint of Cook Communication Ministries [Biblesoft].

10. Leaders have a right to request prayer when it pertains to their Kingdom mandate or assignment, not for their own personal needs or indulgences like a vacation in Hawaii, a family cruise, a new car, or a bigger house.

CHAPTER 9

KINGDOM INTERCESSION

W e discussed the subject of intercession in the previous chapter as it relates to being the biblical responsibility of every Kingdom citizen. We mentioned that in their biblical context the words *intercession* and *intercessor*—words rarely ever used in Scripture—are without the usual religious baggage or fanciful intimations usually projected upon them in Christendom today. When examined from the original Greek and Hebrew, both of which carry very similar connotations, the word *intercession* carries the basic idea of a petition made in any general sense, and the word *intercessor* describes someone who makes contact with God for the purpose of entreating or petitioning Him. Both terms imply a "meeting" with God or a close proximity to His presence.

In this particular chapter we are going to discuss intercession as a spiritual principle from a Kingdom dimension, without limiting it to the traditional understanding of prayer. And once again we will refer to the prophet Isaiah.

Justice is turned back,
and righteousness stands far away;
for truth has stumbled in the public squares,
and uprightness cannot enter.
Truth is lacking,
and he who departs from evil makes himself a prey.

The LORD saw it, and it displeased him
that there was no justice.
He saw that there was no man,
and wondered that there was no one to intercede;
then his own arm brought him salvation,
and his righteousness upheld him.
He put on righteousness as a breastplate,
and a helmet of salvation on his head;
he put on garments of vengeance for clothing,
and wrapped himself in zeal as a cloak.
(Isaiah 59:14-17 ESV)

This is one of those chapters that needs to be read in its entirety in order to comprehend the full gravity and context of what Isaiah is seeking to prophetically communicate. It follows on the heels of Isaiah's rebuke regarding the error and corruption that had permeated the Israelites' religious practices, rendering their prayer and fasting initiatives dysfunctional and ineffective (Is. 58).

Isaiah begins his argument by reminding this religious company that God is neither deaf nor impotent in executing His salvation on their behalf (v. 1). The prevailing issue that either prevented or delayed God's action in this instance—similar to what was described in the previous chapter of Isaiah about their fasting (Is. 58)—was not a lack of earnest prayer, but their iniquity and sin that had created an impenetrable barrier that alienated them from God (v. 2).

Interestingly, of the many sins identified by Isaiah, including lies (vs. 3, 4, 13), wickedness or perversity of the tongue (vs. 3, 13), dishonesty or unfairness (v. 4), violence (v. 6), murder or bloodshed (v. 7), iniquitous thoughts (v. 7), destructive ways (v. 7), crookedness (v. 8), departure from God (v. 13), and oppression (v. 13), injustice is the issue most predominantly mentioned, in addition to falsehood or a lack of truth (vs. 4, 8, 9, 11, 14, 15).

186

This was the same religious company, mind you, that was notorious for requesting of God *"ordinances of justice,"* yet they were exceedingly incapable of executing true justice on a personal, social, or religious level (Is. 58:2 NKJV). Their ethical standards had been totally degraded, leaving them without any moral compass. As a people entrenched in such injustice, they displayed a hypocrisy similar to the type prevalent in many churches today—such as when leaders favor or promote people to positions of leadership based largely upon the size of their financial contributions to the church, their natural likeability, or their willingness to flatter, personally cater to, or brown-nose the leaders (favoritism); when the senior pastor shows special favor to close friends by promoting them or allowing them special privileges not afforded to other members (cronyism); when the church or ministry is run like a family business where the family members of the senior minister/pastor are afforded greater opportunities, privileges, positions, and power than the other members (nepotism); or when churches demonstrate a greater preference toward those of their own race, culture or class (racism and chauvinism). How dare we cry out or call out to God for justice when we have forsaken justice in our own lives and communities through favoritism, cronyism, nepotism, chauvinism, and various other forms of discrimination or inequity?

IDENTIFICATIONAL REPENTANCE

Isaiah calls the people to a recognition of their own responsibility during this time of moral crisis, which is seemingly exacerbated by God's silence and apparent disregard. He identifies himself with the sin, blindness, and moral depravity of the nation (Is. 59:9-15).

This identificational aspect of Isaiah's pronouncement is what many believe to be the primary ingredient for effective intercession. However, this assumption is not entirely accurate unless *intercession* is interpreted to refer *only* to the act of prayer in the traditional religious sense. Biblically speaking, it is a clearly established fact, or rather, truth, that this is not the case because prayer can never operate within a vacuum. We have stated several times throughout this book that prayer is nullified without obedience!

MORE REQUIRED THAN PRAYER

The text plainly states that God was displeased by what He saw regarding the injustice (v. 15). His displeasure was not as a result of any assumed lack of prayer. The undeniable fact is that this was a praying and fasting religious company. The first two verses of the chapter confirm that the current conditions in Israel were not a result of any scarcity in the act of prayer. The previous chapter attests to them being engaged in prayer and fasting on a regular basis. It would be reasonable to assume that many of the people earnestly interceded in prayer for the nation as well.

GOD IS LOOKING FOR SOMEONE TO RAISE UP A RIGHTEOUS STANDARD TO OPPOSE INJUSTICE, STEM THE TIDE OF UNRIGHTEOUSNESS, AND IGNITE A REFORMATION THROUGH AN ACCURATE LIFESTYLE OR WITNESS.

Therefore, when God indicates that He could find *"no man,"* and then wonders at the fact that there was *"no one to intercede,"* He clearly could not have been referring to prayer or intercession in the usual, religious sense of the word. The only reasonable interpretation is that God was looking for someone to raise up a righteous standard to oppose injustice, stem the tide of unrighteousness, and ignite a reformation through his or her accurate lifestyle or witness. God was searching for a person who would elevate truth above falsehood, bring sight to the blind, and possibly defend the interests of the poor, weak, or oppressed. He was not necessarily looking for anyone to "change the world," only to resist the status-quo and impact his or her sphere of influence. God needed someone who would dare to be different and boldly proclaim the truth without fear of suffering rejection or persecution (v. 15). When intercessory prayer is built upon such a foundation, it becomes potent and effective. When these principles are ignored, it becomes utterly useless!

THE PRINCIPLE OF RECONCILIATION

One of the English definitions for the word *intercede* that is not usually communicated through any of the original Hebrew or Greek words is "to intervene between parties with a view to reconciling differences," or "to act as a mediator in a dispute."[1] You will notice from this English definition that the primary connotation is not prayer in the usual sense of the word. The primary focus here is on reconciliation.

THE ACT OF PRAYER ALONE CAN NEVER ADDRESS THE ISSUE OF SIN OR BRING TRUE RECONCILIATION.

To reconcile two parties, one first has to resolve the issue(s) that caused the faction or separation to begin with, before any attempt can be made to restore the relationship. Peace and reconciliation will be futile unless these issues are resolved. If someone committed an offense against another party such as rear-ending their vehicle, he would have to pay damages in the form of a settlement in order to compensate for his wrongdoing. He may also be required to desist from any further offensive action or provocation (such as reckless tailgating) if any meaningful reconciliation is to be achieved or maintained. If the offensive act is pardoned and the respective parties reconciled, peace will only exist between them so long as the offense is never repeated. Once repeated, the process begins all over again and the fracture potentially becomes more severe, making reconciliation much more difficult.

The intermediary person who seeks to transact this reconciliation is considered a functional intercessor. The intercessor's primary purpose is not to plead the case of the offending party, for any pleading is only a means to an end. The goal is always to restore harmony to the fractured relationship, with the expectation that there will be true repentance and contrition in the heart of the offender.

When this principle is applied to our current text, it creates a much better understanding of God's expectations as it pertains to intercession in such a context. God wanted a man who could lift a righteous standard to convict the people of their sins. Light uncovers darkness, truth reveals error or falsehood, and righteousness exposes unrighteousness. Sometimes all that is needed is a spark to ignite the flames.

The act of prayer alone could never have addressed these issues or brought true reconciliation in the situation described in Isaiah 59 because the problem didn't stem from God. God was not the One at fault. He didn't move; the people of Israel did! He was not the offender; they were! It was their own sin, iniquity, and injustice that had separated them from God and His goodness. The best that could have been accomplished by merely petitioning or pleading with God in prayer for Israel would have been delayed judgment, nothing more. The sin issue would have remained unresolved and the people would still have been left without a righteous standard or a beacon of light that would guide them to safety.

It is a sad and unfortunate commentary indeed that during this time of moral crisis, depravity, and injustice, and despite the abundance of religious prayers, fastings, petitions, decrees, and "binding and loosing" in pseudo-spiritual warfare, God is still unable to find a true intercessor in their midst. All the people are stumbling in blindness. On account of this deficiency, God is left with no other option but to initiate their salvation through His own zeal, power, and righteousness, clothing Himself like a warrior in what is considered by some to be a messianic prefiguring of the salvation wrought by Christ (vs. 16, 17).

JESUS THE INTERCESSOR

Therefore I will divide him a portion with the many,
and he shall divide the spoil with the strong,
because he poured out his soul to death
and was numbered with the transgressors;
yet he bore the sin of many,
and makes intercession for the transgressors.
(Isaiah 53:12 ESV)

Who is to condemn? Christ Jesus is the one who died—more than that, who was raised—who is at the right hand of God, who indeed is interceding for us. (Romans 8:34 ESV)

Consequently, he is able to save to the uttermost those who draw near to God through him, since he always lives to make intercession for them. (Hebrews 7:25 ESV)

Jesus is without a doubt the ultimate intercessor. While Jesus' intercession refers primarily to His mediatorial aspect in securing our redemption, rather than to a traditional or religious understanding of prayer,[2] there are principles in these verses that can inform every aspect of intercession—including prayer!

In the Isaiah 53 account—one that is considered by many to be one of the most profound messianic prophecies in Scripture—Jesus is pictured as an intercessor who *"makes intercession for the transgressors."* This ministry of intercession is reiterated and confirmed by Paul in the New Testament; however, we often miss the subtle but profound implications of Jesus' intercession.

Jesus could never have transacted our redemption and reconciliation to God through intercession by remaining in heaven and petitioning the Father on our behalf. Jesus was literally in the presence of the Father, yet remaining in His Father's presence without sacrificing His life and establishing a new and righteous standard on earth would not have been beneficial for us. We know that if the Father was going to listen to anyone it would be His Son, but remaining in heaven petitioning God for our sins would have done very little to accomplish any reconciliation between us and God (John 11:41-42). The issue was never getting God to hear and forgive; the issue was sin and the resulting consequences.

JESUS COULD NEVER HAVE TRANSACTED OUR REDEMPTION AND RECONCILIATION TO GOD THROUGH INTERCESSION BY REMAINING IN HEAVEN AND PETITIONING THE FATHER ON OUR BEHALF.

Jesus had to be willing to leave the Father's side and initiate contact with the lost. He had to be willing to be planted in a dry place and shine His light in the midst of utter darkness (Is. 53:2; John 1:4-5). He had to be willing to endure suffering, pain, rejection, and chastisement from those who were spiritually and morally blind—people who were offended and resistant to His righteous message, morals, manhood, and ministry (Is. 53:3-9).[3] He had to be willing to die and give Himself in complete sacrifice (Is. 53:12). This is the immutable principle of intercession.

THE DEMANDS OF INTERCESSION

We can claim to be intercessors all we want to, but if all we do is soak in the presence of God, calling out to Him day and night for mercy on behalf of the people without ever investing ourselves to reach the very people we claim to be praying for, our "intercession" is futile and vain. With regard to prayer, the principle is always that we are to do everything we *can* do while expecting God to do everything we *can't* do!

A true intercessor is willing to put his life on the line for the person he is praying for.[4] She is willing to invest not only her time in prayer but her energy and resources as well. There should be no disconnection between what is said in the closet and what is actually done toward the cause. If our hands and our feet are not ready and willing to follow our words, then what use are our words at all? If your prayer or intercession doesn't move *you* to action, don't expect it to move God either!

I have witnessed churches, prayer groups, and individual believers crying out to God for the lost, most often with the unrealistic expectation that God will somehow direct the lost to their churches where they can respond to an "altar call" and get saved. But there's a reason why Jesus instructed His disciples to *"pray earnestly to the Lord of the harvest to send out laborers into His harvest,"* rather than to "pray earnestly to the Lord of the laborers to send the harvest to the laborers."

There is nothing wrong with the harvest other than it needs to be reaped. There is nothing more that the Lord can do for them. The problem lies with the laborers. Interestingly, the audience that Jesus is addressing here is His disciples—ones who were already actively engaged in reaching the harvest. Therefore, the only ones truly qualified and authorized to prayerfully intercede to the Lord regarding the need for laborers are those who are willing to fulfill their own prayers by laboring themselves (Matt. 9:37-38; Luke 10:1-2).

The principle Jesus established is simple: If we're not willing to labor, we're not qualified to pray (or intercede)! If we're not willing to go, we can't expect them to come! It doesn't matter how much prayer, shouting, spiritual "labor," or emotional excitement we exert, until we are willing to invest ourselves completely in the fulfillment of our petitions by doing everything within our power that is required, we will continue to experience impotence in our intercession.

IF YOUR PRAYER OR INTERCESSION DOESN'T MOVE YOU TO ACTION, DON'T EXPECT IT TO MOVE GOD EITHER!

When we follow Jesus' example, it creates a double edged sword in that not only are our prayers or intercessions more potent, but our hearts become more connected, softened, and engaged, making it more easier for us to invest ourselves more completely.

PRACTICAL CONSIDERATIONS

The practical implications of this cannot be ignored. For example, when praying for a foreign nation, we should be prepared to go ourselves, if at all possible. If not practically possible, we should be committed to supporting those who can (e.g. missionaries, apostolic teams, missions). When praying for our own nation's peace or prosperity, we should be doing everything possible to create an environment conducive to what we are praying for. This includes voting during all local and general elections for the candidates we believe would best serve our countries, states, or cities; working hard without cheating our employers by extended lunch hours, prolonged breaks, or a slothful work ethic; honestly paying our taxes without seeking avenues or loopholes to defraud the government; being truthful, just, and honest in our business dealings; and living lives of moral uprightness and integrity that seek to be a blessing to the nation rather than just being leeches with a spirit of entitlement or greed.

Whatever it is that we are inclined to pray or intercede for must be accompanied by the corresponding faith action required for its fulfillment. We must be willing to step out and go, do, or become in conjunction with our prayers of intercession.

REBUILDING THE WALL
AND REPAIRING THE BREACH

"I looked for someone who might rebuild the wall of righteousness that guards the land. I searched for someone to stand in the gap in the wall so I wouldn't have to destroy the land, but I found no one. So now I will pour out my fury on them, consuming them with the fire of my anger. I will heap on their heads the full penalty for all their sins. I, the Sovereign LORD, have spoken!" (Ezekiel 22:30-31 NLT)

This very definitive text, while not explicitly using the term *intercession* or any of its related forms, is recognized by many to be one of the primary references for intercessory prayer. While this is certainly true, it would be inaccurate to assume that this passage primarily refers to intercessory prayer in the traditional, religious sense of identificational repentance or petitions for mercy so that God would stay His hand of judgment. In fact, one of the reasons we say that this particular text is definitive is because it clearly identifies the main issues of concern while giving insight into the true nature and function of intercession.

The spiritual and moral climate of the nation of Israel during Ezekiel's writing was in many ways very similar to that which Isaiah encountered during his ministry. One could also argue that Israel's sin, corruption, and social injustices had grown progressively worse. By Ezekiel's time, the nation's internal decay was at its highest. Their "cup of iniquity" had become so full that God was now ready to dispense

195

divine judgment for the serious defilements and ethical impurities that served to permeate every human institution among them, ranging from the individual and family to civil government and religion. Their long list of spiritual, ethical, and moral defilements included idolatry, indicative of impure worship (vs. 3-4, 9); murder or bloodshed, usually associated with greed, selfishness, or injustice (vs. 3-4, 6, 9, 12-13, 27); dishonoring of parents (vs. 7, 10); oppression of the stranger, fatherless, and widow (vs. 7, 29); profaning of the Sabbath (v. 8, 26); gossip, false accusation, or slander (v. 9); premeditated wickedness or licentiousness (v. 9); sexual perversion, including fornication, adultery, and incest (vs. 10-11); and extortion, exploitation, and profiteering (vs. 12-13).

As the prophet Ezekiel issues this divine reprimand against Jerusalem for her many sins, he identifies four specific categories of people within the wider community:

> And the word of the LORD came to me: "Son of man, say to her, You are a land that is not cleansed or rained upon in the day of indignation. The conspiracy of her **prophets** in her midst is like a roaring lion tearing the prey; they have devoured human lives; they have taken treasure and precious things; they have made many widows in her midst. Her **priests** have done violence to my law and have profaned my holy things. They have made no distinction between the holy and the common, neither have they taught the difference between the unclean and the clean, and they have disregarded my Sabbaths, so that I am profaned among them. Her **princes** in her midst are like wolves tearing the prey, shedding blood, destroying lives to get dishonest gain. And her **prophets** have smeared whitewash for them, seeing false visions and divining lies for them, saying, 'Thus says the Lord GOD,' when the LORD has not spoken. The **people** of the land have practiced extortion and committed robbery.

They have oppressed the poor and needy, and have extorted
from the sojourner without justice.
(Ezekiel 22:23-29, ESV; emphasis mine)

1. Princes (rulers or leaders)—vs. 6, 27
2. Prophets (those functioning in prophetic ministry)—vs. 25, 28
3. Priests (ministers, ministries, elders, or pastors)—v. 26
4. People (people in general, typifying church members or Christians)—v. 29

Note that the leaders themselves (princes, prophets, and priests) were responsible for modeling, and therefore reproducing, their error and corruption in the people. Those responsible for setting the standard of righteousness, morality, and ethical purity were themselves incapable of fulfilling God's righteous demands due to their own internal deficiencies and lax ethical standards. They were consumed by their own self-interest, greed, and self-indulgence.

The language and metaphors used in the original Hebrew—"roaring lion tearing the prey" and "wolves tearing the prey"—describe the ferocious, merciless, violent, and predatory nature of these leaders intent on building systems of extraction while pursuing their own personal satisfaction and dishonest gain. Every single leader was defiled, seeking to make himself fat on the sheep he was called to feed and protect (vs. 25, 27).

The priests or spiritual leaders who were responsible for teaching God's laws and truth were themselves blind and ignorant, lacking true discernment, and unable to accurately distinguish between the holy and profane. In other words, they were blinded by religious conformity, lacking any valid spiritual sight or understanding regarding true correctness. In spite of their prayers, sacrifices, and regular priestly ministrations, they still possessed no revelation or understanding regarding what was clean (sanctioned and approved by God) or unclean (rejected and condemned by God). Their spiritual perception and judgment was dubious at best because they possessed no valid comprehension of truth (v. 26).

The prophetic ministry in existence among them was a pathetic display of deceit, divination, and falsehood.[5] With numerous presumptuous prophecies resulting from an inaccurate ethical foundation, their emphasis was on flattery, making people feel good, and telling people what they wanted to hear, thus strengthening them in error, false confidence, and false hope. Their desire to be accepted, popular, and wealthy overshadowed their desire for truth; therefore, they celebrated and whitewashed error with presumptuous lies (v. 28).

The common people, therefore, were no better. The law of Genesis dictates that *like produces like* (Gen. 1:11-12, 21-25). Inclined to follow in the footsteps of their leaders, the people began to oppress those weaker than themselves (the poor and needy), including the strangers or foreigners, who did not enjoy the same rights or privileges as regular citizens and could be easily exploited. The oppressed had now become the oppressors (v. 29).

The people were like sheep without a shepherd, void of any accurate example in leadership that could point them toward truth. This was similar to the situation that existed in Jesus' day (Matt. 9:35-38).

Against such a spiritual and historical backdrop the prophet Ezekiel makes his famed but sad prophetic commentary regarding the Lord's inability—after having carefully surveyed all of the city's inhabitants— to find what is generally believed to be an *intercessor* to prevent its destruction. Fortunately for us, the text is very clear and precise regarding the situation or condition that precipitated the exigency of intercession—and it wasn't a lack of prayer according to the traditional understanding or usage.

THE CONSEQUENCES OF SIN

Sin has consequences. Often what we refer to as a "curse" or "judgment" is simply the natural outcome of sin and disobedience after it has run its full course. The reason God gave us laws and commandments was not so that He could boss us around or control our lives.[6] He gave these laws to protect us from the consequences of our own wrong actions or behavior, similarly to the way traffic signals are meant to direct the flow of traffic and prevent anyone from killing or injuring himself or herself or others.

> *THE REASON GOD GAVE US LAWS AND COMMANDMENTS WAS NOT SO THAT HE COULD BOSS US AROUND OR CONTROL OUR LIVES. HE GAVE THESE LAWS TO PROTECT US.*

When the inhabitants of Jerusalem forsook God's laws and defiled themselves spiritually, ethically, and morally by breaking every single one of God's commandments, they inevitably created a *"gap"* or breach in their perimeter hedge or *"wall"* of protection. This left them vulnerable to be overtaken or overthrown both from without as well as from within.[7] To remedy or correct this severe breach, gap, or fracture existing within the spiritual fabric of the nation, God requires someone qualified enough to repair or rebuild the dilapidated wall that had been broken down as a result of sin and unrighteousness. He needs someone to seal and secure the breach that has compromised their defense and safety.

ADDRESSING THE SIN ISSUE

It stands to reason, therefore, that since the wall was broken down or breached as a result of sin and unrighteousness, the only obvious remedy for rebuilding the wall and repairing the breach would be to address the sin issue with an accurate architecture of holiness and righteousness.

Prayerlessness did not cause the breach—it is quite obvious from the text that the usual religious activities continued to occur, including prayer. A lack of intercessory prayer did not cause the breach either; therefore, it would be ridiculous to assume that intercessory prayer in the traditional sense would be the solution to fixing it. The issues being identified here could never be addressed by traditional prayer alone, no matter how sincere or desperate, yet this has been the primary emphasis of intercession today.

The way intercessory prayer is understood and practiced today is no different from what a large segment of the medical society and pharmaceutical companies practice: They treat or mask the symptoms rather than formulating a cure. We seek only to avert or delay impending judgment by approaching God and crying out in repentance on behalf of a sinful people, without ever placing any emphasis on approaching these sinful people to remind them of God's righteous standards and values, including the inevitable consequences if they continue on a path of disobedience. This does not mean that we should never cry out to God on behalf of sinful mankind for mercy, but we should understand that doing so while neglecting the other only provides a temporary fix or delays the inevitable, since the issues requiring God's mercy have never been addressed. Representing God's cause before the people is not the responsibility of prophets alone. We are all called to be a prophetic people.

THE INTERCESSION OF ABRAHAM AND MOSES

Have you ever stopped to consider that despite all of Moses' intercessory pleas—as noble as they were—on behalf of the people of Israel in the wilderness, God still ended up destroying them (Ex. 32:9-14; Num. 14:11-24; 26:63-65; 32:10-13)?[8] Why do you suppose this was? Why did God still have to destroy Sodom and Gomorrah even after Abraham earnestly pleaded with Him not to do so (Gen. 18:16-33)?[9] Was it because God was rash or running low on mercy that day? Was it because of the lack of a prayer intercessor? No! God destroyed these nations because the cause of the offense or breach—sin—had never been addressed or resolved.

Moses was a true intercessor in that he not only went before God on behalf of the people, but he also stood before the people on behalf of God. However, the people still incurred God's judgment, and they even provoked Moses into incurring upon himself the same (Num. 20:1-13; 27:12-14; Deut. 1:34-37; 3:23-27; 34:1-5; Ps. 106:23-33). Moses did his job well, but he was unable to adequately repair the breach due to the people's own stubbornness, disobedience, and rebellion. Sometimes the best form of intercession is simply allowing God to have His way in the first place, since we can be confident in the fact that God is never hasty or recklessly impulsive. Even Abraham finally relented after realizing the futility of pursuing mercy on behalf of Sodom and Gomorrah, whose wickedness was so pervasive that not even ten righteous people could be found.[10]

GOD'S REDEMPTIVE PURPOSE IN JUDGMENT

Similar conditions appear to have existed in Jerusalem and Judah during the time of Ezekiel when God surveyed the land to find someone who could rebuild the wall and repair the breach. Consider the fact that the prophet Jeremiah, who was an earlier contemporary of Ezekiel (meaning that while their ministries eventually intersected, Jeremiah's ministry began much earlier than Ezekiel's), also ministered and prophesied to the people as a prophetic reformer while setting a righteous standard, yet Jeremiah was instructed by God to no longer pray or make intercession for them (Jer. 6:16-20; 11:14-17; 14:11-12). Consider also that the prophet Ezekiel was a man of truth, sent to confront the perverted mentalities, inaccurate internal architecture, and corrupt ethical values of the offending princes, prophets, priests, and people with warnings of God's impending judgment. Yet Ezekiel, too, would be ignored (Ezek. 3:4-7; 17-21; 33:1-20). It is safe to assume that as far as

God was concerned, judgment was already the foregone conclusion because the people were unrepentant.

Recognizing that the people were completely resistant to any reformation initiative, and that there was absolutely no one of any spiritual stature, power, or influence who could turn the nation from its present apostasy or course of injustice, God had already implemented a plan to purify or refine them as silver through the fiery furnace of affliction. What may have been perceived as God's judgment was actually His redemptive purpose being fulfilled (Ezek. 22:17-22).

RELIGIOUS PRAYER IS NOT THE ANSWER

No amount of praying would have been successful in swaying God in this instance because it was not what He required. We usually interpret this text in Ezekiel 22 as referring primarily to a call for prayer, due to the wording found in most English translations that commonly render the phrase *"stand in the gap in the wall"* as "stand in the gap before Me." While it would be difficult to argue against a certain level of prayer being implied by this phrase, the clearly defined subject and predicate of the entire clause will not fully support that assumption. If sin is the issue that caused a gap or breach in the wall to begin with, and standing in that gap is considered synonymous with standing before God, the most obvious implication is that personal integrity or right standing with God (righteousness) has the capacity to create a protective canopy over a city or nation, acting as a wall of defense and a salt-like preservative or purifying agent (Matt. 5:13).

In that sense, when God looked at Jerusalem, the first thing He would see despite the prevailing wickedness was the righteous.[11] The righteous would be standing *before* God as a protective barrier, preventing Him from executing His full judgment. Had just one wicked person repented, it would have restored the integrity of the invisible wall to a certain degree, and may have convinced God that there was still hope for this people without Him having to directly intervene.

Intercessory petitions for mercy in the context of prevailing wickedness may have their place, but their effectiveness is only in delaying certain judgment for a season. In addition, they are powerless unless issued from a place of righteousness and personal integrity. We (the saints) have had a lot of people willing to pray in such a context, but not very many willing to position themselves in a manner where they can biblically confront the issues by first looking in the mirror to correct themselves before they attempt to correct others.

TRUE KINGDOM INTERCESSION OCCURS WHEN OUR RIGHTEOUSNESS IS DISPLAYED BEFORE GOD AND OUR NATION, NOT WHEN WE OFFER UP RELIGIOUS PETITIONS ASKING GOD FOR MERCY WHILE IGNORING THE SIN ISSUE.

We need to remember that our ability as Kingdom citizens in the earth to act like salt—a natural preservative—is not as a result of our religious prayers, but on account of our righteous obedience (Matt. 5:13-16). Similarly, true Kingdom intercession occurs when our righteousness is displayed before God and our nation, not when we offer up religious petitions asking God for mercy while ignoring the sin issue. True intercession demands that we raise a righteous standard. Are we willing to sacrifice, go, get involved, and do whatever it takes to be the answer? Are we willing to confront our own hypocrisy when necessary? This can mean recognizing that any intercession for the nation regarding the legalization of same-sex marriages and the redefinition of family will first demand true repentance on our part for dishonoring the sacred covenant of marriage and having a very lax approach towards divorce.[12]

It means addressing the injustices in our churches before petitioning God to address the injustices in the nation.

We live in a day not much different from Ezekiel's day with empty religious ritual, rampant hypocrisy and falsehood, shameful ethical standards, amaurotic spiritual leaders consumed with selfishness and greed,[13] false fatidic flatterers otherwise known as "prophets," and numerous forms of injustice and oppression. To advance God's Kingdom against such a diabolically opposing principle will require militant soldiers who are willing to engage the powers of darkness by accurately representing God before the people and calling their attention to the offenses that they have committed against Him. This does not mean that we should be critical or judgmental toward them, but that we should confront the hypocrisy in our own lives first. Then our lives, more than our words, can become a testimony or witness of truth.

KEY PRINCIPLES

1. Reconciliation is the primary objective of intercession.
2. The act of prayer alone can never address the issue of sin or bring true reconciliation.
3. Jesus could never have transacted our redemption and reconciliation to God through intercession by remaining in heaven and petitioning the Father on our behalf.
4. The principle of intercession demands that we do everything we *can* do while expecting God to do everything we *can't* do.
5. A true intercessor is willing to put his life on the line for the person he is praying for.
6. If your prayer or intercession doesn't move *you* to action, don't expect it to move God either!
7. If we're not willing to labor, we're not qualified to pray (or intercede)!
8. Whatever it is that we are inclined to pray or intercede for must be accompanied by the corresponding faith action required for its fulfillment.
9. Sin has consequences.
10. The reason God gave us laws and commandments was not so that He could boss us around or control our lives. They were given for our protection.
11. Representing God's cause before the people is not the responsibility of prophets alone. We are all called to be a prophetic people.
12. Sometimes the best form of intercession is simply allowing God to have His way in the first place.

13. Intercessory petitions for mercy in the context of prevailing wickedness may have their place, but their effectiveness is only in delaying certain judgment for a season.

14. True Kingdom intercession occurs when our righteousness is displayed before God and our nation, not when we offer up religious petitions asking God for mercy while ignoring the sin issue.

15. True intercession demands that we raise a righteous standard.

ENDNOTES

1. "Intercede." *Webster's II New Riverside University Dictionary* (Boston, MA: Houghton Mifflin Company, 1994).

2. A careful study of the scriptures that describe Jesus' intercessory ministry in their various contexts seems to indicate a *positional* rather than a *practical* dimension to Jesus' intercession. His intercession is defined by the mediatorial aspect whereby He stands as the intermediary between humankind and God, bridging the gap between us and the Father. It does not necessarily imply prayer in the usual, practical sense of the word.

3. See Dr. Bill Hamon's 10 M's for maturing and maintaining ministry listed in his book, *Prophets, Pitfalls and Principles*.

4. Putting our lives on the line does not imply becoming anybody's "savior." We are not called to sacrifice ourselves for anyone's sins or seek to take upon ourselves another's sickness or disease. There is only one Mediator between God and men, the Man Christ Jesus (1 Tim. 2:5).

5. Both Ezekiel and Jeremiah were excluded from this prophetic company even though they were both prophets and Jeremiah was considered to be a contemporary of the time. As the exceptions to the common rule, they were never numbered among the transgressors.

6. Far from being controlling, God's desire has always been to share His power and authority with humankind, rather than to keep it for Himself (Luke 9:1; 10:19; 19:17; Rev. 2:26).

7. Scripture seems to indicate that there is an invisible hedge or wall of protection placed around those who fear God and keep His commandments. This hedge appears to cover not only the individual himself, but also his family and property (Job 1:8-10).

8. Moses was a true intercessor in that not only did he plead the people's cause before God, but he actively pleaded and promoted God's cause before the people.

9. Note that the primary requirement or condition for Sodom and Gomorrah to be spared was never finding the right number of

intercessory prayer warriors but finding a minimal number of righteous people in the land.

10. With the exception of Lot and his household, the cities of Sodom and Gomorrah were rotten to the core. They were destroyed not only because of the pervasiveness of wickedness among them, but also because of the pandemic absence of righteousness and good.

11. God was fully aware of all the wickedness taking place in Jerusalem, but His search was only for the righteous.

12. The violation of God's sacred marriage covenant (including fornication, adultery, and divorce) is the primary root cause for the homosexuality epidemic in a nation; however, it is beyond the scope of this book to address this issue any further.

13. Amaurosis is a partial or complete loss of sight or blindness of the eye, without any externally perceptible change in the physical eye itself. Therefore, amaurotic leaders are those who only *appear* to see, but in fact are actually blind from an internal dimension.

CHAPTER 10

THE MODEL PRAYER: VERTICAL PRIORITIES

As we come to the closing chapters of this book, many should have received considerable insight and understanding regarding the true *science* or technology behind how prayer works. Hopefully it has become quite evident that biblical prayer is much more than a spiritual exercise—it is a lifestyle! The principles that we have discussed thus far are of immense importance to cultivating an accurate and effective prayer life. However, with this understanding must come an accurate, practical application of *how* to pray. We will attempt to address this particular issue in these final three chapters by using the famous prayer Jesus taught to His disciples as a model.

> *In this manner, therefore, pray: Our Father in heaven, Hallowed be Your name. Your kingdom come. Your will be done on earth as it is in heaven. Give us this day our daily bread. And forgive us our debts, as we forgive our debtors. And do not lead us into temptation, But deliver us from the evil one. For Yours is the kingdom and the power and the glory forever. Amen.* (Matthew 6:9-13 NKJV)

"The Lord's Prayer,"[1] as it is often referred to, is perhaps the most known and recognized prayer in all of Scripture, memorized and recited by people across all religions, including those who are not even overtly religious. It is highly unlikely that Jesus ever intended this prayer to be an empty recitation of words in any liturgical manner. On the contrary, His intent was to upgrade His disciples' understanding, as well as the focus and architecture of their prayer initiatives, so that they accurately expressed the true architecture and values of God's Kingdom.

These disciples were all Jews who had been introduced to prayer in its various religious forms from birth. Yet despite their familiarity with this very common religious exercise—including what had been modeled before them all of their lives by the established religious leaders—they had recognized a striking difference in the way Jesus prayed, as well as an undeniable deficiency or incompetency in their own prayers. These recognitions prompted their request to be taught (Luke 11:1).[2]

In response to such an obvious and desperate need, where the efficacy as well as the integrity of prayer had been seriously degraded as a result of religious tradition, Jesus begins to teach and delineate the foundational principles upon which true prayer must be built. In doing so He furnishes a blueprint not only to prayer but also to true Kingdom technology in the earth. He provides us not only the correct architecture of prayer but also the core values upon which our lives should be built.

There is a proven principle that if you ever want to discover the level of faith, maturity, theology, or value system governing a person's life, just listen to that person pray. It is no different here: The Divine Architect reveals His theology in this model prayer, constructed of vertical priorities, which become imperative to prayer's success.

OUR FATHER IN HEAVEN

One of the most basic, foundational, and practical aspects of prayer is *who* we should pray to—and it is not Jesus. Jesus Himself testifies, as does the entire scriptural record, to the fact that the *Father* is the One to whom we are to pray. This may seem like a moot point for some, but to violate this command is to express ignorance regarding the Godhead and contempt for the divine order and ranking system expressly demonstrated therein. Examine the biblical record from cover to cover and you will be hard pressed to find even a single instance of prayer being directed either to Jesus or to the Holy Spirit. This principle does not make either of Them inferior or in any way less divine. It does, however, clearly affirm a principle of divine order even in the Godhead, where equality of person does not necessarily imply equality of rank, authority, or position.

Jesus never instructed anyone to pray to Him, whether before or after His ascension into heaven. His clearly defined assignment or objective was *always* to submit Himself to His Father's wishes and promote His Father's interests to humankind. Jesus came to provide a way to the *Father,* not to Himself. In fact, Jesus never came on His own initiative— He was sent, thus making Him subordinate to the Sender (John 7:16-18, 28-29; 8:26-29, 42, 49-50; 12:49-50; 14:6, 10, 24, 28, 31; 15:10, 15-16).

The Holy Spirit operates by the same principle. He never came to glorify Himself or to seek our worship. Rather, His mission is to glorify Jesus and to empower our worship. Like Jesus, the Holy Spirit didn't come on His own initiative but was sent by Jesus and the Father, making Him subordinate to both (John 14:16-17, 26; 15:26; 16:7-15).

JESUS NEVER INSTRUCTED ANYONE TO PRAY TO HIM, WHETHER BEFORE OR AFTER HIS ASCENSION INTO HEAVEN.

We are, therefore, instructed to pray to the *Father* in the name or authority of Jesus. We pray *through* Jesus, not *to* Jesus, just as we pray *with* the Spirit and not *to* the Spirit. If you are one of the many who has been ignorantly praying to Jesus or the Holy Spirit, take heart. You have now been made aware of the truth and can adjust your prayers accordingly. However, if you choose to purposely continue in this error, you are now without excuse (Matt. 6:6; John 15:16; Rom: 8:26; 1 Cor. 14:14-15).

Everything in the Kingdom begins and ends with the Father, which precludes any tendency toward self. For this reason, our prayers should be primarily focused upon accomplishing His intent rather than our own. Many of us have been led to believe through false teaching and doctrines of devils that the Kingdom of God revolves around us, our needs, or our abilities to access heaven's resources in the *now* by faith. But this is a clear violation of Scripture and everything that the Kingdom represents. This corruption of emphasis, focus, and values will be discussed in greater detail as we progress further in this chapter.

When many of us read the word *Father* in Matthew 6:9, we immediately conjure up images of someone who provides for us, someone we can always count on or approach without reservation with a particular need or desire—after all, He owns all things! While all this may be true to a certain degree, this willingness or ability to provide was not the primary connotation that Jesus was seeking to communicate to His disciples.

The exact term that Jesus uses for *Father* in this instance was the Aramaic word *Abba*.[3] This word carried very profound and revolutionary implications even for the Jews, as it conveys a sense of genuine familial relationship and deep personal intimacy above all else. Up until this time it was uncommon for the Jews to relate to God on such a deep and personal level.[4] With the addition of the word *our* ("Our Father"), it is clear that the primary emphasis in this context is not on the Father's inherent ability to supply our needs, but on our relational intimacy with Him—not just on a personal level, but from a corporate dimension as well.

Prayer functions best from a place of personal intimacy. It is not *needs-driven* but *presence-focused*. Therefore, since God does not abide on earth but in heaven, the onus is on us to ascend to His level in our mentality rather than to constantly endeavor to bring God down to our own level. Our Father (the King) and His Kingdom are not of human or earthly origin; therefore, everything that pertains to this Kingdom is antithetical or diametrically opposed to earthly and human philosophy or thinking. From a humanistic standpoint we are often consumed with personal comfort, but from a heavenly perspective His Kingdom is of paramount importance. When our minds are renewed and our philosophies are reformed to match His, we experience greater intimacy with God and higher potency in prayer (Amos 3:3).

> *PRAYER FUNCTIONS BEST FROM A PLACE OF PERSONAL INTIMACY. IT IS NOT NEEDS-DRIVEN BUT PRESENCE-FOCUSED.*

Since Jesus was obviously addressing a corporate company of disciples when He taught this prayer, the same principle applies to corporate prayer gatherings as well. A true Kingdom community is defined not just by our ability to commune with each other while within the comfortable confines of a church facility, but by our ability to personally and corporately commune with the Father as we seek His presence above all else.

HALLOWED BE YOUR NAME

The most common misconception regarding the phrase *"Hallowed be Your name"* is that it is an ascription of praise. While praising the name of God can definitely be regarded as one component of *hallowing* His name, and by extension, of prayer, a much higher principle is being communicated by this phrase.

The word *hallowed* is translated from the Greek word **hagiázō**, meaning "to make holy or sanctify" (as opposed to defile or make common); "to regard and venerate as holy"[5]; or "to regard with respect, honor, and reverence." Another way of saying it would be, "Set apart Your holy name." Or "May Your name be kept holy." Or "Let Your name be venerated (reverenced or held in the highest regard) and esteemed as holy everywhere as You receive due honor from all people."

To understand the full implication of this declaration or request, we must first understand the relationship between a person and his or her name from the Hebraic perspective. Names carried a much more profound significance in the Hebrew culture of biblical times than they do in our Western culture today.

For instance, soon after the death of Samuel while David was still on the run from Saul, David encountered a rich man by the name of *Nabal* to whom he had sent some of his young men for food supplies. According to the text, Nabal had a wife of wisdom and good understanding, but Nabal himself is described as harsh, impudent, foolish, and wicked. After Nabal insulted David and incurred his wrath, David was intent on destroying Nabal's entire household. However, Nabal's wife Abigail hatched a wise plan to diffuse the critical situation and pacify David. As Abigail stood before David and in the gap for her household, she made a profound statement regarding her husband: *"For as his name is, so is he: Nabal is his name and folly is with him."* Nabal's name was indicative of his true person or character. His name literally means "fool" or "foolish," and he was no different from his name (1 Sam. 25:1-25).

In a similar way, the name of God is virtually indistinguishable from His person or character. They cannot be separated. Therefore, to *hallow* God's name is to literally hallow or make holy His very person, identity, or character in the earth and in the eyes of all people.

The opposite of hallowing God's name would be to impugn or profane it. This profanation of God's name or misrepresentation of His true person and character is accomplished through the sin and disobedience of His people (Num. 20:11-12; Jer. 34:12-16; Amos 2:7).

*"Therefore say to the house of Israel, 'Thus says the Lord God: "I do not do this for your sake, O house of Israel, but for My holy name's sake, which you have **profaned** among the nations wherever you went. And I will **sanctify** (hallow) My great name, which has been **profaned** among the nations, which you have **profaned** in their midst; and the nations shall know that I am the Lord," says the Lord God, "when I am **hallowed** in you before their eyes. For I will take you from among the nations, gather you out of all countries, and bring you into your own land. Then I will sprinkle clean water on you, and you shall be clean; I will cleanse you from all your filthiness and from all your idols. I will give you a new heart and put a new spirit within you; I will take the heart of stone out of your flesh and give you a heart of flesh. I will put My Spirit within you and cause you to walk in My statutes, and you will keep My judgments and do them." '"*

(Ezekiel 36:22-27 NKJV; emphasis and parenthesis mine)

The nation of Israel had been disinherited and dispossessed on account of the people's sin and disobedience in rebelling against God. As they were scattered in captivity and defeat across the nations, it reflected negatively upon God, who was seen either as impotent and incapable or unreliable and unfaithful in His care for them. In addition, the Israelites continued in their adulterous and evil ways even while in captivity, thus misrepresenting and profaning the name of God even further (Ezek. 36:1-21).

In order to prevent any further profanation of His holy name among the nations, God decides to initiate Israel's complete restoration, based upon His own name and reputation rather than any merit of their own. By doing so He would not only vindicate or *hallow* His great name before Israel, but He would also demonstrate to the nations that He is indeed the omnipotent and faithful God.

The words *sanctify* and *hallowed* are therefore contrasted in the text against the profanity brought about as a result of Israel's corruption and sin, including the consequences thereof. Since God's name could only be profaned by His people, it follows that God's name could only be sanctified or hallowed by His chosen people as well. God's name could not be hallowed independently from the people called by it. Just as God's name reveals His person or character, God's person or character is revealed by His people. A king is known not only by his kingdom, but by the quality of his people or citizens.

> *TO HALLOW GOD'S NAME IS TO MAKE HOLY HIS VERY PERSON, IDENTITY, OR CHARACTER IN THE EARTH AND IN THE EYES OF ALL PEOPLE.*

Therefore, before God's name could be sanctified among the peoples and nations of the earth, it first had to be sanctified *in* His own people (v. 23). This would require God gathering and assembling them from every foreign nation or country where they had been previously scattered and then cleansing them with the *"water"* of His Word.[6] By giving them a *"new heart"* and a *"new spirit"* He would effectively be correcting their corrupt internal architecture, configuration, and value system—issues responsible for the profanation of His name to begin with. The result would be that God's name would be hallowed *in* them so that His name could be hallowed *through* them (vs. 24-27).

The significance of this principle with regard to a life of prayer cannot be overstated. In petitioning the Father to *hallow* His name, we are, in effect, demonstrating a recognition and submission to His Lordship where His will and desire takes complete precedence in our lives. It means a surrender to His purpose and an acknowledgment that there can be things in our hearts and lives that not only defile, but can also serve to obscure the true image and character of God to the world around us. Hallowing His name indicates we desire for God to remove these impediments and purify our hearts, minds, desires, and motives so that we become accurate reflections and intelligent representations of our God.

This is not necessarily a desire to be pardoned for known sins, as such a request is made later on in the prayer. Rather, it is a cry for holiness, desiring for the wood, hay, stubble, dross, and chaff to be consumed within our lives and communities so that we become an accurate Kingdom people. Rather than an ascription of praise, it becomes an aspiration for true worship—not as a religious activity where we praise Him or sing some songs and then live according to our own imaginations the rest of the time, but where our very lives become a pattern of worship where His nature, character, culture, and values are revealed.

When God's people are "scattered," fractured, or splintered into factions, it becomes counterproductive to God's Kingdom and serves to profane rather than hallow His name before the people. Therefore, on a corporate level, unity is a requirement for effective prayer, as everyone is connected to God and His purposes, as well as to each other.[7] God's Kingdom must first come *in* us before it can be accurately displayed *through* us.

Interestingly, Jesus' prayer recorded in the seventeenth chapter of John (please refer to John 17 now before proceeding) corresponds very closely to the principles we have discussed thus far from the model prayer taught to His disciples. Jesus addresses His prayer directly to the *Father*. And instead of focusing on personal or carnal needs and desires, Jesus' emphasis is upon glorifying the Father in three ways: through His personal obedience and complete sacrifice on the cross (vs. 1-5)[8]; through sanctification of His corporate Kingdom community of disciples with the word of truth (vs. 6-19); and through the unity of all current and future believers (vs. 20-26). Each of these three areas of emphasis in Jesus' prayer conforms to the principle of *hallowing* His name.

YOUR KINGDOM COME

The word *Kingdom* is translated from the Greek word **basileía**, meaning "royal dominion" or "the king's dominion."[9] It refers to the rule, reign, and realm of a king. God's Kingdom represented the primary message of Jesus when He walked the earth, and it has become one of the most popular topics in Christianity today. Ironically, much confusion and misunderstanding has arisen due to teachings emanating from divergent views on the topic. Before we attempt to identify these conflicting views, however, attention must be called to the pattern or priority emphasized within this model prayer thus far.

A. ***Our Father*** represents the object of our prayer. He is to be our primary passion and pursuit.

B. ***Hallowed be Your name*** represents the priority of our prayer, which is to make *His* name great, venerated, and holy—not ours! It is not "hallowed be *my* name"! God's name alone is to be hallowed. Our names, our reputations, and our images are irrelevant (Phil. 2:5-11).

C. ***Your Kingdom come*** represents the primary mission, which is His Kingdom rather than our own. It is not "my kingdom come" or "my church come"! We are not to seek or build our personal kingdoms, and we are not to preach or proclaim the gospel of our churches, denominations, or networks. We are to preach the gospel of God's Kingdom!

Kingdom means it is all about Him and not about us—*His* rule...*His* reign...*His* dominion! The vertical precedence here is unmistakable. When we make the Kingdom of God about us, our needs, or our inheritance from a humanistic mentality, we distort and corrupt the understanding of a true Kingdom concept.

Using the word *Kingdom* doesn't necessarily make anyone genuinely Kingdom. There are many people who employ this very popular term today who may have a completely divergent point of view from what the Scriptures actually teach. Since our theology of the Kingdom of God undoubtedly affects the quality and direction of our prayers, we will briefly discuss the three main conflicting views on the subject in order to define an accurate prayer focus.

1. The Political or Utopian Kingdom

Many of the Jews of Jesus' day believed that the Messiah would come to establish a Davidic-like Kingdom in Jerusalem that would have no end. They expected a political overthrow that would liberate Israel from Rome's control and dominion forever. Even the original twelve apostles ascribed to this incorrect view after having spent over three years with Jesus and having heard numerous teachings on the Kingdom (Acts 1:6).

Some of Jesus' actions were wrongly interpreted to support this view because:

a. He sought to arm His disciples (Luke 22:36-37).
b. He enlisted zealots as disciples (Mark. 3:16-19; Luke 6:15).[10]
c. He made reference to "taking up the cross," which was a symbol of zealot sacrifice (Mark 8:34; 10:21).[11]
d. He was crucified as a political rebel—a "wannabe" or pseudo-king seeking to undermine Rome and usurp authority (Mark 15:26).

Similarly today, there are many who believe and teach that Jesus is setting up an earthly kingdom where Christians will rise to prominence and leadership in business, government, media, education, arts and entertainment, family, and religion, thus resulting in a somewhat utopian society. I personally am not a follower of the Seven Mountain movement (this doesn't mean that I'm a critic of it either); however, I'm inclined to believe that this belief is nothing more than a gross misrepresentation or misconstruction of the original "seven mountain" mandate and message where the emphasis should be on influence from any level.[12]

Jesus ministered to basically every sector of society, yet it is clear from Scripture that His mission and priority was never to convert the established leadership or have them replaced by His followers. Therefore, any attempt to pray or petition God on such a level where we require Christians to occupy seats of power as a valid expression of Kingdom is inaccurate at best.

When Jesus proclaimed to the Pharisees that the Kingdom of God was already amongst them or in their midst, nothing had ostensibly changed in Israel's political condition or in any of the other "seven mountains." The Jews were still under the control of the Romans, and the ungodly or wicked were still in power. Even Zacchaeus, the chief tax collector, was still unconverted at this time.

> *Now when He was asked by the Pharisees when the kingdom of God would come, He answered them and said, "The kingdom of God does not come with observation; nor will they say, 'See here!' or 'See there!' For indeed, the kingdom of God is within you."* (Luke 17:20-21 NKJV)

It is clear that the Kingdom Jesus is referring to here is neither external, nor physical, nor political, but is of an internal or spiritual dimension with hidden or invisible architecture. It cannot be defined by external conditions or by those who occupy earthly positions of authority. Therefore, having a "Christian" record label, school, college, bank, recreational center, hospital, etc., and attaching the word *Kingdom* to it does not necessarily make it Kingdom. God's Kingdom cannot be defined by anything we can externally build or outwardly produce! This means building a bigger church building or facility is not Kingdom, so why should it be the priority of our personal or corporate prayer initiatives? Obtaining wealth or finances is not Kingdom, so why make it our primary concern? Having a "Christian" leader occupy the highest seat of government is not Kingdom, so why such a misguided emphasis? While these things may arguably serve to help facilitate a Kingdom objective, in and of themselves they are not Kingdom.

GOD'S KINGDOM CANNOT BE DEFINED BY ANYTHING WE CAN EXTERNALLY BUILD OR OUTWARDLY PRODUCE!

Examine Jesus' prayer in the seventeenth chapter of John again—which should truly be titled "The Lord's Prayer"—and you will discover that His prayer was predominantly *Kingdom*. Jesus revealed a Kingdom dynamic to His prayer where earthly externals similar to those mentioned above were considered nonessential to powerful Kingdom advance.

The Principle of Leaven

Jesus' Kingdom strategy was simple: He reproduced Himself—including His culture, values, wisdom, character, ministry, and anointing—in a dozen disciples (seemingly insignificant people). He then had them also reproduce themselves in others until, like leaven, God's Kingdom impacted the whole earth.

If you know anything about leaven (or yeast), you know it is never placed at the top of the other ingredients. In fact, placing it at the top significantly compromises its effectiveness. Leaven does its best work when it is hidden within the substance it is affecting, thereby allowing it to permeate the whole. When it has finished its work it becomes virtually indistinguishable from the substance itself, completely undetectable to the human eye. Therefore, no one is able to observe it or say, "Here it is!" or "There it is!" (Matt. 13:33; Luke 17:20-21).

God has always been quite capable of influencing nations despite who occupies the chief seats of government, and He usually accomplishes this through the ministry and influence of the seemingly insignificant.

Joseph was able to exert arguably his greatest influence over Egypt while as a prisoner rather than a prince (Gen. 41).[13] Daniel, also, was able to reveal profound Kingdom insight and shift the nation into a recognition of the one true God while still a captive in Babylon (Dan. 2; 6). The three young Hebrew captives—Shadrach, Meshach, and Abednego—exerted similar influence over the nation (Dan. 3). It was never God's intention for any of these men to occupy the highest seat or position of power in order to promote His purposes in the nation. God's purpose and Kingdom would be advanced from a place of insignificance (or without occupying the top position). The same principle can be seen in the nameless slave/servant girl of Naaman's household, who, in seeking the best interest of her captors, was able to effectively influence the Syrian general so that he experienced a genuine encounter with God (2 Kings 5:1-19).

The Kingdom of God is not defined by who occupies earthly positions of authority. God's Kingdom is advanced regardless! When we truly understand this principle, our prayers will be less likely to miss the mark with meaningless externals or vain human substitutions for what is truly Kingdom.

2. The Spiritual and Present Kingdom

This particular view places an overemphasis on the spiritual dimension of the Kingdom, relegating it to the human heart, revivals, or other spiritual activity, while denying the practical as well as the eschatological dimensions of Jesus' teachings.

Many sincere believers promote a message of revival and pray fervently for it. However, revival was never Jesus' mission. Jesus never came to revive Jewish religion or practice in order to make it more alive and acceptable to God. Rather, He came to completely replace and reform it! Therefore, revival cannot be equated with the Kingdom of God. Revival can be good for reigniting the fire and passion in dead religion, or for creating an environment for supernatural encounters or experiences, but it is not the Kingdom.

The temptation to substitute the supernatural for the Kingdom of God is ever present. While Jesus clearly indicated that the supernatural has the ability to validate or confirm the presence of His Kingdom, it is a mistake to assume that supernatural experiences *are* His Kingdom (Matt. 12:28).

In addition, while the Kingdom of God is most definitely supernatural, the Kingdom of God is not the source of all supernatural activity.

False Christs Equals False Kingdoms

> *Then if anyone says to you, 'Look, here is the Christ!' or 'There!' do not believe it. For false christs and false prophets will rise and show great signs and wonders to deceive, if possible, even the elect. See, I have told you beforehand. Therefore if they say to you, 'Look, He is in the desert!' do not go out; or 'Look, He is in the inner rooms!' do not believe it.* (Matthew 24:23-26)

The primary issue being addressed in this text is deception. The activity of "false christs" and "false prophets" with great (counterfeit) signs and wonders, as distinguished from the true, is indicative of a false kingdom. Therefore, when we make the Kingdom of God simply the operation of spiritual phenomena or supernatural signs and activity, without taking the time to look beyond the supernatural experience to discern the governing principle operating behind it, we will be deceived into embracing a false or counterfeit kingdom.

ANY OVEREMPHASIS ON THE SUPERNATURAL MAKES US A PRIME CANDIDATE FOR DECEPTION.

False christs and false kingdoms outwardly appear just like Christ and His Kingdom, but they lack the internal architecture, values, and culture that truly define God's Kingdom. Therefore, any overemphasis on the supernatural makes us a prime candidate for deception.

Many today are proclaiming, "Look here! This is Kingdom!" or "Look there! That is Kingdom!" when the things they are pointing to have absolutely no connection to anything genuinely Kingdom.

The Error of Promoting a Powerless Kingdom Message

Conversely, in an effort to counteract the error and overemphasis of those who blindly or foolishly pursue supernatural manifestations, some have quenched the Spirit's fire and now preach or promote a powerless "Kingdom" message. This, too, is error! It doesn't matter how well we're able to articulate the principles of the Kingdom or effectively address the core internal issues of the heart if we show no outward evidence of its power. The Kingdom of God is not fully preached unless and until it is preached with signs, wonders, and miracles!

John the Baptist preached the Kingdom of God, yet worked no miracles, because His situation was unique. He was called to prepare the way for the Miracle Worker—Jesus—which caused him to be ever conscious of fulfilling a diminished role in this regard (John 3:30). In John's case, working miracles would have been counterproductive to His assignment of preparing the way for Jesus, and it would have distracted from His true purpose. With the large following John already had, miracles would have made him appear to be the messiah. While the previous statements are purely conjecture, what we do know for certain

224

is that John was never the standard. In other words, God never intended for us to make John's miracle-less ministry the pattern for Kingdom expression among His saints today. According to Jesus, he that is *least* in the Kingdom of Heaven is greater than John, making him more of a platform than a pattern for Kingdom activity (Matt. 11:11).[14]

Jesus gave His audience the right to disbelieve Him if He could not produce the Father's (miraculous) works. He also said that His followers would do greater works than He did. So why should anyone believe us when we fail to produce them?

> *If I do not do the works of My Father, do not believe Me; but if I do, though you do not believe Me, believe the works, that you may know and believe that the Father is in Me, and I in Him.* (John 10:37-38 NKJV)[15]

Correct and Incorrect Petitions Regarding the Supernatural

In light of this spiritual aspect of the Kingdom and its close relationship to the supernatural, it seems appropriate to petition God for a greater demonstration of His supernatural power in conjunction with the gospel of the Kingdom being preached (Acts 4:29-30). However, any form of preoccupation or obsession with supernatural experiences above and beyond this in seeking God for angelic manifestations, unusual spiritual phenomena, or so-called "glory encounters" is a clear violation of the Kingdom of God by not *holding fast to the Head* (Col. 2:18-19).

Neither Jesus, the apostles, nor any of the early believers ever petitioned God in such a manner. The several references Jesus made to *"glory"* in His prayer in John 17 had absolutely no connection to pursuing supernatural experiences according to the common connotation of the word today. And even Moses' famous prayer—*"show me Your glory"*—should be interpreted according to its context and not as an attempt to solicit God into doing something grand or spectacular (Ex. 33:18).[16]

3. The Postponed or Future Kingdom

This particular view overemphasizes the eschatological dimension of the Kingdom and promotes a mentality of "holding on" till the last day. It reasons that the world is basically "going to hell in a hand-basket" and only a righteous remnant will remain unspotted from the world as the antichrist takes over.

Made popular by both the Christian as well as the secular media—including bestselling books and movies portraying the complete dominance of satan during the end times—this view has postponed the Kingdom of God until sometime in the hereafter, believing that it is not *now* but future.

This apparent tension or contradiction between the Kingdom of God *now* and the Kingdom of God *not yet* is present throughout the Scriptures. Both principles are valid, and they should be understood as mutually inclusive. Even though the overwhelming scriptural support is in favor of the futuristic view, the Kingdom of God is both *present* and *continuing*, while at the same time *future* and *culminating* (Matt. 5:19-20; 7:21-23; 8:11-12; 12:28; 25:31-46; Mark 14:25; Luke 11:2, 20; 17:20-21).

Any truth or principle taken to the extreme inevitably causes us to wind up in error, and it is no different with the futuristic view. This view frequently promotes the Church as weak and powerless, waiting to be raptured and delivered from the onslaught of satan. By emphasizing this one aspect of the Kingdom—its future culmination—at the expense of the others, its proponents have created a sense of apathy, complacency, and indifference with regard to the Kingdom of God being forcefully advanced in the earth. This strips our prayer of the faith, fervency, and urgency needed to apprehend in the *now*, being contented instead with a passive acceptance of *what is* in favor of *what should be*. We become helpless spectators interpreting signs in light of our eschatological beliefs, instead of powerfully active participants fully engaged in implementing key initiatives for Kingdom advance.

However, this does not mean that we should be foolish, presumptuous, or naïve in our prayers by forgetting that the Kingdom of God has certain futuristic implications that make certain things impossible for us to fully attain in the present. Some of these are:

a. Immortality—we can still die. (1 Cor. 15:24-26; 50-57).
b. The absence of sorrow and suffering—there is still death, tears, sickness, and pain. (Rev. 21:4).
c. Absolute peace—we still war against principalities and powers. (Eph. 6:10-12).
d. Kingdom consummation—the kingdom of this world has not yet become the Kingdom of our Lord. (Rev. 11:15).[17]
e. Undiminished sight—we still *"see though a glass darkly."* (1 Cor. 13:9-12).
f. Completeness, perfection, and maturity—God's Kingdom Community has not been fully perfected or matured, thus the need for ascension gift ministries. (Eph. 4:11-16).
g. New heaven and earth—we are still awaiting the new. (Rev. 21:1-2).

To ignore this futuristic dimension of the Kingdom, therefore, would lead to false hope and disillusionment. We must pray intelligently, understanding that the petition *"your Kingdom come"* carries with it very present implications in the *now* as well, such as:

a. Victory over death—death has already been defeated to a certain degree, allowing us to deliver victims from its power by raising them from the dead. (Matt. 10:8; John 5:24; 8:51; Rom. 5:21).
b. Eternal life—inclusive of miracles, healing, joy, provision, etc. (Mark 16:17-18; John 3:16; 15:11; 1 Pet. 2:24).
c. Authentic peace—not dependent upon outward circumstances (John 14:27; 16:33; Phil. 4:7; Col. 3:15).

d. Victory over sin and satan—both have already been defeated. (Luke 10:18; 11:20-22; Rom. 6:12-14).

e. Kingdom present-continuous—God's Kingdom is already in our midst and advancing. (Matt. 13:33; Luke 17:21).

f. Progressive sight—our sight is progressively increasing. (Mark 8:22-25).

g. Progressive maturation and development—we are being transformed into the image of God, from glory to glory. (2 Cor. 3:18).

YOUR WILL BE DONE

The clearly established pattern of vertical priority remains consistent in this next clause. It immediately identifies the governing principle and the primary objective or requirement of the previous petition, *"Your Kingdom come."* They are the two sides of the same coin.

The word *will* is translated from the Greek word ***thélēma*** (thel-ay-mah), meaning "active volition, wish, or good pleasure."[18] It is "not to be conceived as a demand, but as an expression or inclination of pleasure towards that which is liked, that which pleases and creates joy. When it denotes God's will, it signifies His gracious disposition towards something."[19]

In other words, above and beyond this clause communicating a sense of total submission or allegiance to God and His righteous demands, it emphasizes a desire to satisfy God's good pleasure and bring Him joy even beyond the legalistic constraints of what is required by command.

The best example of this can be found in Jesus' Gethsemane prayer where He cried, *"Not My will but Yours be done"* (Luke 22:42). Jesus was under no legal obligation to drink that bitter cup of suffering and death because He had done no wrong. He could have sought His own pleasure or satisfaction by passing on the cup and returning to His Father in heaven in a much easier and more "respectful" way. However, because His desire was to glorify the Father and bring Him pleasure and joy, He willingly submitted to the Father's *will* in both prayer and obedience.

The opposite of this principle is effectively portrayed by the Second Timothy 3:1-4 company, those who are so consumed by their own selfish desires that they establish a form of religion that focuses upon outward displays of righteousness, with complete disregard for the heart of the Father and what brings Him pleasure.

The petition *"Your will be done"* is, therefore, a death sentence to every form of selfish pursuit, indulgence, or ambition, as the primary emphasis becomes God's sole pleasure. This is the foundation of true Kingdom architecture. The goal is not what *we* wish for, or what *we* think is good for *us*, or what brings *us* pleasure. It becomes all about Him and His delight. This principle is interwoven throughout the entirety of the Jesus' John 17 prayer.

GOD'S WILL CAN ONLY BE ACCOMPLISHED IN OUR LIVES TO THE DEGREE THAT WE ARE HEARING AND OBEYING.

We should note at this point that there is a clear implication in this petition regarding participation. God's will is obviously not automatic, thus the reason we pray this prayer. If it was, there would be no need to pray. Consequently, God requires our participation on a micro level in order to bring His will to pass, even though on a macro level His will is seemingly inevitable. This means that with or without us God's will shall be accomplished, but He needs or prefers our participation in order to impact our spheres on a micro level, as well as hasten the "inevitable" on a macro level. The need for our participation reflects one of those

229

biblical tensions between God's sovereignty and human responsibility. They both work in tandem.

To make such a petition also means that we are not just praying a religious prayer or making a prophetic declaration with no practical relevance to our lives or communities. On the contrary, the petitioner is consciously aware of specific issues both individually and corporately that serve to militate against God's good pleasure, and he or she is earnestly seeking to address these issues by willingly surrendering personal comfort or desire while participating with God.

Since it is impossible to fulfill this declaration in ignorance, it is imperative that we are ever consciously pursuing a greater knowledge of Him both in Word and in relationship, so that we are better able to discern His *will* and good pleasure. God's will can only be accomplished in our lives to the degree that we are hearing and obeying.

ON EARTH AS IT IS IN HEAVEN

If the previous two petitions were considered to be two sides of the same coin, then this particular petition can be considered as providing insight into the specific territory or province where the coin was made. Heaven becomes the consummate prototype or model through which all Kingdom activity and divine intent or pleasure is to be reflected on earth. The clear assumption is that we are both knowledgeable and familiar with this territory.

Many Bible scholars and theologians are perplexed with regard to the subject of heaven, beset by a high degree of uncertainty due to its vastly spiritual nature. However, we understand from Scripture that the word *heaven* is used to refer to three distinctly separate domains, thus the reason for its frequent appearance in the plural. These domains are:

1. The atmosphere above the earth and under the sky where the birds fly (Lam. 4:19) and where the rain (Deut. 11:11), snow (Is. 55:10), dew (Dan. 4:23), frost (Job 38:29), wind (Ps. 135:7),

clouds (Ps. 147:8), thunder (1 Sam. 2:10), and hail (Job. 38:22) all originate.

2. Outer space where the stars, sun, moon, and planets reside (Gen. 1:8, 14-16; Deut. 17:3; Is. 40:22; Jer. 33:25; Nah. 3:16).

3. Where God dwells, also known as the "third" heaven (1 Kings 8:27, 30, 39, 43, 49; 2 Chron. 6:21, 30; 30:27; 2 Cor. 12:2-4).

These three domains can be broken down even further into two somewhat interrelated yet contradistinct concepts, namely:

1. The *physical reality* beyond the earth and extending upward throughout the far reaches of space.[20]

2. The *spiritual reality* where God abides.[21]

The *heaven* Jesus is referring to in this model prayer is obviously not of a physical nature but refers specifically to the spiritual reality where God abides. Therefore, we need never be concerned with studying the first two heavens—meaning the physical reality—for any signs or astrological phenomenon in order to clue us in to God's determination and intent for the earth. Jesus' command to *"watch and pray"* was never intended to be a license for observing signs or dabbling in numbers and dates in any form of mantic or divinatory way. Rather, it was an exhortation to be vigilant and alert with regard to the posture of our hearts and the tactics of the enemy, as well as diligent and dutiful in our Kingdom responsibilities (Matt. 26:41; Mark 13:33-37; 14:38; Luke 21:34-36).

To better understand this spiritual reality Jesus is referring to, it would be beneficial to do a brief word study on the word *heaven*. The word *heaven* is translated from the Greek word **ouranos** (oo-ran-os), meaning literally "that which is elevated or raised up." It occurs 284 times in the New Testament, about one-third of the time in the plural form. Its Hebrew equivalent, **šāmayîm**, is a plural form that carries a similar meaning of "heights" or "elevations."[22] This vertical imagery of height or elevation is consistent in both Hebrew and Greek, thus making this principle of immense importance to our understanding of heaven.

While this principle is quite easy to grasp from a purely physical standpoint as it relates to the sky or outer space, it becomes quite confusing when applied to the place that God dwells. The tendency to lose sight of the spiritual nature of this realm is common when viewed from a purely spatial or physical point of reference. Our natural physics do not apply there, and human limitations of time and space are rendered obsolete.

> *IT IS IMPOSSIBLE TO EFFECTIVELY PRAY OR EXECUTE GOD'S WILL AND PLEASURE IN THE EARTH FROM AN EARTHLY OR HUMAN PERSPECTIVE.*

Heaven is not some lofty place spatially far away, beyond the outer reaches of the physical heavens or incomprehensible vastness of the universe, from which we are separated by both time and space. More accurately, *heaven* refers to a highly elevated *spiritual* realm or dimension that is far superior to earth's present existence (Ps. 14:2; 80:14; 102:19; John 6:33, 38, 41-42; Acts 1:2, 10-11).

In other words, the height or elevation being described in this context is not a spatial or physical one but a spiritual one. It describes a higher, more superior form of life; a higher standard of living. Just as God is always present with us, so is heaven, even though they both exist in a more elevated spiritual realm.

This implies that there is no human or earthly point of reference for the previous two petitions *("Your Kingdom come, Your will be done")* beyond Jesus and the Scriptures. There is no earthly paradigm that we can point to and say, "This is Kingdom!" or "That is Kingdom!" Since heaven is the *spiritual* model or blueprint, we have to rely upon spiritual insight and understanding. It is impossible to effectively pray or execute God's will and pleasure in the earth from an earthly or human perspective. Our human priorities, religious practices, and earthly paradigms are incapable of reproducing heaven's architecture on earth. Inferior human systems can never substitute for heaven's spiritual model or ideal.

Like Noah, we are being called upon to build something that has never before existed (an ark or boat), in preparation for something that has never before been seen (rain and flood). Therefore, we can no longer continue to pray as we have in the past, falling into the rut of what we have become accustomed to. The people of Noah's day were too consumed with the normal affairs and routine business of life to recognize their error or what was coming. We cannot continue to be consumed with the same, seeking only for God to bless our churches, our services, our meetings, our members, our menus, and our messages (Luke 17:26-27; Heb. 11:7; 1 Pet. 3:20).

Heaven consists of much more than personal blessing or maintaining the religious status quo. It is based upon an elevated level of thinking, a heightened sense of value, and a highly superior moral standard of living. It is based upon the very nature of God Himself. Therefore, we do the Kingdom of Heaven a great injustice by focusing on our petty issues. Instead, we should be crying out to God in prayer for a greater dimension of wisdom and sight so that we can more fully comprehend the true nature and architecture of this elevated spiritual realm called heaven (Is. 55:8-9).

God's desire has always been for His people to flow or operate seamlessly between both realms in a synchronous fashion, which is a principle the New Testament frequently alludes to. He never intended for there to be any form of difference, disparity, or disconnect between the physical and the spiritual or between heaven and earth (1 Cor. 7:24; Eph. 1:3; 2:6; Col. 3:1-3).

The Garden of Eden

The original model for this seamless connection can be found in Adam and Eve in the Garden of Eden. From a purely archaeological perspective, this garden has never been found. The reason for this, I believe, is because it was not a purely physical place. It was the place— or rather, portal—where heaven and earth were so seamlessly connected and intertwined that they were virtually indistinguishable from each other.[23]

For example, in both the second and third chapters of Genesis this garden was said to contain the *tree of life* in its *"midst"* (Gen. 2:8-9; 3:22-24). We know from John's Revelation of Jesus Christ that the tree of life exists in the *"midst of the Paradise of God"* in heaven (Rev. 2:7; 22:2, 14).

Also, the very presence of *cherubim*—heavenly angelic creatures— guarding the way to both the garden and tree of life after man's expulsion is clear evidence of this indistinguishable and profound union or connection between heaven and earth. This is because cherubim (plural) in Scripture are *always* closely associated with the manifest presence or dwelling place of God (2 Sam. 6:2; 1 Kings 8:6-7; 2 Kings 19:15; 1 Chron. 13:6; Ps. 80:1; 99:1; Is. 37:16; Ezek. 10:1-20).

In light of this discovery, we can infer that when Adam sinned, he did, in fact, fall from *heaven*. We know that Adam did not "fall" from the earth, because the word *fall* implies a plummeting, lowering, declension, or downward degradation and deterioration from a formerly higher state. Since humankind is still earthly, in all respects, the obvious implication is that man fell from a higher, heavenly dimension.

The Link Between Heaven and Dominion

Some, including myself in the past, have ignorantly attempted to create a fallacious dichotomy between heaven and dominion by stating that Adam only fell from the latter without ever occupying a legitimate place in the former. However, the truth is that *heaven* and *dominion* are two sides of the same coin, inseparably linked together to form a whole.

In other words, Adam never fell from some ethereal realm located somewhere over the rainbow, beyond the outer boundaries of what is normally referred to as the universe. Adam fell from a highly elevated spiritual dimension called *heaven*—the very abode of God, a place of communing daily in His manifest presence, a spiritual reality infinitely superior to earth's present existence.

ADAM'S DOMINION WAS LOST BECAUSE HIS POSITION IN HEAVEN WAS LOST.

Consequently, it was *only* from this highly elevated position that Adam could effectively exercise his dominion over the earth. His very ability to undertake as well as to complete the daunting task of naming all the creatures on earth was based upon his elevated heavenly perspective and clear insight into that realm. Adam had no earthly frame of reference by which to name this almost innumerable host of varying species. However, considering that earth was a clear, visible reflection of the unseen realm of heaven where similar creatures existed, it follows that Adam would use heaven as his frame of reference and name the creatures accordingly (Is. 65:17-25; Ezek. 1:4-10; 10:14-15; Rev. 4:6-7; 5:11-13; 19:11, 14).

A few years back (and maybe still today), some were teaching that most humans only used ten percent or less of their brain capacity, with the remaining ninety percent or more remaining dormant or untapped. While this assumption has now been "proven" false by the majority of scientific and neurological professionals worldwide, I am of the opinion that there is still a measure of truth to the original claim.[24] This is because man is essentially a spirit being, created to live and operate from a higher, heavenly spiritual dimension, which to a very large degree we have become totally unconscious of and unresponsive to.[25] We now find it extremely difficult to see or hear God, or even to perceive spiritual things—abilities that were once quite natural and effortless to Adam and Eve. We have been demoted to a much lower, fleshly frequency of living, unable to interact with the spiritual realm as easily as we do with the physical, if we are even able to at all. Even animals appear to have a far greater degree of sight or consciousness with regard to this unseen realm, making humanity's condition a truly debased and pitiful one indeed (Num. 22:22-33).

I viewed a medical program on television not too long ago where they interviewed a clairvoyant and proved that various parts of the brain that were otherwise dormant in this particular subject become quite active when introduced to certain paranormal stimuli.[26] While these activities are clearly beyond my very limited (or laughable) scientific knowledge or expertise, no one can honestly deny the fact that our spiritual consciousness has been severely degraded since the fall, making the interface between the spiritual dimension and our natural minds or brains almost implausible in the realm of normalcy (1 Cor. 2:14).

The fact is that Adam could not exercise dominion outside of his heavenly positioning and vantage point, and neither can we. Adam's dominion was lost because his position in heaven was lost. We cannot have one without the other, so to have lost one implies that we have lost the other also.

Therefore, in order for us to exercise dominion through prayer, for the purpose of effectively reproducing or recreating heaven's highly unique spiritual architecture on earth, we will need more than empty, hollow words, high volume petitions, or high-ranking petitioners. Our religious titles do not earn us rank in heaven, and neither do they assure us dominion on earth. We have no legitimate right to make earthly decrees or declarations in prayer unless we have both *seen* and *heard* what heaven is doing and saying, and this extends far beyond our natural understanding of Scripture. Our true authority comes when we are able to ascend into that heavenly dimension where God dwells and obtain spiritual sight.[27]

How Jesus and His Apostles Exercised Dominion

Jesus was able to exercise dominion in the earth and usher in the Kingdom of Heaven through His ability to tap into that high heavenly frequency of *hearing* what the Father was saying and *seeing* what the Father was doing. At a young age, Jesus had a very mature understanding of the scriptures—so much so that it caused Him to astound the formal teachers at the temple in Jerusalem—but even with that wisdom, He wasn't ready to exercise dominion or usher in His Father's Kingdom. He still needed a high degree of spiritual sight to accomplish His assignment (Luke 2:41-50; John 5:19; 8:26-29, 38, 40, 47).

Even Jesus' original twelve apostles were not able to exercise dominion by virtue of their apostleship alone. They required *keys,* which are representative of authority and access, indicating a rite of passage and open access to a highly elevated spiritual realm—the Kingdom of Heaven—from which man had been barred since the fall of Adam.

> *I will give you the keys of the kingdom of heaven; and whatever you bind (declare to be improper and unlawful) on earth must be what is already bound in heaven; and whatever you loose (declare lawful) on earth must be what is already loosed in heaven.* (Matthew 16:19 AMP)

I find it hard to understand how such a very clear and straightforward text could be misinterpreted and misunderstood to the degree that it has in the past. But this error only serves to testify to the previous point—that due to the effects of the fall, it has become very difficult for us to comprehend or accurately process spiritual things, resulting in our carnality and blindness. Even though Jesus is directly addressing Peter in this instance, the principle obviously applies to the entire apostolic company, as well as to every member of the Kingdom Community He is building (Matt. 16:13-18).

While the Greek construction of words being employed in this text has posed significant problems for translators, I believe the Amplified translation captures the true essence of what Jesus is trying to communicate, which is obviously the principle or technology of dominion. In seeking to restore what Adam had lost—humankind's place of dominion in heaven—Jesus is about to give His followers the authority to once again access the elevated position humankind had once occupied through Adam prior to the fall. No matter how much apostolic authority they seemingly had, it was insufficient, because dominion cannot be exercised from an earthly or carnal position.[28]

By receiving access to this new spiritual dimension, Jesus' followers would now be qualified to fulfill Adam's original mandate through a greater level of sight into heaven's activity and architecture. They would be able to *"bind"* and *"loose"*—legislative or governmental terminology meaning to prohibit and forbid (bind) or permit and allow (loose)—on earth what they had *seen* in heaven, thus causing earth to be an accurate reflection of heaven (Gen. 1:27-28).

Heaven Should Determine the Course of Our Prayer

The idea here is not one of asserting our own will or intent over God's in an attempt to cause heaven to align or acquiesce to our requests, a practice that is very common in religious Christianity today. We are not trying to make heaven conform to our will, our pleasure, or our designs. It is God's will and pleasure to be done on earth, not our will and pleasure to be done in heaven. Heaven determines what is to be done on earth; earth does not determine what is to be done in heaven. Heaven is the prototype; therefore, it is heaven's divine architecture that we are seeking to impose upon earth's carnal configurations. We submit to heaven; heaven does not submit to us.

Again, this is a far cry from what is generally practiced today. We expect our prayers to determine heaven's course of action, when it is heaven's course of action that should determine our prayers. When we come before God and the first thing we start doing is belching out personal or corporate requests without any regard for what heaven has determined is the Father's delight, we are operating in error. Such requests are void of any true power and authority, regardless of how eloquent or convincing the petitioner sounds. It doesn't matter what we think we know. It matters little what our theology is. It matters even less what title we carry in front of our names. What matters most is our ability to ascend to that heavenly realm, receive insight into heaven's architecture, and then construct a prayer focus that conforms to heaven's intent so that there is a divine convergence between heaven and earth.

EFFECTIVE DOMINION PRAYER CONSISTS OF MORE SEEING AND LISTENING THAN CRYING AND PLEADING.

This implies patiently (not slothfully, but diligently) waiting on God and seeking His face, allowing Him to elevate us in our mentality and bring us into a new, higher dimension of sight. It implies that effective dominion prayer consists of more seeing and listening than crying and pleading. It involves a posture of submission and a high prophetic frequency in determining God's desire and heaven's design in every situation. Sometimes praying in the Spirit is the most effective method of praying in this regard.

Contrary to the old popular adage, "Don't be so heavenly minded that you are of no earthly good," the more truly *heavenly* minded we are in life, including prayer, the more earthly good we become (Col. 3:2).

Binding and Loosing

Because of the tendency for religious people to create a ritualized formula out of divine principles, it is important that we understand that using the words *bind* and *loose* in prayer doesn't necessarily mean that anything is being forbidden or allowed. There is no inherent "magic" or authority in these words. They simply communicate a principle of government and dominion. This is not "spiritual warfare" terminology in the full practical sense of the words either, so they should not be interpreted as referring directly to "binding and loosing" evil spirits, which has been the general religious perception. These words represent the exercise of authority through an elevated spiritual position of dominion in heaven. When such a spiritual position is not the reality, the words become empty, vacuous, and meaningless.

Spiritual Resistance in Heaven

One final point on the subject of heaven relates to these issues of spiritual warfare and diabolical hindrances. Heaven—the highest or ultimate dimension—should not be assumed to exist or operate without spiritual resistance or opposition. In fact, one of the recurring motifs in Scripture is this sense of spiritual opposition, which occurs even in God's very domain.

For example, we are told a "war" occurs between Michael (and his angels) and the dragon (and his angels) in heaven (Rev. 12:7). A diabolical serpent was present in the Garden of Eden—the very portal of heaven—seeking to oppose God's divine intent. Incidentally, while man was expelled from this garden, synonymous with heaven, the serpent was not. The cherubim were placed to keep man out, not to protect from the serpent or devil (Gen. 3). In addition, the adversary (satan) was present in heaven to accuse and conspire against Job, just as he has made accusations against the other brethren day and night (Job 1:6-12; Rev. 12:10). Jesus is pictured in heaven as one who *"judges and makes war,"* who is followed by *"armies in heaven"* (Rev. 19:11-15).

Then we have the issue of cherubim to consider. Cherubim are pictured in Scripture as celestial creatures who cover, guard, and protect the throne of God. This begs the question: Why does God dwell between them? What does God seemingly require protection from?

There is a lot that we do not know. But what we do know is that while heaven is a place of ultimate peace, it is also a place of opposition and conflict from diabolical forces, at least until the final judgment. This understanding should serve to inform our expectations with regard to prayer and the Kingdom Jesus is establishing. Opposition and conflict does not mean that heaven's architecture is not being fulfilled or that the Kingdom of God is not advancing. Read the eleventh chapter of the Book of Revelation and the seventh chapter of Daniel and you will discover that the Kingdom of God is established in the midst of great persecution, opposition, and darkness, not in a utopia (Rev. 11-12).[29]

ADVERSE HUMAN OR DEMONIC ACTIVITY DOES NOT DISQUALIFY OR INVALIDATE KINGDOM ADVANCE.

While things on the outside may look dark and defeating to us, God's Kingdom is primarily spiritual, not physical. We are not building an earthly kingdom. Therefore, regardless of the darkness, regardless of the opposition, regardless of who sits in power, regardless of the adversity, persecution, or antagonistic government legislation, we are to be faithful and consistent in our callings. We are not praying to undo government legislation, remove ungodly people from power, or preserve our own lives and comfort. We can "bind and loose" evil spirits all we want, but that is not going to get rid of them. In fact, they are of little concern. God's Kingdom is going to come and His will is going to be done regardless of the opposition that hell unleashes or the earth produces. Adverse human or demonic activity does not disqualify or invalidate Kingdom advance.

KEY PRINCIPLES

1. If you ever want to discover the level of faith, maturity, theology, or value system governing a person's life, just listen to that person pray.
2. The Father is the One to whom we are to pray.
3. Jesus never instructed anyone to pray to Him, whether before or after His ascension into heaven.
4. Jesus came to provide a way to the *Father,* not to Himself.
5. We pray *through* Jesus, not *to* Jesus, just as we pray *with* the Spirit and not *to* the Spirit.
6. Everything in the Kingdom begins and ends with the Father.
7. Prayer functions best from a place of personal intimacy. It is not *needs-driven* but *presence-focused.*
8. A true Kingdom community is defined not just by our ability to commune with each other while within the comfortable confines of a church facility, but by our ability to personally and corporately commune with the Father as we seek His presence above all else.
9. The name of God is virtually indistinguishable from His person or character.
10. God's name cannot be hallowed independently from the people called by it.
11. Just as God's name reveals His person or character, God's person or character is revealed by His people.
12. God's Kingdom must first come *in* us before it can be accurately displayed *through* us.
13. Kingdom means it is all about Him and not about us—*His* rule...*His* reign...*His* dominion!

14. When we make the Kingdom of God about us, our needs, or our inheritance from a humanistic mentality, we distort and corrupt the understanding of a true Kingdom concept.

15. Using the word *Kingdom* doesn't necessarily make something genuinely Kingdom.

16. God's Kingdom cannot be defined by anything we can externally build or outwardly produce!

17. God has always been quite capable of influencing nations despite who occupies the chief seats of government, and He usually accomplishes this through the ministry and influence of the seemingly insignificant.

18. The Kingdom of God is not defined by who occupies earthly positions of authority. God's Kingdom is advanced regardless!

19. Revival cannot be equated with the Kingdom of God.

20. While the Kingdom of God is most definitely supernatural, the Kingdom of God is not the source of all supernatural activity.

21. The Kingdom of God is not fully preached unless and until it is preached with signs, wonders, and miracles!

22. God's will is not automatic, thus the reason we pray.

23. God's will can only be accomplished in our lives to the degree that we are hearing and obeying.

24. Our human priorities, religious practices, and earthly paradigms are incapable of reproducing heaven's architecture on earth.

25. When Adam sinned, he did, in fact, fall from *heaven*.

26. *Heaven* and *dominion* are two sides of the same coin, inseparably linked together to form a whole.

27. Adam's dominion was lost because his position in heaven was lost.

28. Our religious titles do not earn us rank in heaven, and neither do they assure us dominion on earth.

29. We have no legitimate right to make earthly decrees or declarations in prayer unless we have both *seen* and *heard* what heaven is doing and saying.

30. God's will and pleasure are to be done on earth, not our will and pleasure to be done in heaven.

31. Opposition and conflict does not mean that heaven's architecture is not being fulfilled or that the Kingdom of God is not advancing.

32. Adverse human or demonic activity does not disqualify or invalidate Kingdom advance.

ENDNOTES

1. "The Lord's Prayer" is technically an incorrect title since there is no evidence that Jesus ever actually prayed this prayer. He was simply teaching His disciples the form and structure of how to pray.

2. Both Jesus and John the Baptist taught their disciples to pray. Most believers today assume that they know how to pray when, in fact, they don't. One of the first and primary areas in need of reformation in Christianity today is prayer, due to the error of religious tradition.

3. Jesus spoke in Aramaic, not Greek. However, His original words were later translated into Greek, thus rendering *Abba* as *patēr*. Except for Mark 14:36, Rom. 8:15, and Gal. 4:6 which retained the original Aramaic term *Abba*, the Greek word *patēr* is most often used.

4. The term *Abba* is used more than 165 times in the four Gospels alone, compared to only 15 times in the entire Old Testament.

5. *The Complete Word Study Dictionary: New Testament*, ed. Spiros Zodhiates Th.D. (Chattanooga, TN: AMG International, 1993), 37.

6. Ephesians 5:25-26.

7. Unity in prayer is only effective when there is first unity with God and His purposes, in addition to unity with each other in the petition being made. Unity in petition alone is useless if it violates the will and purpose of God. The oneness or unity that Jesus prayed for was never carnal or superficial, but was predicated upon oneness with Jesus and the Father rather than just oneness with each other (John 17:20-21).

8. Jesus was never selfishly seeking His own personal glory or recognition. He understood that the Father could never be glorified independently from the Son. Therefore, the glory Jesus sought was the suffering of the cross, resulting in His death, burial, and resurrection, so that the Father could be truly glorified.

9. *The Complete Word Study Dictionary: New Testament*, ed. Spiros Zodhiates Th.D. (Chattanooga, TN: AMG International, 1993), 932.

10. A *zealot* was someone intent on preserving Judaism by uncompromisingly rejecting foreign occupation or rule, even if it meant suffering, dying, or killing to promote their patriotic cause.

11. Robert H. Stein, "Kingdom of God," in *Baker Theological Dictionary of the Bible*, ed. Walter A. Elwell (Grand Rapids, MI: Baker Books, 2000), 451.

12. The "seven mountains" refer to the seven key areas of influence within a nation (business, education, family, arts and entertainment, media, government, and religion). In short, the Seven Mountains movement is about Christians reclaiming these seven spheres or "mountains" of society where they no longer have influence.

13. Joseph was still a prisoner when he interpreted Pharaoh's dreams and provided wisdom and insight for navigating a severe global crisis. His promotion came only after the initial influence he exerted. It is our influence that causes promotion and not our promotion that causes influence.

14. The John principle is that the Kingdom of God is based, built, and founded upon an internal reality rather than upon any outward demonstration or experience. The Jews expected the promised messenger to be Elijah returned in the flesh, or at least someone demonstrating the same spirit and power as Elijah in mighty miracles. John was a fulfillment of this promise, yet the Elijah dimension that he walked in was of an internal nature. Not even his prophesying came anywhere close to Elijah's standard, but it was that powerfully accurate spiritual dimension and principle operating within his life that truly defined him as one walking *"in the spirit and power of Elijah"* (Mal. 4:5; Matt. 11:13-14; 17:10-13; Luke 1:17). Compare against 2 Tim. 3:5.

15. See also John 5:36; 10:25; 14:11.

16. Moses was seeking a greater revelation of God, not a greater manifestation of His power.

17. The word translated *kingdoms* in the English should more accurately be translated *kingdom* (singular) according to the original manuscripts.

18. *The Complete Word Study Dictionary: New Testament*, ed. Spiros Zodhiates Th.D. (Chattanooga, TN: AMG International, 1993), 2307.

19. Ibid.

20. Bradford A. Mullen, "Heaven," in *Baker Theological Dictionary of the Bible*, ed. Walter A. Elwell (Grand Rapids, MI: Baker Books, 2000), 332.

21. Ibid.

22. Ibid.

23. This seamless connection between heaven and earth will be restored in the last day when heaven and earth are made new (Rev. 21:1-5; 9-27; 22:1-5).

24. Science is limited to studying physical phenomena (matter) consistent with our five physical senses. As such, natural science is incapable of gauging the human brain's true potential as it relates to spiritual substance.

25. This apparent disconnection from the spirit world is also known as spiritual death.

26. This was on a Dr. Oz program. Dr. Oz had a device attached to the clairvoyant's head while she was doing her "sensings" in order to map her brain patterns. Please note also that the author does not approve of clairvoyants or any similar type of psychic activity that the Scriptures clearly condemn.

27. Jesus modeled this ascension when He took Peter, James, and John with Him on the mountain to pray. His prayer opened up a portal to the heavenly realm, causing His very appearance to radiate with heaven's glory, similar to the experience of Moses (Ex. 34:29-35; Luke 9:28-36).

28. In Luke's account of the demonized boy whom Jesus' disciples could not deliver, he prefaces the account with a reminder that this was the day after Jesus had taken some of His disciples up with Him on the mountain to pray, which is pertinent to the text. When Jesus ascended to heaven in prayer and became transfigured in heavenly glory, His intention in bringing some of His disciples was not so that they could be mere spectators, but so that they could participate with Him in this experience. By falling asleep during this important training class, they never personally experienced what it means to ascend in prayer and thus were unqualified and incapable of exercising dominion over the

unclean spirit. Their apostleship alone was inadequate to deliver the boy (Luke 9:27-42).

29. One of the mysterious ironies of Scripture is that God, who is the epitome of light, chooses to make His habitation in the midst of thick darkness (1 Chron. 6:1; 1 Kings 8:12; Ps. 97:2; 18:11 KJV).

CHAPTER 11

THE MODEL PRAYER: HORIZONTAL PETITIONS

N ow that we have discovered the foundational priorities, principles, and imperatives related to the subject of prayer, we are now ready to proceed into the second part of our study with clarity regarding where we place our human concerns. Up until this point the emphasis and priority has been clearly on the divine, with a vertical focus upon the Father and what He desires:

A. Our Father in heaven
B. The Father's name being hallowed
C. The Father's Kingdom coming
D. The Father's will and pleasure being accomplished
E. The Father's elevated spiritual domain being the model or prototype

Again, the divine order, emphasis, and priority of prayer—or anything relating to the Kingdom for that matter—is always with the Father. Whenever this biblical precedent is ignored or disregarded, our prayers become shallow, misguided, ineffectual, and perverse. The vertical aspect provides the foundation as well as the operational framework for the horizontal aspect. It serves to regulate our prayers so that they don't become carnal. The horizontal aspect will not work unless the vertical priority is in place.

These horizontal petitions are:

> *Give us this day our daily bread. And forgive us our debts, as we forgive our debtors. And do not lead us into temptation, but deliver us from the evil one. For Yours is the kingdom and the power and the glory forever. Amen.* (Matthew 6:11-13 NKJV)

A. Give us
B. Forgive us
C. Lead us
D. Deliver us

While these horizontal petitions may appear to place the focus entirely back upon us, that is not entirely the case. Every one of these horizontal petitions is contingent upon, and subject to, the foundational vertical priorities. In other words, in order for us as God's people to effectively fulfill our mission of hallowing the name of the Father, establishing His Kingdom, fulfilling His will and pleasure, and accurately building according to heaven's revealed architecture, we will require a large degree of divine assistance. We cannot fulfill this mission by depending upon our own human strength or resources alone.

The foundation always determines the strength and form of the structure; therefore, the vertical aspect continues to dictate and impose its heavenly emphasis upon these human concerns. The emphasis continues to be upon the Father in heaven, though in a more indirect manner. When we lose sight of this governing principle and selfishly choose to place the emphasis back upon ourselves—our needs, wants, prosperity, blessing, welfare, healing, or access to heaven's abundant resource—we are not only violating God's divine order and precedent by dishonoring God, but we become disciples of an antichrist system and promoters of a false kingdom.

WHEN THE EMPHASIS IS SHIFTED FROM WHAT HE WANTS TO WHAT WE WANT, WE HAVE ENTERED INTO A SATANIC KINGDOM.

The Kingdom of God on earth became the kingdom of satan when Adam followed Eve, who had yielded to the serpent's temptation to disregard God's commandment or divine intent (vertical) in preference for satisfying her own personal ambition or desires (horizontal). When the emphasis is shifted from what *He* wants to what *we* want, we have entered into a satanic kingdom (Gen. 3:1-6).

GIVE US THIS DAY OUR DAILY BREAD

This particular petition has created a significant amount of perplexities for Bible interpreters and scholars. This is on account of a Greek compound word translated as "daily" that is found nowhere else in Scripture or in any form of classical Greek. Apparently no corresponding word existed in Greek for whatever Aramaic term Jesus originally used, prompting the writer to seemingly invent his own word. As a result of this, several divergent views have arisen as to what this clause actually means. Rather than take the time to identify these varying views, we shall proceed with what I believe best fits the spirit and context of the text.

Most are in agreement that the word *bread* here is used in a wider sense to symbolically refer to needs in general, whether physical or spiritual, rather than just to bread or food. Therefore, an accurate

251

paraphrase of this somewhat mysterious Greek construct would be, "Give us what we essentially need for today."

Before your flesh becomes too excited and you are tempted to misconstrue this petition as a license for covetousness or a green light for self-indulgence, pay special attention to the words *essentially need*. This petition does not flow out of a selfish desire to accumulate wealth or gratify our carnal desires. It is based upon accessing heaven's limitless resource for a purpose that extends far beyond us. The implications, I believe, are primarily spiritual rather than physical, even though the physical aspect would be difficult to deny. What we *essentially need* implies that which is absolutely necessary or indispensable for the completion of our divinely ordained earthly mission. This could include a perfect heart (1 Chron. 29:18-19), unfailing faith (Luke 22:32), spiritual wisdom and discernment (2 Chron. 1:8-10; Col. 1:9; Jam. 1:5), boldness (Acts 4:24-30), and spiritual sight (Eph. 1:15-23).

In Jesus' personal prayer recorded in John 17, His personal petition addresses the "daily bread" or essential needs of His corporate Kingdom Community in the areas of continual sanctification (John 17:17), genuine unity through oneness with Jesus and the Father (John 17:11, 20-23), and elevated spiritual sight through heavenly occupation with Him in heaven (John 17:24). There is absolutely nothing in Jesus' prayer that is of a purely physical or carnal nature.

The Manna Principle

This spiritual emphasis becomes even more credible considering what many scholars believe to be an obvious allusion to the daily provision of manna for the Israelites. That manna was referred to as *"manna from heaven,"* indicating that it was a heavenly rather than earthly resource. The name *manna* literally means "what is this?" There was no physical or earthly reference for this substance because it represented a spiritual principle. Even Jesus affirmed this spiritual principle when He referred to Himself as the *"true bread* (manna) *from heaven,"* indicating that His origin was not earthly but from above (in heaven). Thus when tempted by the devil to misappropriate prayer and dominion power so as to satisfy what was seemingly His legitimate physical need, Jesus referred to the manna principle by emphasizing that man's true "bread" was spiritual rather than a physical resource—*"every word that proceeds from the mouth of God"* (Ex. 16; Deut. 8:3; Matt. 4:1-4; John 6:31-58; Rev. 2:17).

Consider also Jesus' exhortation to His disciples directly following His teaching on prayer and fasting, where He discourages them against materialism and the accumulation of earthly or temporal treasures. He then follows it with an admonition not to worry or be concerned about the everyday physical needs of life but to instead focus their attention on the (spiritual) Kingdom. Therefore, it becomes quite a convincing proposition that Jesus did not have physical concerns in mind with this particular clause (Matt. 6:19-34).[1]

Seek the Kingdom and Don't Worry

We generally interpret Jesus' teaching to mean that we should pray about our physical needs first and then stop worrying about them. But that is not what He is saying. Jesus takes considerably more time to focus upon the aspect of clothing, making it somewhat of a symbol for all physical provision (Matt. 6:26-34). I believe the reason Jesus does this is to subtly allude to Israel in the wilderness. During their forty-year journey in the wilderness, the Israelites never had to pray for clothing because the Lord supernaturally provided for them by causing their shoes and clothing to never wear, tear, or fall apart. This implies not only supernatural preservation of what they had, but also abundant provision during their journey in the wilderness with wool and leather from their own herds or from the booty of Egypt. They literally could *"take no thought"* regarding what they would wear.[2] God would have done the same for them with food and water, but He purposely allowed them to suffer hunger and thirst in order to test them (Deut. 8:2-6).[3]

Jesus isn't saying that we should first seek the Kingdom and then afterward go ahead and pursue our own human concerns. He is saying that the pursuit of the Kingdom should govern everything in our lives, so that everything in our lives becomes subject to it. Attending to our daily physical needs is His concern, not ours, and He doesn't need to be reminded of it. Our concern is to attend to His Kingdom business. The implication is that all of our practical physical needs are supplied as a natural consequence of us focusing our undivided attention upon the Father's Kingdom priority.

For example, when an employer hires you to do a job, it is usually made clear what your remuneration will be and what type of pay period to expect it (whether weekly, bi-weekly, or monthly). If your pay period is weekly, you can usually expect to receive payment for your work every Friday, as long as you continue to be an employee and fulfill your responsibilities to your employer. You are confident that as long as you have faithfully attended to the employer's business, at the end of the week you will receive payment. There is usually never any doubt regarding whether or not you will receive pay. You don't have to remind your employer every Thursday that payment is due tomorrow. You don't have to ask or petition your employer every week for payment, because it is an automatic process as long as you have clocked in or submitted your hours.

ALL OF OUR PRACTICAL PHYSICAL NEEDS ARE SUPPLIED AS A NATURAL CONSEQUENCE OF US FOCUSING OUR UNDIVIDED ATTENTION UPON THE FATHER'S KINGDOM PRIORITY.

God expects you to have the same kind of confidence (faith) in Him as you demonstrate with your natural employer. If you have been faithfully attending to His Kingdom business, then you should have every confidence in God supplying your every need without having to ask for it. Just as it would be ludicrous for an employee to keep reminding or petitioning his faithful employer regarding payment, it is the same with God. The process is automatic. In fact, any employee who demonstrated such a lack of confidence regarding their employer's willingness or ability to pay would cause offense to the employer and soon be out of a job.

Corporate Community Considerations

Notwithstanding all that is mentioned above, this apparently spiritual emphasis regarding bread or manna in the context of discussion does not completely discount a degree of physical application. The apostle Paul alludes to this manna principle in his letter to the Corinthians, applying it in a particularly physical sense to a financial collection for the saints at Jerusalem. The principle here, however, is not about petitioning God to meet the dire physical needs of the suffering saints at Jerusalem, but about the responsibility of the Corinthian believers to give out of their abundance to supply the brethren's lack so as to balance the scales of provision (2 Cor. 8:8-15; Ex. 16:14-18).

Ironically, this serves to validate the spiritual emphasis even further, extending it beyond the personal level to the corporate or community level as well. When it comes to physical or practical areas of lack within the corporate body, God's expectation is that the bountiful or resourceful members of the community generously supply what is needed without petitioning God to do it. If the entire community of believers is impoverished, as was the case with the saints in Jerusalem, relief should be sought beyond the local community from the broader global community or network. Despite our geographical differences or lack of physical proximity, we are to be a unified, global Kingdom Community with shared resources.

Since Jesus obviously intends for this petition to be used primarily in a corporate manner by the words *"give us,"* the clear charge or obligation is for us to maintain a spiritual rather than carnal focus in all

255

of our corporate prayer gatherings. Jesus, Paul, and the early apostolic leaders understood that the Body of Christ's greatest need was spiritual resource; therefore, they were never distracted by physical or earthly concerns. Our prayers must be conditioned by what is essentially needful for the corporate community to fulfill its heavenly mission, not to maintain its earthly comfort. It will eventually become quite evident to everyone around us whose kingdom we are building by what prayers we are praying.

Accompanying the acceptance of this charge should be a comprehensive understanding that when physical needs exist within the community, the divine expectation and biblical requirement is not prayer but personal responsibility, as we saw in Chapter 3. Every member is responsible for each other, and this responsibility extends even beyond the local community level to a global dimension. When there is a physical need, those with the abilities or required resources to meet that need should step forward and do so without depending on God or someone else to do it. One of the principles of the Kingdom is a departure from personal ownership as each member embraces the principle of shared resource.[4]

The Prodigal Spirit

Of course, each of us is free to disagree with these divine imperatives and choose to interpret this petition as a form of liberty for our own self-indulgence. We may continue, as we have in the past, with a sense of entitlement where our primary focus is upon physical blessing, breakthrough, and increase. Like the wastefully extravagant (prodigal)[5] son—who is symbolic of prodigal Christianity today—the Father may even acquiesce to our requests and divide unto us our earthly inheritance before the appointed time,[6] but it will be to our destruction.[7] The prodigal spirit has an uncircumcised nature, seeking full access and entitlement to earthly blessing, inheritance, and promised resource or possession, while living independently of the Father's authority and will—a clear violation of the principle of heaven itself (Luke 15:11-32).

Conversely, we are not seeking to espouse a theology similar to that of the prodigal's antithetically religious brother, who was unable to recognize or appropriate the practical benefits of being a faithful and obedient son in his father's household, or to acknowledge the tender loving kindness of the father's heart towards him as well as to all those who are called his own. Both of these extreme positions are unsound (2 Chron. 1:11-12; Matt. 6:33).

AND FORGIVE US OUR DEBTS
AS WE FORGIVE OUR DEBTORS

Contained within this petition are several valid presuppositions that accompany the explicit meaning. Firstly, it argues for the ongoing need for forgiveness in the lives of believers. We are still in a perfecting and sanctification process, which implies that we have not yet arrived at that perfect state. As we grow in our knowledge of God and experience greater levels of spiritual sight, we will experience a greater recognition of the defilement in our lives, especially from an internal dimension. We are progressively *becoming* more like Him as we allow the substance of our worship to become more refined. The minute we become lax or lulled into a false sense of confidence or complacency regarding our image or character, we begin to operate according to a Pharisaical principle known as self-righteousness (Luke 18:9-14).

EVERY TIME A KINGDOM CITIZEN CHOOSES TO WILLFULLY INDULGE IN OR PRACTICE SIN, HE OR SHE IS, IN EFFECT, WEAKENING AND ERODING THE VERY FABRIC OF AUTHENTIC PRAYER.

Like David, the cry of our hearts should constantly be that God search us and know us, exposing every area of internal defilement or corruption within our hearts (Ps. 139:23-24). If our time of prayer and communion with God doesn't cause us to be assaulted with a greater revelation of His holiness and a greater recognition of our own sinfulness or weakness, we have not yet seen God or beheld His glory (Job 42:5-6; Is. 6:1-5).

Secondly, since these horizontal petitions are contingent upon, as well as subject to, the vertical aspect of the Father and His Kingdom, it stands to reason that sin is a hindrance or impediment in this regard. Sin serves in a counterproductive measure to undermine the Kingdom, profane the name of the Father, and misrepresent heaven.

Every time a Kingdom citizen chooses to willfully indulge in or practice sin, he or she is, in effect, weakening and eroding the very fabric of authentic prayer. When we have unconfessed sin in our lives, it serves to vigorously oppose God's divine intent within our particular spheres. This is why we should be ever so conscious of allowing God to shine His light into the deep, dark, hidden places of our hearts until we are completely transparent before Him. We may choose to hide sin from our conscious minds or from the sight of others, but its effects remain the same. Sins hidden in our thoughts or hearts may be the easiest to conceal, but their effects can be just as destructive in the end as sins that can be seen in our outward actions.

Many "Christian" leaders and believers today have caught wind of the Kingdom mandate and reformation initiative but have embraced it in a purely carnal dimension. They seek to pursue reformation and transformation in society, government, or what is referred to as the "seven mountains" with no internal transformation or reform having taken place within them. This is folly![8] We have no legitimate right or authority to petition for any genuine societal transformation or reform until the principle of reform has penetrated the darkness of our own hearts and internal configurations. The degree to which we have personally submitted to this spiritual principle and have become reformed and transformed will be the degree to which we have authority to effect this principle in others.

Thirdly, nowhere else in this model prayer is the personal pronoun plural *us*—indicative of a corporate dimension—more meaningful or significant than it is here. Everything that was stated in the previous two points becomes greatly intensified when viewed from this corporate dimension. If there is an ongoing need for forgiveness on a personal level, this dynamic becomes magnified on a corporate level. If personal sin has the ability to undermine heaven's agenda within that individual's specific sphere, then that sphere becomes greatly enlarged or multiplied within the community context. From God's point of view, what we usually regard as "personal" or individual sins should really be accounted as corporate or community transgressions. They may have been committed by an individual in private, but the ripple effect and repercussions are corporate (Josh. 7; 22:20; 1 Cor. 5:1-8; Rev. 2:12-23).

The Culture of Repentance

Incidentally, most corporate prayer gatherings never address this sin issue except during times of crisis. Like the Laodicean community, we become blinded by our public images—our popularity, reputations, physical prosperity, earthly success, powerful events, or large numbers of people—while remaining completely unaware of our corporate blindness, nakedness, and deficiency (Rev. 3:14-22). We become careless and complacent as we depend upon trained "intercessors" to petition God for us and identify the dark spiritual forces seeking to undermine the "vision of the house," without ever having a comprehensive corporate posturing of every member's heart in humility and repentance before God.

When true humility and repentance become the regular culture of a Kingdom community, sin is never allowed to stay hidden and flourish. Self-righteousness, self-deception, and hypocrisy will diminish. Blind spots become opportunities to receive greater sight. There is greater unity in the body, with less carnal accusation and judgment, as each member seeks to deal with the mote or plank in his own eye first before seeking to correct the apparent speck in another's (Matt. 7:3-5). But most important of all, with more correct architecture, God's Kingdom will be more accurately expressed through that community.

Jesus expected this model prayer to be appropriated and practiced on a daily basis, not just during times of crisis. If we wait until the crisis comes, it will be too late. Our prayers then become a superficial demonstration of desperation rather than a genuine exercise of biblical principle, faith, or desire for God. This type of pseudo-repentance is not going to get us anywhere with Him.

Taking Personal Responsibility

I encourage you to go back over the previous points and apply them to a corporate dimension after you have applied them to yourself first. If you are a pastor, elder, or spiritual leader, you are doubly accountable to God for what you have just heard (Jam. 3:1). The community you have been given stewardship over is a reflection of your leadership (or lack thereof).

> *PRAYERS OF GENUINE CONTRITION AND REPENTANCE SHOULD BE A REGULAR STAPLE IN CORPORATE PRAYER GATHERINGS.*

If you are an active member, remember that you are your brother's keeper. Every sin committed by a member is accounted to the community as a whole.[9] This doesn't make you a judge, but it does give you the responsibility to no longer just casually ignore your brother's sins. This doesn't mean that you should go and tell your pastor, elder, or other leader every time you witness your brother or sister commit a transgression. This is an incorrect and ungodly approach when the proper biblical protocol is violated. It simply means you have a biblical responsibility to help build and restore your erring brother back into right standing with God by humbly confronting him personally and confidentially—after you have addressed the issues in your own life first. If that fails, your last resort is to expose the person's behavior to the leadership of the community (Matt. 7:1-5; 18:15-20; Gal. 6:1-2; Jam. 5:19-20).[10]

Every Kingdom community should be consciously aware of this sin principle and ever pressing forward into a greater dimension of corporate perfection. The Pharisees were a religious company that became self-righteous, and it is very easy for a corporate community to fall into this mold. Our desire during corporate gatherings should be to behold Him, not conduct good "church" services. Only in beholding Him are we able to see Him for who He is and ourselves for who we really are, which in turn leads to greater humility and repentance. In this way, prayers of genuine contrition and repentance should be a regular staple in corporate prayer gatherings—not in a rehearsed, repetitious, or mechanical way, but in response to a genuine revelation of Him and a greater understanding of His requirements.

The Father's Mercy and Forgiveness

Explicitly stated in this petition are two fundamental doctrinal principles—the forgiveness of God (vertical, divine) and the forgiveness of man (horizontal, human). An understanding of the former is essential for the effective execution of the latter. The vertical dimension of God's forgiveness toward us is what informs and determines the horizontal aspect of how we are supposed to reciprocally forgive others. Once again, heaven becomes the standard or model to be executed on earth.

The word *forgive* here is translated from the Greek word **aphiēmi**, meaning "to send forth or away, let go from oneself." Metaphorically, it means "to let go from obligation toward oneself," or "to remit." It gives the understanding of letting someone go free and releasing him or her from our power or control to impose any further obligation.[11]

The word *debts* refers to something "owed" and is used synonymously to refer to sin as an "offense" or "trespass that requires reparation" (the original Aramaic word could be translated either way).[12] This understanding of sin as a debt needing to be repaid is conveyed quite effectively by Jesus in His parable of the unforgiving servant.

> *"Therefore the kingdom of heaven is like a certain king who wanted to settle accounts with his servants. And when he had begun to settle accounts, one was brought to him who owed him ten thousand talents. But as he was not able to pay, his master commanded that he be sold, with his wife and children and all that he had, and that payment be made. The servant therefore fell down before him, saying, 'Master, have patience with me, and I will pay you all.' Then the master of that servant was moved with compassion, released him, and forgave him the debt. But that servant went out and found one of his fellow servants who owed him a hundred denarii; and he laid hands on him and took him by the throat, saying, 'Pay me what you owe!' So his fellow servant fell down at his feet and begged him, saying, 'Have patience with me, and I will pay you all.' And he would not, but went and threw him into prison till he should pay the debt. So when his fellow servants saw what had been done, they were very grieved, and came and told their master all that had been done. Then his master, after he had called him, said to him, 'You wicked servant! I forgave you all that debt because you begged me. Should you not also have had compassion on your fellow servant, just as I had pity on you?' And his master was angry, and delivered him to the torturers until he should pay all that was due to him. So My heavenly Father*

also will do to you if each of you, from his heart, does not forgive his brother his trespasses."
(Matthew 18:23-35 NKJV)

We won't take the time to explore this very profound parable in great detail, but we will look at several important principles regarding the subject of forgiveness that it communicates—from both a vertical as well as horizontal dimension—and establish them upon a Kingdom of Heaven framework.

MERCY AND FORGIVENESS CAN NEVER BE DEMANDED, ONLY HUMBLY REQUESTED.

The parable begins from a vertical dimension with a focus upon the mercy and compassion of the king (a type of God) towards his indebted or transgressing servant (typical of all humanity). The king was just in settling his accounts, but this enormous debt incurred by his servant would be virtually impossible for him to pay.[13] Justice demanded that this servant, his family, and everything he owned be sold in lieu of repaying this debt, even though the proceeds still would not cover more than a tiny fraction of what he actually owed. This represents, of course, the impossible debt of sin owed by humankind to God, which justice demands to be repaid. Our sin is deserving of death and causes us, our families, and everything we own to be sold into bondage (Ex. 20:5; 34:7; Num. 14:18; Rom. 6:23).

The servant, understanding his dire predicament, falls on his knees before his master and pleads for mercy. He literally begs for mercy because mercy and forgiveness can never be demanded, only humbly requested. No person has a legal *right* to forgiveness. It cannot be earned

263

because the minute a debt is fulfilled it is reckoned as *paid*. Therefore, when a prisoner is released after having fulfilled his sentence of incarceration, he is not *forgiven*; he simply paid his debt to society by fulfilling his penalty. This principle will become profoundly significant as we continue in this study.

The response of the king to his servant's pleas for mercy identifies the internal governing principle that both defines as well as drives the entire process of forgiveness. The tender heart of the master is one of mercy and compassion; therefore, he *"released him, and forgave him the debt."* The servant is now no longer under any obligation to pay. He is free, with the implication that he is fully restored to his former position as his master's servant. There is no indication of any punishment or requirement to be fulfilled from this point on.

When a person forgives another's debt, as in this instance, it is equivalent to that person paying for the other person's debt himself. The forgiver incurs the cost to be made "whole" again. For example, if I loaned my car to someone who accidentally wrecked it, and I forgave him of the trespass, or debt, he would be released from the costly obligation to repair my car. However, repairs would still need to be done, which I would have to cover personally. If I insisted on him covering the cost for the repairs and anything else associated with the loss of my primary vehicle, such as a rental car, and he did so, he would have repaid his debt to me and forgiveness would no longer apply.

When God sent His only begotten Son, Jesus, to die on the cross for our sins, in effect, He forgave and covered the enormous expense of the debt of man's sins through the death of His Son. He couldn't just pretend that the debt never existed; that would be unjust. It had to be paid. Jesus paid it in full with no further requirement needed from us![14] This is the Kingdom model of forgiveness.

The Unforgiving Servant's Response

The way we digress from this model is aptly portrayed by the servant in this parable. After having personally experienced his master's mercy and compassion toward him in forgiving him of an insurmountable debt, he turns around and exacts judgment on a colleague or peer who owes him a very insignificant amount when compared to what he himself had owed.[15] Even though he has a *legal* right to exact what was owed, he is displayed as violent and aggressive in his actions. When his transgressing colleague falls to his knees and begs for the same mercy he previously requested from his master, he refuses to demonstrate the same mercy or compassion and instead has his indebted colleague thrown into prison until he pays his debt.

It is important to note that this unforgiving servant had every *legal* right to do what he did, minus the acts of violence or aggression. However, his actions were not *moral* or *lawful*. He was unwilling to release the man from his debt or obligation by allowing him to go free after he had received compassionate treatment from his master for a much greater debt.

In light of the fact that this parable follows on the heels of Jesus' teaching regarding the restoration of an erring or transgressing brother from a community context, and the fact that this petition of the model prayer is emphatically corporate by design, it is clear that this subject of forgiveness can and should be addressed in a similar way with regard to the entire community (without ignoring the personal or individual implications).

Comparing God's Forgiveness with Religious Christianity Today

What we find demonstrated by religious Christianity today is a clear contradiction of the principle of forgiveness described above. When a brother or sister falls into error or sin, the religious approach has always been to penalize and discipline instead of forgive and restore.[16] The problem with this approach is that by penalizing or disciplining someone for his error, we are effectively exacting payment or dues for his debt. This is the opposite of the principle of forgiveness.

When God forgives, every penalty for sin is reckoned paid by Jesus on the cross. God doesn't expect any further payment from us. God doesn't forgive and then turn around and inflict punishment upon us. What we misconstrue as God's punishment is simply the natural consequence of sin when it has run its course. In other words, it would be more accurate to say that we are punished *by* our sins instead of *for* our sins. Therefore, when Adam and Eve sinned, the judgments stated were not divine "punishments" per se, even though they may have been prefaced with the words *"I will."* God was simply stating the natural consequences of their actions upon the fabric of the conditions on earth.[17] He never pronounced a "curse" on them; only the serpent received a curse. On the contrary, God's response was to quickly *cover* or clothe Adam and Eve by temporarily atoning for their sins until the fullness of time when the Messiah would be sent to complete the work. Even their expulsion from the garden was an act of mercy (Gen. 3).

WHAT WE MISCONSTRUE AS GOD'S PUNISHMENT IS SIMPLY THE NATURAL CONSEQUENCE OF SIN WHEN IT HAS RUN ITS COURSE.

We see this principle again with David after his sins of adultery and murder. When the prophet Nathan confronts him with God's words of judgment regarding the adversity that is going to come upon him and his household on account of his sinful actions, David repents. The Lord immediately forgives him and rescinds what should have been certain death. However, Scripture historically proves that David would indeed suffer the things God had said, including the death of his child.[18] It is not that God only *partially* forgives him, because there is no such thing. While a financial debt can be only partially forgiven, biblical forgiveness must be complete, or there is no forgiveness at all. This is not a "reduced sentence." David experiences the natural consequences of his actions as stated by God so as to prepare him for what is to come. God cannot and will not overturn the spiritual and physical principle of "sowing and reaping" that governs the earth (Gen. 8:22; 2 Sam. 12:1-15).

When the Pharisees bring unto Jesus a woman caught in adultery, the religious expectation is to impose the legal requirements of the law and penalize her for her sin. However, Jesus emphasizes and demonstrates the principle of forgiveness by reminding her accusers of their own sinfulness and need for mercy. She sinned in a different way than they did, but her debt to God is no greater than their own. When her accusers become convicted by their consciences and leave, Jesus doesn't proceed to list a number of disciplinary measures or requirements for her to be fully restored. His only command is that she go and (from now on[19]) *"sin no more"* (John 8:1-11).

When Zacchaeus was rejected and treated as an outcast by the established religious community on account of his sin, he is embraced by Jesus. After personally meeting with him, Jesus doesn't impose any requirements upon Zacchaeus in order to be restored into complete fellowship. The restitutions Zacchaeus chooses to make are made by his own initiative, not Jesus' command, and they give evidence of a transformed heart (Luke 19:1-10).

When one of Jesus' chief apostles—Peter—denies Jesus not once, but three times (indicative of a complete and total denial), Jesus doesn't impose any disciplinary requirements upon him. He doesn't place Peter on a "time out" or leave of absence from public ministry in order to prove himself before he was "worthy" enough to continue in his apostolic calling (Matt. 26:34, 69-75).[20]

Then, of course, we have the prodigal son, whom we briefly mentioned earlier in this chapter. After having seriously dishonored and offended his father by his wayward and lawless actions, he comes to his senses and decides to return to his father in humility and repentance. The father's compassionate heart is revealed by his loving reaction upon his son's return. While the son's genuine heart of contrition is evident by his willingness to submit to his father's interests as a mere servant rather than as a privileged son, the father places no such terms or conditions upon him. He demonstrates total and complete forgiveness by giving him the honor of a son and restoring him to his former position (Luke 15:11-32).

In a context such as this one, the Pharisaical principle would have been to demote the son to the status of servant until he pays his debt and proves himself worthy to be acknowledged as a son again. I am certain the religious brother would have preferred such a response. As it stands, the father demonstrates a true heart of forgiveness by restoring his disgraced son completely to his former state.[21] This type of response, however, offends a religious mindset.

There can be no forgiveness with imposed penalties. There is no such thing as, "I forgive you, *but...*" or "I'll forgive you, *if...*" Even if the offender repeats the act numerous times we are still expected to completely forgive him or her (Matt. 18:21-22).

When church scandals occur and leaders fall into public disrepute or error, there is usually a public clamor for discipline or justice. However, the world's standard is not the Kingdom's. When a brother or sister falls we are not to judge, discipline, or penalize, which is a Pharisee technology or principle; we are to forgive and restore.[22] Forgiving the way God requires may offend the worldly and religious, but to do otherwise is to offend God Himself.

Different Extremes

This is not the same as simply ignoring someone's indiscretions and permitting them to continue in error—a common but extreme reaction that produces disastrous effects upon the entire community. Instead, it means that we invest ourselves in their lives to help them overcome whatever it is they are dealing with without imposing external penalties in a controlling manner. This requires a mutual submission through relationship, not from an autocratic position. The objective is to restore the person to wholeness spiritually and practically. If the person is unrepentant or poses a risk or liability to other members of the community, the person may need to be removed entirely from fellowship (Matt. 18:8-9; 15-20; 1 Cor. 5:1-13; Gal. 5:13; Eph. 5:21; Phil. 2:3-4).

The opposite extreme is no forgiveness at all, as we observed in the parable of the unforgiving servant. This type of unforgiving mentality is often paraded among the religious as something real or genuine, but it's a counterfeit forgiveness. Like Jacob's sons exhibited when their sister, Dinah, was sexually defiled by the Hivite prince, a false sense of forgiveness is portrayed. Jacob's sons deceitfully gave the impression that they would forgive the transgression of the erring prince and give their already defiled sister to him to be his wife *if* he and every male in his city became circumcised—a sign of covenant, righteousness, obedience, and purification. However, their desire to see these men circumcised was not for the men's purification, restoration, or benefit, but to exact vengeance and judgment upon them by weakening them, killing them, and disinheriting them (Gen. 34).

Jacob did not take kindly to the cruel actions of his sons Simeon and Levi, and he deprived them of his patriarchal blessing (Gen. 49:5-7). The king in the parable we discussed above identified the unforgiving servant as *"wicked"* and dispensed upon him severe judgment (Matt. 18:31-35). This the same way that God views and treats unforgiveness perpetrated by His children or servants (Matt. 6:14-15; Mark 11:25-26; Luke 6:37).

The Neutralizing Effect on Prayer

The fact is that we cannot pray effectively if our relationships are not in order or we hold unforgiveness in our hearts. You may remember that the apostle Peter indicated that the quality of our relationship with our spouse has a direct impact on the effectiveness of our prayers (1 Pet. 3:7). How much more, then, will unforgiveness serve to undermine our personal and/or corporate prayer initiatives? We have no *right* to exercise authority in prayer until we are willing to surrender our *rights* through the act of forgiveness. We cannot expect to receive mercy when we ourselves are unwilling to give it. These areas must be properly addressed before we attempt to commune with God or seek to prayerfully engage in establishing His Kingdom agenda on earth. This is because unforgiveness is diametrically opposed to the architecture of the Kingdom of Heaven and serves to dishonor God, obscure His image, and undermine or impede Kingdom progress (Mark 11:25; Eph. 4:32; 1 Pet. 3:7).

> *WE HAVE NO RIGHT TO EXERCISE AUTHORITY IN PRAYER UNTIL WE ARE WILLING TO SURRENDER OUR RIGHTS THROUGH THE ACT OF FORGIVENESS.*

When a community that claims to know and worship God fails to demonstrate the kind of forgiveness that is required by the Father, we become religious hypocrites whose prayers may appear corporately dynamic and purposeful, but are nevertheless frivolous, futile, and ineffective. By failing to conform to the Father's image in this regard, we are, in effect, operating contrary to His intent and design.

One of the greatest needs we have as a true Kingdom community is a greater revelation of God. When Moses asked to behold God's glory—the full weight and measure of His person—the dimension of God that was proclaimed first and most was His mercy (inclusive of grace, longsuffering, and forgiveness, which are all various aspects of mercy). In other words, the most predominant characteristic or facet of God's nature is His mercy. If this is true with Him, then it should also be true with us as His children and earthly ambassadors (Ex. 33:12-34:9).

AND DO NOT LEAD US INTO TEMPTATION

This particular petition has served to confuse numerous Bible interpreters due to its difficult wording. Taken at face value, it seems to imply that God can somehow lead us into temptation or sin. However, we know that this is clearly not the case because it contradicts the very nature of God as revealed through His Word, and also because the Scriptures are very explicit regarding the fact that God does not tempt anyone, much less lead anyone into temptation. We are tempted when we succumb to our own human ambitions, passions, or desires, thereby causing us to become enticed into sin (Jam. 1:13-15).

Incorrect Interpretations

To overcome this obvious theological hurdle with regard to God somehow leading us into temptation, some have chosen to interpret the word *temptation* as referring to tests, trials, or adversity.[23] They render the clause as somewhat of an injunction against future or eschatological testing, meaning "do not lead us into testing" or "do not allow us to suffer adversity," but this itself is a clear violation of Scripture.

THERE IS NO BIBLICAL BASIS TO SUPPORT THE ERRONEOUS INTERPRETATION OF PETITIONING GOD TO ESCAPE SUFFERING OR ADVERSITY.

The truth of the matter is that while God will never lead us into temptation to sin, He does, however, sometimes lead us into times of testing in order to strengthen and prove us. It was God who led Abraham to Mount Moriah to be tested (Gen. 22:1-19). It was God who led the nation of Israel for forty years in the wilderness in order to test and prove them (Deut. 8:2). And it was the Holy Spirit who led Jesus into the wilderness to be tested and tempted by the devil (Matt. 4:1-11).[24] Any attempt for these people to pray against or subvert such testing would have been counterproductive to their own spiritual development and

271

contradictory to the divine will and purpose of God. Therefore, it would be ludicrous to believe that Jesus is espousing such a notion that so clearly contradicts the main tenets of prayer, including the vertical aspects upon which every one of the horizontal petitions are hinged.

There is also no biblical basis to support the erroneous interpretation of petitioning God to escape suffering or adversity. Such a petition is not focused upon divine purpose but upon carnal comfort. Jesus never prayed this way, so why would He encourage His disciples to do what He never did? The very premise of such a petition is diabolical in nature, as evidenced by Jesus' response to Peter when he attempted to dissuade Jesus from pursuing a path of suffering (Matt. 16:21-23).

When Jesus commanded His disciples to *"watch and pray"* that they may be *"counted worthy (have strength) to escape all these things"* regarding what was to come, He was not endorsing an "escape" mentality made popular by religious Christianity or implying that we should pray to escape eschatological adversity.[25] He commanded them to watch and pray so that they would have the spiritual strength, internal fortitude, and divine resource necessary to escape or be delivered from the internal contamination that would engulf, devour, and define earth's inhabitants prior to His return (Luke 21:34-36).

The Correct Approach

In order to understand the true meaning of this petition, we first have to take into account the clear implication and recognition that it is, in fact, God who is doing the leading. This suggests that the petitioner's heart is postured in humble submission toward God. This particular petition follows quite naturally on the heels of the preceding petition asking God for forgiveness from personal and corporate transgressions, indicating a progression of continuity in thought. Therefore, the only reasonable interpretation for this clause is that a truly contrite heart, which has no desire or intention to continue displeasing God, acknowledges the need for God's leadership in order to avoid unnecessary temptation and the entrapment of sin.

In other words, this petition is an acknowledgment of personal as well as corporate weakness, blindness, and insufficiency. It is saying to God, "You have to lead us and You have to navigate for us because we cannot lead or navigate ourselves without falling into personal (or corporate) error or failure." To paraphrase the clause, it is saying to God, "Lead us (me) so we (I) do not get in the flesh and end up succumbing to temptation" (Matt. 26:41; Gal. 5:16-18).

The Need for Daily Divine Guidance

This is not a "once-and-for-all" religious prayer that we pray rarely or occasionally when we are in a quandary, have encountered a fork in the road, or are in desperate need for divine direction. Neither is it a religious ritual that we repeat liturgically or mechanically, as often as possible, without any internal consistency or substance. This prayer conveys a reality similar to the manna principle where there is a *daily* recognition of one's need for divine direction in order to be preserved from the entrapments of temptation and sin. We need progressive revelation, direction, and divine navigation, and this places a requirement upon us to accurately position and posture ourselves to hear His directives and be led. We cannot depend on yesterday's manna— yesterday's revelation or course of direction—because it may have become outdated and begun to stink (Ex. 16:4, 16-20; Deut. 8:3; Matt. 4:4).

The Pharisees became internally sinful and corrupt because they chose to anchor themselves upon what God did "yesterday" and the way He led them previously. They possessed no genuine desire or receptivity for the current speaking and leading of God beyond Moses, thereby causing them to become enticed and entrapped in the sin of religious tradition. Most religious Christian denominations have fallen into the same trap, having become enticed into error and sin due to their internal resistance to being currently and progressively *led* (Matt. 15:1-9).

The Kingdom of God is not static or stagnant; it progresses continuously and vigorously. This implies continuous migration and forward movement rather than a false sense of "arrival." The minute we become settled or complacent regarding what we previously heard, or the way we were previously led, we have already precariously positioned ourselves upon the precipice of error. Stagnation always breeds filth and corruption, which is why we can never allow ourselves to become overly confident or complacent regarding what we have heard from God. Our hearts must forever be conditioned toward following Him *daily* as a requirement for our very survival.

THE KINGDOM OF GOD IS NOT STATIC OR STAGNANT; IT PROGRESSES CONTINUOUSLY AND VIGOROUSLY.

Again, the operating system for this type of prayer is a heart postured in total humility and surrender. These are not empty religious words that we pray before corporate religious gatherings or business meetings and then hold tightly to our own personal agendas. If our hearts were never accurately postured to submit to God's direction and leadership prior to the meeting or event, before we even formulated an agenda, then praying a prayer such as this just before we officially start is just a vain display of religious piety. This petition is a prayer of total surrender to the leadership of God through His Holy Spirit, made because we truly recognize and understand the utter futility of trusting in ourselves despite our high achievements, education, wisdom, reputations, social status, talents, gifting, titles, positions, or whatever else we may feel inclined to humanly trust in.

To pray this way requires an emptying of ourselves, similar to the way Jesus totally emptied Himself of all human sustenance during His time of fasting prior to being tempted by the devil. He was able to withstand the devil's temptations not because of His own human strength or ability but because of His total dependence upon God and the Holy Spirit. He was able to defeat the enemy and overcome temptation because He was led by the Spirit rather than by His own human or fleshly desires (Matt. 4:1-11).

The Temptation of Leaders

Leaders especially are often prone to trusting in their own human strength or in worldly systems or devices. King David, the priests, and the elders of Israel all succumbed to the temptation of following the worldly (Philistine) example of transporting the Ark of the Covenant upon a manmade cart. This resulted in the sin and ultimate untimely death of Uzzah, the man who was driving it. In the same way, church leaders today succumb to worldly architecture, marketing schemes, leadership structures, methods, and devices in order to build churches and attempt to manufacture "God's presence" (1 Sam. 6; 2 Sam. 6:1-8; 1 Chron. 13).

The sad thing about this is that we then turn around and petition God to bless and direct us in what we are doing, but our hearts were never fully surrendered to Him to begin with. This makes our petitions an insincere demonstration of vain religion, and what we are building becomes a contradiction of every preceding petition. Until we are ready to lay down our plans, programs, designs, goals, vision, agendas, human expectations, and traditions, we are not yet qualified to pray this prayer. We must have a recognition of our own deficiency (as well as the world's) that activates an internal disposition of absolute surrender to God's determination and intent, prompting us to desperately cry out to Him for His leadership every step of the way and for deliverance from every temptation toward evil.

BUT DELIVER US FROM EVIL

This final petition is closely linked and connected to the preceding one, and it is once again dependent upon God's leadership. Many of the modern translations, including the New King James, have rendered this clause in such a way that it refers to satan as the patriarch or personification of evil that we require deliverance from with the term "evil one." However, the old King James Version remains the closest to the original manuscripts by excluding the "one" after the evil, thus rendering the clause, *"but deliver us from evil."*

This may seem like an insignificant point, but it is not. This is not a cry to God to save or rescue us from satan as if he is some formidable or unconquerable enemy. This type of misconception is precisely the reason why we often find so many sincere, but poorly informed, believers who focus an inordinate amount of time and attention in prayer on addressing satan or "binding and loosing" demon spirits, many times fictitiously inventing their own. I have often wondered at the end of certain corporate prayer gatherings exactly who it was we were supposedly praying to, because the words *satan, devil, demon,* etc., came up so often that I thought perhaps we might have been praying to them instead of to God.

Satan didn't storm into the Garden of Eden and somehow try to wrestle earth's dominion away from Adam, since he knew he could never win that battle. In fact, the serpent's tactic was to deceive Eve as the weaker vessel because he knew he would never get over that easily with Adam. The point is that neither Adam nor Eve could have been overcome by a head-on confrontation or brute force. The serpent's only advantage was to gain a foothold through deception. Rather than being formidable or unconquerable, our enemy is weak, but he is very cunning. His ability to deceive is second to none; however, it is completely neutralized against us as long as we are being led by God and not trusting in ourselves (Rom. 6:16; 16:20; 1 Tim. 2:14; Rev. 12:9).

We have made the devil a god and have ascribed to him more honor and recognition than he deserves. Your car probably didn't break down because of the devil. Perhaps it was because you never (or rarely) changed your oil or neglected to have maintenance performed during the years you have been driving it. It may not have been the devil to blame for your automobile accident, but the fact that you chose to ignore safety guidelines or restrictions imposed in the form of a speed limit. Maybe the financial lack or hardship you have been experiencing is really not an "attack" of the devil, but the natural outcome of your own mismanagement, mishandling, and misappropriation of funds. And the overwhelming heaviness you felt during the church service last evening may have had nothing to do with witchcraft or heightened demonic activity, but your own hardened heart, prayerlessness, or internal rebellion against God.

> *THE DEVIL NEVER HAS BEEN, NOR WILL HE EVER BE, THE MAIN ISSUE THAT WE AS A KINGDOM COMMUNITY ARE CONTENDING AGAINST.*

The devil never has been, nor will he ever be, the main issue that we as a Kingdom community are contending against. The finished work of Jesus on the cross effectively took care of that issue. We are not the ones who need to be rescued from him; he is the one who needs to be rescued from us! We are the ones who *crush* satan's head, not the other way around. We destroy him; he does not destroy us (Rom. 16:20).

The Internal Dimension of Evil

When this clause is read as God originally intended, we see a petition made to God to deliver His people from every degree or dimension of evil that surrounds us, especially as it relates to the issues of sin and temptation, which is the natural flow of thought in this instance. Of special emphasis here, I believe, is that internal dimension of evil, since the internal dimension is what provides temptation the hook with which to draw us away and give birth to sin.

277

> *But each one is tempted when he is drawn away by his own desires and enticed. Then, when desire has conceived, it gives birth to sin; and sin, when it is full-grown, brings forth death.* (James 1:14-15 NKJV)

According to James, temptation is fueled by our own evil desires. These evil seeds of desire may seem tiny and insignificant to us because they are hidden from others' sight, deep inside the darkness of our own hearts. But their true potential is only revealed after the maturation process when desire gives birth to sin and sin gives birth to death. One tiny seed has the potential to produce a mighty harvest. A seed has the potential to create not just another tree but a literal forest. Therefore, it is not the evil that exists without or outside us that should be our greatest concern, but the evil that resides within our own hearts and provides satan an access point into our lives (2 Cor. 2:9-11; Eph. 4:27).[26]

When Jesus made the statement regarding *"the ruler of this world"* coming and having or finding *"nothing in Me,"* He was declaring that no evil desire or corrupt internal principle was operating within Him that satan could use to his advantage (John 14:30). There was no hook of temptation that the enemy could use to gain an advantage over Him. It didn't matter what kind of external pressure or conditions were brought to bear upon Jesus as long as His internal condition remained uncompromised and sound. This principle provides a better context for understanding the petition now before us.

You will notice in the principle described by James above that temptation is manifested by a "drawing away." This is significant because the word *deliver* in our current petition is translated from the Greek word **rhúomai**, which conveys the idea of not only salvation, rescue, protection, and deliverance, but more importantly of a drawing to oneself and away from someone or something else. In other words, by employing the word *deliver* in this petition, the petitioner is asking God to *draw us away from the evil that would seek to draw us away from God.*

This internal conflict of polarized passions or influences is a normal occurrence for believers. A continual battle is raging within us between the Spirit of God and our own evil tendencies toward sin. By praying this prayer we are seeking to energize that accurate internal dimension, to deny our flesh, and to yield to the Holy Spirit. Once again it is an acknowledgment of our own personal or corporate weakness, as we petition God to deliver—free, save, rescue, protect, and preserve—us from every internal as well as external element of evil by drawing us to Himself.

Internal Submission and Guidance

Everything in this petition is hinged upon the preceding one. In other words, we should not expect any deliverance from evil until we are first willing to be led by God (Matt. 26:41; John 6:63; Rom. 7:4-8:17; Gal. 6:8; Jam. 4:7).

The degree to which we are willing to submit to God and be led is the degree to which we will walk in freedom and deliverance. It doesn't matter what pastor, preacher, prophet, or "man of faith" lays hands on us and speaks deliverance; we cannot "cast out" uncrucified flesh or the inherent evil working within our members.[27] It doesn't matter how many people we have pray. The victory comes when *we* pray and receive the fresh manna of His Word, humbly posture our hearts before God, and then submit to His guidance by yielding to the Holy Spirit.

Whomever you choose to yield to becomes the dominant force in your life.

Most stubborn people who are set in their ways and have become more inclined to follow after their evil passions or desires will choose to substitute external forms of direction for internal guidance. A thief will justify his stealing by praying, "Lord, if You don't want me to steal anymore, please don't have anyone place their belongings anywhere close to me where I can reach them or have my neighbor leave her door open." Or a fornicator might pray, "Lord, if You don't want me to end up in sexual sin, please don't make my girlfriend (or boyfriend) come to my apartment when I'm alone." When it comes to a corporate assembly or church, the leaders might pray something like this, "Lord, if it is not Your will that we continue upon this particular path or direction, send us a prophet whom we trust to tell us so." They deceive themselves into believing that they are submitting to God's leadership and direction, when in fact they are not.

Neither of these examples mentioned above represent petitioners who are willing to allow God to deal with the inaccurate internal principles operating within their hearts. They were unwilling to allow God to touch and deliver them at the core. Therefore, self-deception crept in and caused them to portray a form of godliness through their religious petitions, without any true internal submission. This helped to ease their consciences from the sinful guilt. But if they were really genuinely submitted to God's leadership and direction for true deliverance, the thief would have confessed and surrendered to God his covetousness, the fornicator would allow God to deal with the lust, and the church leaders would have confessed their doubt and blindness, relinquished their tight hold on the reigns of leadership, and waited on God for divine directives.

THE DEGREE TO WHICH WE ARE WILLING TO SUBMIT TO GOD AND BE LED IS THE DEGREE TO WHICH WE WILL WALK IN FREEDOM AND DELIVERANCE.

The children of Israel were delivered from Egypt after over four hundred years of bondage, but the sinful culture of the Egyptians had become so ingrained in them after so much time that even after their physical departure from the land, they were still inclined toward the evil tendencies that became embedded in them there. The reason God had to lead this vast company by means of a pillar of fire and cloud—external signs or phenomena—was not just so He could demonstrate to Egypt and the surrounding nations His miraculous power, but it was also because the children of Israel had no internal capacity to be led spiritually otherwise.

God gave numerous laws and external requirements or restrictions to the Israelites as a newly established nation of people because they were internally lawless. Had God not done so and He had left them to their own ways, this would have quickly accelerated their deterioration and destruction as a nation. But external requirements or controls were incapable of reining in the corrupt evil tendencies they had adopted from Egypt and the surrounding nations. Over and over again they rebelled against God. Over and over again they were consumed and overwhelmed by evil. And over and over again they chose to acclimate themselves to the corrupt customs and cultures that had been practiced by the heathen nations around them.

The point is that lack of internal governance requires external control, but external control or "guidance" can never substitute for internal discipline or direction. That which is within you will eventually make its way outside of you. Depending on external conditions, circumstances, or directives to be led by God and escape evil is fallacious, foolish, and futile. We will always have a tendency toward compromise when these external limitations are temporarily suspended or removed. For example, most of us are inclined to violate the speed limit when no authorities are around, but we willingly conform when they are present (Jer. 31:31-33; Heb. 8:7-13).

The evil that is in the world will have no power to overcome or overwhelm us as long as we are willing to address the evil that is resident within our own hearts and willingly submit to God's leadership and direction from an internal dimension (John 14:30).

As we pray these two final petitions of Jesus' model prayer, asking God to lead us away from temptation and to deliver us from evil, we are echoing Jesus' own personal prayer for His disciples.

281

Now I am no longer in the world, but these are in the world, and I come to You. Holy Father, keep through Your name those whom You have given Me, that they may be one as We are. While I was with them in the world, I kept them in Your name. Those whom You gave Me I have kept; and none of them is lost except the son of perdition, that the Scripture might be fulfilled. But now I come to You, and these things I speak in the world, that they may have My joy fulfilled in themselves. I have given them Your word; and the world has hated them because they are not of the world, just as I am not of the world. I do not pray that You should take them out of the world, but that You should keep them from the evil one.[28] (John 17:11-15 NKJV)

DOXOLOGY

For Yours is the Kingdom and the power and the glory forever. Amen.

This closing portion of Jesus' model prayer is unique to Matthew's gospel record. It is excluded in Luke's account as well as in many earlier manuscripts, thus leading many to believe that it was not part of Jesus' original model prayer, but a later scribal appendage that should be omitted even though there is no theological inconsistency in the words.[29]

While this may be true, there is no possible way for any of us to confirm this for sure. Regardless of where the words of this doxology may have truly originated, the fact is that it comes full circle in returning the clear emphasis in a vertical dimension back to God. This is reason enough to argue for its inclusion and relevance as part of this prayer.

Everything in the Kingdom of Heaven begins and ends with the Father. Affirming once again that it is His Kingdom and not ours that we are seeking to establish in the earth makes a perfect way to conclude the prayer. It is His power and authority that makes prayer effectual. And it is His glory that we are seeking to pursue rather than our own.

IT IS VERY DIFFICULT TO MISS THE MARK IN PRAYER WHEN THE FATHER AND HIS KINGDOM REMAIN FRONT AND CENTER OF EVERYTHING WE DO AND EVERY PETITION WE MAKE.

I tire of any form of prayer that leaves us with a greater awareness of ourselves than of God. I reject every corporate religious prayer exercise that chooses to remain fixated upon personal needs or carnal horizontal petitions without an elevated vertical recognition of the splendor and majesty of God. Everything we say and do in prayer must point back to Him and reflect these three main vertical areas of concern—His Kingdom and dominion; His rule, power, and authority; and His glory and honor. This should not just be the case *some* of the time, but *all* of the time, as implied by the word *forever*.

Even though this doxology is officially missing in Jesus' own personal prayer recorded in John 17, the principle of this elevated recognition of the Father remains consistent throughout the entirety of His prayer, and it is conspicuously present toward the close of it (John 17:25-26).

It is very difficult to miss the mark in prayer when the Father and His Kingdom remain front and center of everything we do and every petition we make. The minute we lose sight of the Father and begin focusing upon ourselves and what we carnally desire, error and corruption enter in. Remember, the foundational purpose of prayer is for the execution of the Father's will and purpose in the earth, not our own. As we proceed

283

into the final chapter, we will discover how to reformulate our own personal and corporate prayer initiatives according to the model Jesus taught so that it accomplishes this purpose.

KEY PRINCIPLES

1. The divine order, emphasis, and priority of prayer—or anything relating to the Kingdom for that matter—is always with the Father.

2. Every horizontal petition is contingent upon, and subject to, the foundational vertical priorities.

3. When the emphasis is shifted from what *He* wants to what *we* want, we have entered into a satanic kingdom.

4. All of our practical physical needs are supplied as a natural consequence of us focusing our undivided attention upon the Father's Kingdom priority.

5. Our prayers must be conditioned by what is essentially needful for the corporate community to fulfill its heavenly mission, not to maintain its earthly comfort.

6. One of the principles of the Kingdom is a departure from personal ownership as each member embraces the principle of shared resource.

7. The prodigal spirit has an uncircumcised nature, seeking full access and entitlement to earthly blessing, inheritance, and promised resources or possession, while living independently of the Father's authority and will.

8. If our time of prayer and communion with God doesn't cause us to be assaulted with a greater revelation of His holiness and a greater recognition of our own sinfulness or weakness, we have not yet seen God or beheld His glory.

9. Every time a Kingdom citizen chooses to willfully indulge in or practice sin, he or she is, in effect, weakening and eroding the very fabric of authentic prayer.

10. The degree to which we have become reformed and transformed will be the degree to which we have authority to effect reformation and transformation in others.

11. The vertical dimension of God's forgiveness toward us is what informs and determines the horizontal aspect of how we are supposed to reciprocally forgive others.

12. Forgiveness can never be demanded, only humbly requested. No person has a legal *right* to forgiveness.

13. God doesn't forgive and then turn around and inflict punishment upon us.

14. While a financial debt can be partially forgiven, biblical forgiveness must be complete, or there is no forgiveness at all.

15. We cannot pray effectively if our relationships are not in order or we hold unforgiveness in our hearts.

16. We have no *right* to exercise authority in prayer until we are willing to surrender our *rights* through the act of forgiveness.

17. The most predominant characteristic or facet of God's nature is His mercy.

18. God will never lead us into temptation to sin. He does, however, sometimes lead us into times of testing in order to strengthen and prove us.

19. The Kingdom of God is not static or stagnant; it progresses continuously and vigorously.

20. The devil never has been, nor will he ever be, the main issue that we as a Kingdom community are contending against.

21. It is not the evil that exists without or outside us that should be our greatest concern, but the evil that resides within our own hearts and provides satan an access point into our lives.

22. The degree to which we are willing to submit to God and be led is the degree to which we will walk in freedom and deliverance.

23. Whomever you choose to yield to becomes the dominant force in your life.

24. Lack of internal governance requires external control, but external control or "guidance" can never substitute for internal discipline or direction.

ENDNOTES

1. In Luke's account of Jesus' teaching on *The Model Prayer*, he follows this teaching with an admonition to *ask, seek,* and *knock*—obvious references to prayer—but with an apparently physical emphasis using various types of food. However, these physical analogies are explained in the end in the context of clearly spiritual or divine resource—the Holy Spirit. Our persistent seeking in prayer should be for the apprehension of spiritual things (Luke 11:5-13).

2. Matt. 6:25, 31 KJV.

3. Jesus was tested in a similar way, but He responded accurately (Matt. 4:1-4).

4. Not to be confused with socialism, which is government imposed. While certain elements may appear to be similar, the architecture is not. This is Kingdom architecture, not social reform.

5. Note that the word *prodigal* refers to someone who is wastefully extravagant by either spending his money recklessly or mismanaging his resources in pursuit of a lavish lifestyle. It does not refer, as is often misused in religious circles, to a departed or estranged loved one.

6. Jewish cultural protocol dictates that it must be the father who initiates this division and transfer of inheritance before he approaches death's door, not the son.

7. See also Num. 11; Ps. 78:27-31; 106:13-15.

8. Outward (religious) conformity minus an inward (spiritual) principle equals a counterfeit kingdom.

9. Remember that Achan's sin was accounted as Israel's sin, thus causing the nation to be defeated by their enemies (Josh. 7:1, 10-13).

10. False accusation, gossip, slander, and judgment are counterproductive to the spirit of restoration. The objective here is to *cover* and not expose, unless exposure is absolutely necessary for the sake of the community (Matt. 18:8-9).

11. *The Complete Word Study Dictionary: New Testament*, ed. Spiros Zodhiates Th.D. (Chattanooga, TN: AMG International, 1993), 863.

12. Ibid., 3783.

13. *"Ten thousand talents"* is a hyperbole for an impossible or insurmountable debt. According to the ESV Study Bible, it is equivalent to approximately 6 billion U.S. dollars.

14. We are completely justified through Christ's sacrifice on the cross; however, we are still expected to confess and repent of known transgressions (Matt. 6:12; 1 John 1:9).

15. *"A hundred denarii,"* though large, is contrasted against a much larger amount to show its relative insignificance. According to the ESV Study Bible, it is equivalent to approximately twelve thousand U.S. dollars.

16. While the process of restoration may occasionally entail a certain measure of discipline, discipline is never to become the driving philosophy or goal.

17. The fact that these conditions still exist upon the earth and afflict the righteous just as much as the wicked is proof that these are natural consequences and not a sign of God's displeasure with us or punishment for sin.

18. The death of the child is proof of the consequences of sin upon one's household. God had no choice but to kill the child in order to protect the honor of His name.

19. These additional words are found in various manuscripts.

20. The seriousness and gravity of Peter's sin of denial is often overlooked. This was no mere trifle, and it could have resulted in him being denied access to both the Father and heaven had he not repented (Matt. 10:32-33; Luke 12:8-9).

21. True forgiveness requires full restoration. The person's state or position after the transgression must be the same as his state or position prior to it in order for the forgiveness to be complete and genuine.

22. God administers discipline as an expression of love, not as an execution of justice or recompense for sin. Godly discipline looks *forward* to preventing the person's destruction; religious discipline looks *backward* to punishing the person for his or her error (Heb. 12:3-11; 1 Cor. 5:5).

23. The Greek word **peirasmós**, which is translated as *temptation*, can also be translated in this way depending upon the context.

24. God led Jesus to the test, but it was the devil who sought to lure and tempt Jesus into sin.

25. The *escape* principle communicated in Scripture is not one of "fleeing away" in defeat, but rather of spiritual or internal endurance in victory (1 Cor. 10:13).

26. Note that in Luke 22:31-32, when satan desired to have Peter so that he could *"sift you (him) as wheat,"* Jesus' response was not to gather the other disciples around Peter and pray a "blood line" over him. Neither did He and His disciples enter into any pseudo-spiritual warfare of "binding or loosing" the enemy for this diabolical assault planned against their brother. Jesus never focuses His prayer on addressing satan because he was not their main concern. Jesus' prayer is focused solely upon the internal architecture of Peter's faith to withstand this diabolical onslaught—in other words, the *internal* dimension of evil.

27. This does not diminish the need for deliverance from demonic activity in someone's life.

28. The term *evil one* is once again an incorrect translation. The original manuscripts omit the "one," which makes the KJV rendering more accurate, true, and consistent with the original—*"keep them from the evil."* While some may argue that the original Greek word for *evil* (*ponērós*) can be translated either way, the biblical context will not fully support this view of making satan the subject. It communicates a theology that is flawed and diverts our attention from the real issues.

29. Many of the more modern Bible translations have ascribed to this view and have omitted this doxology altogether.

CHAPTER 12

THE NEED FOR REFORMATION

A

s we come to the conclusion of this book, it is my desire that not only will you come into a more accurate understanding of prayer, but that the Holy Spirit will quicken you to pray more effectively and intelligently than you have in the past. The religious traditions and inaccurate models we have inherited from our Christian forefathers are in desperate need of reform. The technology of prayer must be grasped by every Kingdom citizen if we hope to accelerate Kingdom advance, propel toward the finish, and hasten Jesus' return.

Both Jesus and John the Baptist taught their disciples to pray for a reason, even though the Jews were well acquainted with the common religious exercise of prayer (Luke 11:1). John the Baptist was the forerunner and Jesus was the Architect of a new heavenly Kingdom sent to replace the formal structures of religious Judaism. With this new Kingdom came an entirely new operating system, with architecture that was of an internal design. The religious prayer dynamics the Jews had grown accustomed to had been severely degraded and corrupted through centuries of syncretism, apostasy, and pagan influence, especially with regard to Baal worship. Whatever these Jews felt they knew or understood about prayer from past generations was either inconsistent with God's Kingdom or largely outdated and in need of reform. This new Kingdom being introduced operated by a much higher standard, and it required radical revisions in the way the Jews understood and practiced prayer. This is why Jesus and John taught their disciples—to upgrade them in current Kingdom technology and reform them in their understanding and practice of prayer.

BOTH JESUS AND JOHN THE BAPTIST TAUGHT THEIR DISCIPLES TO PRAY FOR A REASON, EVEN THOUGH THE JEWS WERE WELL ACQUAINTED WITH THE COMMON RELIGIOUS EXERCISE OF PRAYER.

The Jews and religious leaders were in need of understanding and reform then, just as we are in need of understanding and reform today. Our prayers have been largely ineffectual because we have been praying amiss. God is now seeking to deliver us from our internal blindness and ignorance. May the eyes of our understanding be enlightened as we learn to conform to Jesus' accurate model.

FOLLOWING THE PATTERN

Those of us who have allowed God to make these internal adjustments within us are now ready to proceed in a more practical sense to formulating our vocal prayer petitions according to the prescribed model and pattern taught by Jesus. To help you do this I have created an example below. Note that this is only an example to help guide you in applying the principles of the Model Prayer in your own personal or corporate context. The prayer below was formulated according to Jesus' model, but it also carries a personal dimension in that it addresses certain issues that are spiritually organic and relevant to me in my present earthly context. For you, some of these issues may be a little different, but the overall context should continue to capture the Father's desire and intent.

The corporate element of the prayer is maintained throughout so that it can be used in a corporate worship environment, the same as Jesus' Model Prayer. Just keep in mind that these—as in the prayer Jesus taught—are more than just words. If the internal posture of your heart doesn't correspond with the words below, all you're doing is reciting empty words.

May this prayer and the technology discussed in this book become instruments to help shift you into greater Kingdom alignment, upgrade you from the old religious standard, and accelerate the coming of our Lord.

Prayer

Father in heaven, we come to You now because we know we can approach you boldly through the blood of Jesus, Your Son. We who were once alienated from You have now been drawn close, and we are able to call you "Father." You are our Eternal Daddy. You sacrificed Your only begotten Son for us so we could be reconciled to You and intimately connected to our very source of life.

Your presence is our delight. Your person is our pursuit. Nothing else truly matters beside You. It is in You and You only that we live and move and have our being. You are more needful than the air that we breathe, or the food and water that we consume in our bodies. You have become our joy and our delight, and our desire is only to worship You. Our focus and our gaze will remain upon You.

Let Your name be exalted within us. Let your name be reverenced, honored, and magnified among the nations. We desire to reflect Your glory. We desire to make You known among the heathen. We desire to be an accurate reflection and intelligent representation of You among all people. Be glorified within the full volume and context of our existence and in the entire length and breadth of our individual and corporate spheres.

293

Consume the wood, hay, dross, stubble, and chaff in our lives as a Kingdom community called by Your name. Remove every element within us that would seek to obscure or distort Your true image and likeness to the world around us. Give us a new heart and a new spirit. Sanctify us as You sanctify Your great name. Make us one in You just as You are one with Your Son. Make Your people of one heart—Your heart. Make us of one mind—Your mind. Let us be of one spirit—Your Spirit. Remove every fracture, faction, and friction that has kept us apart and sought to militate against any genuine experience of unity.

Let Your Kingdom come! Let the full measure of the very culture of heaven permeate and transform our lives and community so that we, in turn, become a holy leaven that permeates the entire earth. Fill the earth with Your glory as the waters cover the sea. Let Your Kingdom influence be brought to bear upon every mountain of society, including government, media, education, business, family, entertainment, and religion. May we as Your people learn to exert Kingdom influence even from a place of obscurity or insignificance. Let Your Kingdom first come in us so that Your Kingdom could be powerfully demonstrated through us in great power, signs, wonders, and miracles.

Reform our hearts and minds with Your Kingdom architecture. We reject the Pharisaical principle of cleaning only the outside of the cup by seeking external reform. We adamantly refuse the foolishness and hypocrisy of pursuing external change without internal transformation. We desire Your rule, Your reign, and Your government within our hearts. We abdicate every personal throne in favor of You.

We understand that Your Kingdom is spiritual in nature; therefore, we are not moved by the external conditions taking place around us. Your Kingdom is not defined by earthly rulers who occupy positions of authority but do not fear Your name. You were able to humble and bend the great king Nebuchadnezzar to Your will, and there is no human authority on earth who can escape Your piercing gaze and influence.

Every other kingdom must bow to your Kingdom. Every human will must conform to Your own. It is Your will and pleasure that we seek, so let Your will be done in our lives, communities, and nations. We give ourselves completely to Your delight. We refuse to limit ourselves to the moral requirements of the law. We refuse to restrict ourselves to the boundaries of religious obligations. We reject the status quo! Our passion for You is real, and it propels us beyond what is common, normal, or acceptable. There is no limit that we will not exceed to bring You pleasure.

Like our father Abraham on Mount Moriah, we surrender every Isaac, every selfish pursuit, and every personal ambition. We choose to conform to what You have determined brings You joy. We refuse to walk any longer in ignorance or to stumble along anymore in blindness.

Open our eyes and give us sight. Open up new portals to the place where You reside and teach us to ascend to that elevated spiritual position where You are. Give us the spiritual wisdom, understanding, knowledge, and insight necessary to comprehend the true architecture of heaven so that we can effectively reproduce it in the earth. Restore unto us the ability that Adam once had to effortlessly interface and interact with both realms.

We believe that we can and should be able to hear You, see You, and interact with You effortlessly. We believe that we can be totally prophetic effortlessly, without having to stress or strain to hear Your voice. Jesus was able to progressively see what You were doing and hear what You were saying, and we believe that You have given that same ability to us. You gave to the original apostles, and by extension Your entire Kingdom Community, keys of authority and access to that place where You reside so that we can truly exercise dominion in the earth. We refuse to live or operate any more beneath the potential You paid such a hefty price to procure for us.

Reunite heaven and earth once again! Restore unto us the garden that was once lost through Adam. Let there be no division, no dichotomy, no disparity, no difference, and no form of divergence or disconnect between heaven and earth. Let the two become one!

295

Give us the divine resource necessary to establish Your Kingdom and bring Your will and pleasure to pass on earth. We cannot fulfill this assignment on our own. We need Your grace, we need Your power, we need Your wisdom.

Lord, like Solomon, we recognize that our greatest need is not wealth, recognition, or earthly power. In order to accurately build and lead we need Your wisdom. You said through Solomon that it is by wisdom that a house is built, by understanding it is established, and by knowledge its chambers are filled; so fill our hearts with Your wisdom. Grant unto us the spirit of wisdom and revelation in the knowledge of You. Cause the eyes of our understanding to be enlightened so that we may know what is the hope of Your calling and the exceeding riches of the glory of Your inheritance in the saints. Deliver us from our own personal blindness and ignorance as we seek to tap into that dimension of Your omniscient grace. You said that if we asked that You would give, so we receive it by faith.

We thank You for the daily manna of Your Spirit and for the fresh revelation, insight, and understanding of Your Word. We thank You for what we heard from You yesterday, but we are desperate to hear from You again today. Baptize us afresh! Fill us to overflowing with Your Holy Spirit. We are not content to just speak in tongues. We are not content with just being able to prophesy. We want the full measure, the full reality, and the full experience that both meets and surpasses what our ancient brothers and sisters experienced in the Book of Acts.

Forgive us for trusting in religion. Forgive us for trusting in tradition. Forgive us for our selfishness, self-righteousness, and attitudes of self-sufficiency. Forgive us for our pride, stubbornness, and rebellion. Search us and know our hearts, try us and know our thoughts, and see if there is any wicked way in us—any internal area of corruption and defilement—and lead us in the way everlasting. Purify us as the sons of Levi that we may offer up our offerings unto You in righteousness. Create in us a clean heart and renew a right spirit within us.

Forgive us where we have failed to demonstrate Your love, kindness, and mercy to others. Where we have hated our brother or sister and failed to demonstrate the same mercy and compassion that You have shown unto us as sinners, we repent. We reject the religious principle of penalizing and punishing others for their errors. We reject the carnal mentality of holding fast to our rights and seeking to enforce them upon others in order to exact from them their debts. We understand that though society may reckon our actions as legal, You continue to view them as lawless.

We bless those who have cursed us or have sought to invoke evil upon us. We pray that You will bless and prosper them. We commit ourselves to do good to those who hate us. We pray also for those who have used us, betrayed us, and persecuted us. We forgive them, and we ask that You will forgive them also because they are ignorant of what they do.

Show us Your glory like Moses and cause us to behold Your mercy, longsuffering, forgiveness, and compassion. We desire to reflect Your image and glory to the world.

Like Moses we ask that You will lead us and go before us, to navigate us unto our destiny. There are many diverse traps and pitfalls of temptation that we cannot escape or avoid without Your leadership and guidance. We acknowledge our personal and corporate weakness, blindness, and insufficiency. Your Word declares that the steps of a righteous man are ordered by the Lord, so order our steps in righteousness as Your people submit to Your lead. Enlarge our steps under us so that our feet do not slip.

We refuse to settle. We refuse to build a permanent habitation or resting place upon any previous, current, or even future revelation or point of direction You have given to us until we arrive safely at the finish and the consummation of all things. We understand that Your Kingdom is not static or stagnant but continuously and vigorously progressive, so migrate us beyond the entrapments of worldliness and religious tradition.

We humble ourselves and lay our crowns of earthly achievements at Your feet. We posture our hearts in total surrender and submission to Your ways. We refuse to trust any longer in our human wisdom or ability, manmade programs and constructs, or any other thing we may have substituted for Your divine leadership and guidance.

Deliver us from every evil tendency toward sin. Liberate us from every internal element of evil or corruption. Let there be no ungodly principle operating within our hearts that the enemy can use to hook or entice us in order to gain an unfair advantage over us. Draw us away from the evil that would seek to draw us away from You.

We are in the world but we are not of it; therefore, we refuse to be defined by this world's evil character, customs, or culture. We reject its corrupt systems and methodologies in favor of Your divine architecture. We understand that though we are fully sanctified in spirit, there is still a process of sanctification taking place within our hearts. We are not yet perfect, so we understand that there may be areas in our lives and community that are not yet fully submitted to You. There are polarized passions doing battle within us as the spirit and the flesh wage war within our members. Save us from ourselves, and may Your strength be made perfect in our own personal and corporate weakness. We give thanks to You, God, for You have given us the victory through our Lord Jesus Christ.

We thank You, Father, for hearing our prayer, because it is Your Kingdom and Your Kingdom alone that we seek. It is by Your power and authority alone that Your will is accomplished, and it is You alone who deserves all glory, honor, and praise. Amen.

KEY PRINCIPLES

1. The religious traditions and inaccurate models we have inherited from our Christian forefathers are in desperate need of reform.
2. Both Jesus and John the Baptist taught their disciples to pray.
3. John the Baptist was the forerunner and Jesus was the Architect of a new heavenly Kingdom.
4. The Kingdom Jesus introduced functions by an entirely different operating system from religious Judaism, with architecture that is of an internal design.
5. The religious prayer dynamics the Jews had grown accustomed to had been severely degraded and corrupted through centuries of syncretism, apostasy, and pagan influence.
6. The internal posture of our hearts must correspond with the words we pray if our prayers are to be effective.

To order books and other resources by
Robert Paul
or to make contact for ministry requests
please use the information provided below

Kingdom Ambassadors International
177 Apostles Way, Box J
Santa Rosa Beach, FL 32459
1-888-NOW-4KAI (1-888-669-4524)

Email:
ambassadors@kaiembassy.com or
invitation@kaiembassy.com

Visit us on the web:
www.kaiembassy.com
www.facebook.com/kaiembassy
www.twitter.com/KAIEmbassy7

Made in the USA
Charleston, SC
20 November 2013